Who Needs SHAKESPEARE?

Who Needs SHAKESPEARE?

by Sidney Finkelstein

INTERNATIONAL PUBLISHERS New York

ACKNOWLEDGEMENTS

The publishers wish to thank the authors and publishers of the following for permission to quote from their works.

Verdi by F. Werfel and P. Stefan, © AMS Press Edition, 1973; *Medieval Panorama* by G.G. Coulton, © Cambridge University Press, 1947; *What Happens In Hamlet* by J.D. Wilson, © by Cambridge University Press, 1967; *Life in Shakespeare's England* by J.D. Wilson, © by Cambridge University Press, 1949; *An Approach To Shakespeare* © 1960, 1967 by D.A. Traversi; © 1956 by Doubleday & Company, Inc.; *Meaning In The Visual Arts* © 1955 by Erwin Panofsky, by permission of Doubleday & Company, Inc; *Africa and Africans* © 1964 by Paul Bohannan, by permission of Doubleday & Company, Inc.; *Shakespearean Criticism* by Samuel Taylor Coleridge, Ed. with an intro. by T.M. Raysor, *Everyman's Library Edition,* published by E.P. Dutton & Co., Inc; T.S. Eliot's essays *"Dante"* and *"Hamlet" Selected Essays,* by permission of Harcourt Brace Jovanovich, Inc; *Religion and the Rise of Capitalism* by R.H. Tawney, by permission of Harcourt Brace Jovanovich, Inc; *The Wheel Of Fire* by G.W. Knight © Harper & Row Publishers; *Shakespeare* by Mark Van Doren, permission granted by Holt, Rinehart and Winston, Inc. Publishers; *Shakespeare:* A Survey by E.K. Chambers, by permission of MacMillan Publishing Co., Inc; *The Hidden Persuaders* published by David McKay Co., Inc; *The New Poets* by M.L. Rosenthal by permission of Oxford University Press; *Characters of Shakespeare's Plays* by W. Hazlitt, by permission of Oxford University Press; *Shakespearean Tragedy* by A.C. Bradley, by permission of St. Martin's Press, Inc., MacMillan & Co., Ltd; *Political and Comic Characters of Shakespeare* by J. Palmer, by permission of St. Martin's Press, Inc., MacMillan & Co., Ltd.

ISBN 0-7178-0315-5 (cloth); 0-7178-316-3 (paperback)
Library of Congress Catalog Card Number 73-77647

© 1973 by International Publishers Co., Inc.
First Edition 1973

Printed in the United States of America

Contents

Who Needs SHAKESPEARE?

1

WHO NEEDS SHAKESPEARE

Humanism and Politics

WHO needs Shakespeare? Apparently the stage needs him, for he is the most performed dramatist of our time. There has hardly been a period since his death in 1616 when his plays have not been shown. Not always in the form in which he wrote them, because it became recurrent practice to change them to fit the times. The plays that were produced in the 17th century were rewritten; in the 18th and 19th centuries they were drastically cut and rearranged. Today the "improvements" often consist of shifting settings, costumes and atmosphere into those of an age later than Shakespeare's in the attempt to establish him simply as a student of abstract character who could have produced his plays in any age and had no integral relationship with his own.

Producers and critics often ascribe to Shakespeare a primary concern with one or another of the special problems that preoccupy modern writers. Thus we are offered a Freudian Shakespeare who, whatever he seems to be discussing, is actually writing of the Oedipus complex; a Jungian Shakespeare devoted to myths stemming from a "collective unconscious"; an existentialist Shakespeare whose thesis is that the world is forever absurd; a philologist Shakespeare devoted to purifying the English language.

Motion pictures have entered the competition by providing interpretations that are at odds with the playwright's own words. The Old Vic's stage production of *Troilus and Cressida* adopted World War I costumes that robbed the play of Shakespeare's crucial analysis of medieval chivalry. In Peter Brook's *King Lear,* which moved from the stage to the cinema, Lear speaks and acts like a death's-head in the latter part of the play, thus nullifying the resurgence of his character that is one of the most wonderful and significant elements in the play. Zefferelli's *Romeo and Juliet* transforms Shakespeare's villainous Tybalt into a noble personage, Mercutio into an inept clown, and Romeo and Juliet into squalling brats—cancelling out the heroism revealed in Juliet's later scenes. His *Much Ado About Nothing* updates the costumes a couple of centuries and, among other things, nullifies the 16th-century charm of Dogberry and his followers. Polanski's *Macbeth* contributes nudes and scenes of violence, and by adding a scene at the end where Donalbain seeks out the witches, moves the play into an existentialist frame.

The influential poet and critic, the late T. S. Eliot, gave a historical reason for Shakespeare's great stature, at the same time removing him from history:

> To pass on to posterity one's own language, more highly developed, more refined, and more precise than it was before one wrote it, that is the supreme possible achievement of the poet as poet. Of course a really supreme poet makes poetry also more difficult for his successors, but the simple fact of his supremacy, and the price literature must pay for having a Dante or a Shakespeare, is that it can have only one. Later poets must find something else to do, and be content if the things left to do are lesser things.[1]

It is hard to believe, however, that writers after Shakespeare who were also masters of the English language, like Donne, Pope, Keats, Dickens and Hardy, were rendered impotent because of the wonders he had wrought or felt weakened by their rivalry with him. Nor did they make language, rather than the reality they projected through it, their primary concern. As life has changed, people's minds have changed and, along with them, their language. Later writers reshaped Shakespeare's language in order that it would follow the usage of their own times and express their own sensibilities. From Eliot's remarks one would have to conclude that to bring forth a new Shakespeare we would have to create a wholly new language—an impossible task. Eliot would appear to be looking for some overriding, fateful reason outside himself that made him find "lesser things" to do than Shakespeare. He blames the existence of a writer 350 years ago for his own limitations.

It is Shakespeare, the social thinker and the writer who dealt with politics in its deepest sense—concern with the theory and practice of government and the state of civic morality—who is the center of the present study. The perception and grasp with which he met the challenge of his own times made him a giant among artists. Later ages could not ignore him for they, too, were confronted by many of the questions he raised; and today, when the answers are finally at hand, he still remains a constant source of inspiration.

The England of 1564 in which Shakespeare was born was medieval in its political institutions and in much of its thought. That is, it was ruled by a monarch with absolute powers, presumably approved by God. Below the monarch was a group of aristocratic families who were also great landowners, and thought of themselves as sharing in the lineage of kings. Some were selected by the monarch to be members of a ruling state council. There was a class of gentlemen—knights, squires and possessors of coats of arms—gentry who lived off the land and despised labor or trade. Sometimes they held government or court posts; while among the lesser gentry the local justices of the peace were to be found. At the bottom of the social ladder, with no rights in their own government, was the great mass of the population—the laboring peasantry. Rising out of the masses when they accumulated a little money were the merchants, traders, small manufacturers, skilled artisans, and small independent farmers. They had scarcely more rights than the peasantry, and their ambition generally was to own substantial land, buy themselves a coat of arms and enter the ranks of the gentry.

The House of Commons, representing the smaller gentry, met

very irregularly, when called by the monarch, and usually for the purpose of raising men and women for a war. Relatively few people could read and write. There were printed books and pamphlets but no newspapers, and the most powerful medium of public communication was oratory—notably that of the great preachers. S. T. Bindoff writes of the mid-16th century, "For everyone who read Brinkelow or Crowley, a hundred must have listened to Hugh Latimer."[2]

But there were forces developing which could not continue to exist under these institutions and were straining them to the breaking point. A considerable increase in commerce, manufacturing and trade brought with it a fluidity among social classes, so that some people with money could become peers, and some noblemen and gentry were to turn to commerce. The growth of internal trade demanded a free flow of commodities throughout a nobleman's domain (held almost as independent territories) and increased the pressure for the establishment of a unified nation, at the price of limiting the power of the nobility. The growth of external trade as well as the scramble for American gold required something of a unified effort, and since the sacrifices of the commoners were needed, it became more difficult to continue to look upon them as nonentities.

The concept of an independent nation was alien to the medieval and feudal mind. Theoretically the Holy Roman Emperor and the Pope ruled the local kings, who, in turn, ruled their nobles and barons, and so on down to the peasantry. But the feudal lords and barons considered themselves virtually independent rulers of their own domains, and they maintained their own retinues. In wars, the king had to appeal to them for troops, led by the lords and barons themselves. They as well as the king could increase their estates by wars and marriages. The languages and customs of the land from which they drew revenue mattered little to them, and a monarch's revenues came from his own private land. The language of politics, education, religion and official culture was Latin.

But national languages were growing among the common people. From the 13th century on, this was accelerated, as the increasing oppression of the peasantry by the money-hungry nobility sparked rebellions. Since the king was often looked upon with contempt or used as a cat's-paw by the great nobles, the idea grew among the peasantry and the more moneyed "nobodies" of the cities that a strong king might be their protector against the nobility. This was by no means a stable solution, for if a strong king should arise who could assert his powers over the nobility, he could also eventually use them for his own purposes.

The first form of national unity arose under a strong monarch. Around the 16th century, nations were established in France and Spain, for example—from which a rich literature in the common people's language developed.

In France, the kings were able to assert their strength against such virtually independent centers as the Duchy of Burgundy; they could also run the French Catholic Church in relative independence of the Pope. French literature, national in feeling, flourished with Ronsard, Rabelais and Montaigne.

In Spain, the Moors were expelled and Castille was united with Aragon by means of a royal marriage. In the new nation Spanish literature soon flourished, helped along by the gold of the Americas. The Spanish kings could win independence from the Empire and Pope by the simple process of taking them over or dominating them. Assisting them were the great banking families like the Fuggers and the Welsers. The Fuggers, writes R. H. Tawney, "provided the funds with which Charles V bought the imperial crown, after an election conducted with the publicity of an auction and the morals of a gambling hell."[3] And at the same time revolt against Spain flared in the Netherlands, resulting in the formation in the 17th century of another independent nation, the Dutch Republic.

Everywhere in Europe national movements were stirring, but not everywhere was it possible for them to come to fruition. In Italy, independent city-states like Florence and Venice had grown alongside of Rome, where the Papacy dwelt. They were ruled by an oligarchy of merchants and bankers who eventually, like the Medici, made themselves into a nobility. There, the great art of the Renaissance flourished. But a small city-state remained weak, as perceived by the astute observer and diplomat Machiavelli in the early 16th century. He sought for political unity, to avoid enslavement by those whom he called "barbarians," the French and Spanish. But such unity arrived only long afterwards—in the nineteenth century—and meanwhile the power of the Italian city-states was broken by French and Spanish invasion. In Germany, the possibility of national unity was destroyed when the middle class joined the nobility to crush the great peasant revolt of 1525, and the middle class was later devastated by the wars among the nobles in the 17th century known as the "Thirty Years War." Germany remained divided into many petty principalities and stayed economically backward until well into the 19th century.

In the early 16th century England could be considered to have become an independent nation. In the "Wars of the Roses," between 1455 and 1485, the great noble families of York and Plantagenet decimated each other in struggles for the throne. This was the subject matter of what was probably Shakespeare's first set of plays, the tetralogy consisting of the three parts of *Henry VI* and *Richard III.* Then Henry VII, beating off rebellions, established on the debris of the conflict a strong Tudor dynasty. In the 1530's Henry VIII broke with the Roman Catholic Church, setting up an independent Church of England with himself at its head. What might have led to the change in Henry's thinking was his desire for divorce, which the Pope refused, and his greed to enrich himself by seizing the church lands and selling them. But his break with the Roman Church spurred forces into motion that were more important than his own desires. By selling the seized church lands, he created a new gentry and nobility that was bound to the throne and was less feudal and more commercial-minded than the old order. Moreover, the merchants and manufacturers welcomed the move to independence.

Elizabeth became Queen in 1558, the year that England lost its last French possession, the port of Calais. She drew income from the crown-controlled monopolies of various forms of manufacturing and trade and she encouraged piracy against Spanish ships bearing gold from the Americas. France and Spain were engaged in intrigues against the English crown, and this fired the growing patriotism in England. The defeat of the attempted invasion in

1588 by the Spanish Armada unleashed a great outburst of pride in the independent English nation.

Shakespeare deeply felt this national pride, and it is indicative of his stature as a human being as well as of his development as an artist that he dwelt on its human values and expanded what was socially progressive in it. He was no chauvinist; he did not deride other peoples in comparison to Englishmen. To him the formation of the nation meant internal peace and an expansion of human kinship. The bloody rivalry of the old-line, feudal-minded nobility, with their own armed bands, he felt, should be brought under control. And he insisted that the common people, especially the unlettered peasantry, were a living part of the nation and had to be considered and treated as human beings.

Shakespeare's attitude toward the common people is widely misunderstood. It must be seen in the framework of the medieval England of his time rather than as it becomes when distorted by the updating to which his plays have been subjected. For his period, the ignorance that characterized the common people was a social fact of life. In a more modern setting, this may often appear to be stupidity, but this is neither Shakespeare's intention nor feeling. He insists on the people's humanity, and though he may use them as material for laughter, it is with kindness and sympathy. It was, of course, inconceivable to him that they could ever become rulers of the nation; but they were part of it; they were wounded, suffered and died in its wars.

In *Henry V*, in which the flame of nationalism burns brightly, Shakespeare writes the powerful, haunting speech of a common soldier, Michael Williams, on what it means to die in a war. And if the people are frequently his clowns, as his art develops he gives this clownishness a double aspect. On the one hand, it entertains the masters and, on the other, it becomes a form of defense against their blows and even a criticism of their own stupidity. Thus the Fool in *King Lear,* in the first part of the play, is the King's sharpest and truest critic.

With the growth of the essentially progressive national feeling, Shakespeare moved into a wide-ranging battle of ideas. For the people had begun to feel the weight of medieval attitudes, born of medieval institutions, on their lives. And Shakespeare began to ask questions in his plays about such ideas as, for example, honor. Could its meaning be restricted to the confines of the family honor of the nobility? Honor, in this sense, might have its lofty side of courage and gallantry, but could its exercise be restricted to the confines of the nobility? Did it not deprive those who prized honor from engaging in useful occupations or trade; exalt fighting and killing as it pitted family against family, dividing the state and causing bloodshed among the ordinary people? Was it not now outmoded, and should not a deeper concept of honor be sought in human relations?

A king was obviously necessary to rule the state. But to whom was the king responsible? It could not be to God alone, for that would remove his acts from public scrutiny. It could not be to the nobility, for they disregarded and exploited the people and saw themselves as potential kings. Then could it be to the nation and its great mass of people? Were there principles of conduct involving the need for happiness of the great mass of people incumbent on a ruler? Thus Shakespeare's national feeling became a compelling factor in the development of his human- ism—his social thought and politics.

Humanism had risen in the Italian cities in the 14th century with the avid appreciation and study of the classics of Ancient Greece and Rome, from a viewpoint different from that of the earlier Middle Ages. Scholars were less interested in finding the pagan precursors of Christian theological doctrine than in dwell- ing upon their regard for the stature of the human being and on their love of life and nature. Even before this time, humanistic influences had existed in the Middle Ages but, like nationalism, they had been regarded as hearsay. Now, however, humanism began to flower openly, encouraged by the great growth in middle-class trade and manufacture and the possibilities of social progress. It was a reaction against the dominant medieval man as an impotent being, living in a vale of tears, redeemable only if he was a loyal servant of God, after which he was rewarded in death. Humanism began the study of real people, the application of reason to human affairs, and the possibility of human perfec- tibility. As it developed from the Italian poet Petrarch (1394–74), to Erasmus (1466–1546) in the Netherlands, the emphasis moved away from the ancient past to an exposure of contemporary social evils and church abuses. With Sir Thomas More (1478–1535), in England it expanded to a vision of a utopian commonwealth in which all would share the labor and enjoyments of life; there would be no rich and poor since there would be no need for money.

As a theory of social reform, humanism rested on an appeal to the good will of princes. Thus it was bound to fail. With the passage of centuries, social progress in the form of inventions, expanded manufacture of goods, and the rise of the capitalist middle class to state power, was carried on with the most flagrant greed. In consequence, humanism tended to become a set of precepts restricted to personal life. As Erwin Panofsky today defines it:

> It is not so much a movement as an attitude, which can be defined as the conviction of the dignity of man based on the insistence on human values (rationality and freedom) and the acceptance of human limitations (fallibility and frailty): from this, two postulates result—responsibility and tolerance.

Implied here is a withdrawal from an ugly society. A person who is convinced of the dignity of man can be tolerant of different views from his own. But can he be tolerant of militarism? Or widespread public lying by supposedly responsible authorities. Or the spread of poverty and misery? Yet humanism remains a vision of human possibilities, although the problem is less to alter society by teaching people to be humanists than to discover the real forces operating in society and master them so that people can be liberated to live in a truly human way.

To Shakespeare, humanism was a social force, opened up by changes in society and prospects of continuing change, and it impelled him to a study of people in their social relations that resulted in his becoming a social and political dramatist. For how could he feel responsible for human suffering without concerning himself with the way in which people were governed and sought their freedom? His great virtue as an artist is that he based his vision of what people could be on a firm grasp of what they already were. In this process he became not merely a follower of humanist thought but its great developer, carrying it into new directions. His plays give no visionary answers impossible for the time, like Sir Thomas More's *Utopia*, but they raised profound questions.

The social conditions surrounding Shakespeare—medieval institutions stretched almost to the breaking point by the new forces rising within them—helped him to discover his own powers and rise to a rich fulfillment of them.

Son of a Stratford-on-Avon glovemaker and merchant, who was successful enough to become a town official and who yearned to get a coat of arms, Shakespeare himself never got a university education. He married a woman older than he, who was pregnant with his child. In an earlier time he might have become a local schoolteacher or a clerk to some nobleman. But at this period there were broader opportunities in London, and there he went—probably in the late 1580's. Theater was being welcomed as a highly popular form of entertainment. Medieval in its framework, it stemmed from the old religious miracle and morality plays put on by the town guilds, and from performances by traveling companies of mountebanks, comedians and acrobats. Such a traveling group appears in *Hamlet*. Thanks to the lively and enormously increasing population of London and to the rise of many social questions in the air, acting companies now began to settle down in one place and take up serious issues. Shakespeare was able to work as an actor in an established company and also to rewrite old plays for his company's repertory. In this process he discovered in himself a talent for writing plays of his own, and in a few years he rose to become the most popular playwright in London.

Shakespeare's company was successful enough to build its own theater, outside the city limits in order to escape the censorship of puritanical city officials. This theater was still medieval in framework, resembling the courtyard of an inn, with a stage jutting out into the audience and no front curtain. But Shakespeare could make the conventions this stage demanded part of his creative thinking, for he saw the stage as representing an open door to the audience. The audience was not bound by narrow class prejudice; it embraced many classes from gentlemen to apprentices, and this was an added inspiration. Queen Elizabeth's policies of encouraging manufacture and trade and strengthening her position against the older feudal noble families encouraged a relative freedom of ideas. Of course, there were varying levels of intelligence in the audience and many fools among them—not necessarily determined by their class position.

To some extent Shakespeare's acting company was a cooperative form of middle-class business enterprise. For although a company had to have some nobleman's sponsorship (his was that of the Lord Chamberlain), its actual support came from the audience who bought admissions. And while the theater had to make money, commercialism in the form of a standard formula for creating works as sellable commodities had not yet made its appearance. There was, furthermore, a community of spirit in the company. (It was two of Shakespeare's associates who, after his death, produced the First Folio, the complete printed edition of his plays.)

Shakespeare also wrote poems, which he dedicated to various noblemen to gain their patronage, but he was still a nonentity so far as they were concerned; fortunately, he did not depend upon them for money. In some respects, inevitably, his thinking was medieval; he could conceive no form of government more advanced than that of an absolute monarch; he had no strong convictions as to whether witches and ghosts actually existed. And although he was a realist, he could not describe his own country directly in terms of the issues he raised in his plays.

Among the many Elizabethan plays, some of them did deal with what was presumably contemporary life, but only in its more personal aspects, while they skirted the existing government and its issues. It was only a succession of later revolutions in history that were to make independence in literature possible. In the form of the history of other countries, however, or in writing of far places and distant times, he could indirectly point up issues of challenging cogency to the England and the government of his own time.

If Shakespeare became the great political dramatist of his day, it does not mean that his plays abound in political treatises that can be understood as reflecting his own thinking. Nor does it mean that his subject matter was kings and administrators who can be called political leaders. Others in his time dealt with such figures, too, but their plays are not at all political. Shakespeare himself wrote one tragedy in his early years, *Titus Adronicus,* with noble characters and no political cast of thought at all. When we call Shakespeare a political dramatist, we mean that he deals with government administrators in their capacity as governors of the state and makes the state's problems central to the play. Thus the content of the play becomes political in that the way the people are governed becomes crucial to him, and this includes such apparently personal concerns as honor, morality, love and the acquisition of money.

A comparatively early tragedy like *Romeo and Juliet* may deal overwhelmingly with young love, but central to it and determining the action are the city-state of Verona and the relation of its governmental needs to the two feuding old-line noble families. A comparatively early comedy like *The Merchant of Venice* may deal with a ready-made story of the attempt of a Jew to outwit a Christian, but in the course of the play Shakespeare examines the character of the government of Venice and makes it central to the development of the play.

Shakespeare is keenly conscious of the conflict between old and new ideas in his time, and he becomes profoundly aware of the dependence of ideas on social classes. This does not mean that he thinks of class in the way a 19th or 20th century Marxist would. What it means is that he has grasped how the thinking of people is conditioned, if not controlled, by their social status or interests. And thus he can treat the most intimate matters and show that they also are class and political questions.

The conflict of old and new in society also becomes a conflict within the mind, and in Shakespeare this generates a new level of realism on which people are not simply angels or sinners, saints or monsters; they are human beings, like his listeners. The problem is to understand why they do what they do. The realism of this search does not, of course, mean that his characters are scrupulously recreated from real life in every detail nor that they can be considered to be "real" people of whom his plays provide a partial biography. They are what he makes them, but he gives them a complex mentality that relates to the complexities of the world outside them—a mentality of conflict. They have strengths and weaknesses, courage and fears, humane and selfish impulses. Out of this complexity some factors predominate that result in action and may often have unexpected results, reacting back on the characters in such manner that an individual's actions and thoughts become part of a social picture.

This quality Shakespeare exhibits in the treatment of characters has been misinterpreted as a triumph of individualism. Thus D. A. Traversi writes:

> If the *Divine Comedy* sums up and unifies the discoveries of a whole period of European civilization, its science, its politics, its philosophy, and its religion. Shakespeare's great series of plays is a synthesis of the experience of the *individual;* as such, it is supreme.[5]

Naturally, if one ignores or refuses to take seriously the society that Shakespeare recreates in his plays, they will appear to be nonsocial. But one of the characteristics of the abundance of characters in a Shakespeare play is that through them he is creating a society in which individuals play their role and are shaped by the traditions of that society, the opportunities for growth it gives them and the demands it makes upon them. They are bound to that society by the influence it has exerted on their ways of living and of thinking. They oppose some aspects of it because of collectively generated activities that do not bend to their individual needs or desires. Shakespeare's men and women are immersed in their society; their outer life, along with their internal reactions, are two sides of the same truth. If his humanization does not always make the unloveable characters more loveable, it makes them more understandable.

His power to create characters who think in terms of social realities developed slowly, but it can already be glimpsed in his earliest plays, as in the trilogy of *Henry VI* (which may not be altogether his own). The trilogy deals with the Wars of the Roses.

In Part I of this trilogy, Joan la Pucelle, known to the French as Jeanne d'Arc, makes her appearance. Shakespeare, an English patriot, sees her as the enemy and accepts the legend that she is a witch. Yet he also humanizes her with the remarkable insight that his own feelings about his country can also be felt by others about their own. Joan makes an impassioned plea to the Duke of Burgundy to join with Charles of France:

> Look on thy country, look on fertile France,
> And see the cities and the towns defaced by wasting ruin of
>   the cruel foe.
> As looks the mother on her lowly babe
> When death doth close his tender dying eyes,
> See, see the pining malady of France;
> Behold the wounds, the most unnatural wounds,
> Which thou thyself hast given her woeful breast,
> O, turn thy edged sword another way;
> Strike those that hurt, and hurt not those that help.
>
> *Act III, Scene 3*[6]

Thus Joan also speaks for a nation.

In Part III of this trilogy Shakespeare gives the hunchbacked Richard, Duke of Gloucester (who will afterwards become Richard III), a powerful, revealing dialogue. Some of it reads like Marlowe, Shakespeare's great predecessor, who had died young and violently. Marlowe, in *The Jew of Malta,* has created a monster figure, the Jew Barabas, a merchant of extraordinary wealth who uses it to manipulate governments (which was actually being done at that time by the great Christian banking families). In this anti-Semitic play, Marlow has Barabas say:

> We Jews can fawn like spaniels when we please;
> And when we grin we bite; yet are our looks
> As innocent and harmless as a lamb's.
>
> *Act II.*

Richard, in his soliloquy, says:

> Why I can smile, and murther whiles I smile,
> And cry 'Content' to that which grieves my heart,
> And wet my cheeks with artificial tears,
> And frame my face to all occasions.

But in this monologue Richard is also humanized, made more understandable. His deformity—he is a hunchback, with a withered arm and unequal legs—preys on his mind. He feels despised. How could one as ugly as he succeed, for example, in a love affair?

Why, love foreswore me in my mother's womb;
And, for I should not deal in her soft laws,
She did corrupt frail nature with some bribe,
To shrink mine arm up like a withered shrub;
To make an envious mountain on my back,
Where sits deformity to mock my body;
To shape my legs of an unequal size;
To disproportion me in every part,
Like to a chaos, or an unlicked bear-whelp
That carries no impression like the dam.

Act III, Scene 2.

Shakespeare in these early plays, while he writes excellent poetry, has not yet acquired the power to develop this psychological damage into a penetrating characterization, but he does make Richard somewhat more understandable. The speech that opens the next play, *Richard III,* repeats the thought:

And therefore, since I cannot prove a lover
To entertain these fair well-spoken days,
I am determined to prove a villain,
And have the idle pleasures of these days.

This scene gains an awesome power because Richard, though loathsome, is not depicted as a monster, and the other evil characters are all human beings, each of whom come alive as individuals. In the play, besides Richard, we find old Queen Margaret, widow of Henry VI, who herself is a murderess, now scorned by the others, while her harsh curses hang over the play; the Duke of Buckingham, a weak man turned evil by ambition, who joins with Richard to help him seize the throne. When the Duke asks for his promised reward, Richard tells him, "I am not in the giving vein today." There are two unnamed murderers who are commissioned by Richard to kill his brother, the Duke of Clarence. (One of them is afflicted by conscience.) Even Lady Anne, widow of the Prince of Wales, is a human if bitter characterization. Shakespeare explores the problem of how she let herself be flattered into marrying the man who killed her husband (she is later discarded by him.)

In this picture of the old order of nobility at its most murderous, there are practically no characters of any importance who are admirable human beings. Richmond, who conquers Richard and becomes Henry VII, enters too late to be given a full characterization. But already in this early play Shakespeare is not so much passing judgment on evildoers as he is creating, on a higher level, a society in which the members claw at one another and, in the end, engineer their own destruction. This is the beginning of his many investigations into the politics of power and his search for a new morality.

Therefore, in answer to the question that begins this chapter, "Who Needs Shakespeare?" we all need him—not in any mystic way, as a writer with miraculous powers that have since been lost; or one to whom we turn for relaxation and a dream life; or as one who has pleased his public by writing down to them, at the same time writing over their heads to us about the eternal verities that he was somehow able to capture better than any one since. We need him as an artist who, writing in the early or prerevolutionary stage of capitalism, grasped that changes were under way and put foremost in his work a concern for human values. Himself a "nobody," in that he had no political rights; a servant of the aristocracy who could nevertheless operate as an independent businessman and artist, he was as critical of incipient capitalist currents as he was of the old feudal-minded order. He carried his concern for human values into the consideration of the central issues of the day, and in so doing encompassed in his art a range of characters from the highest strata to the lowest. He raised questions that capitalism, even with all the revolutions (which began in the 1640's, after his death), was not able to answer, and that are still on the agenda today. And now that capitalism in crisis becomes more savagely corrupt and inhuman and is being challenged by the rise of socialism, we need his humanity to illuminate these questions and to assure us that they are still central to the solutions that pave the way to human happiness.

2

ARISTOCRATIC PERSONS AND DEMOCRATIC IMAGERY

Love's Labour Lost
and the Imagery of
the Sonnets and Plays

POETRY has been the most popular and beloved of the literary arts but also at times the most abstruse, difficult and unpopular. At key moments in history a genius has risen to restore its popular character, extending its influence by using the language shared by most of the people of the land. Thus Dante, at a time when the language of "learned" writing was Latin, turned to the "vulgar" Italian language of Florence for his great *Commedia.* And when many writers were using a highly ornamental and affected English in the belief that it gave them literary distinction, Shakespeare turned for his great poetry to what Dr. Johnson later called the language "of the common intercourse of life" . . . a language used by "those who speak only to be understood, without ambition or elegance." One of Shakespeare's early comedies, *Love's Labour Lost,* holds special interest in this respect because it is among other things a study in the use of language.

The plot is relatively simple: The leading characters, the King of Navarre and his three noblemen friends, are taking a "vacation" from matters of state. The King pledges that he and his friends will devote themselves for three years to studying, living in austerity and renouncing any consort with women. One of these nobles, Biron, is cynical about such a program, but he takes the oath along with the others. On to the Scene come the Princess of France and three of her ladies, to take up some affairs of state. The four men are immediately stricken with love. Surreptitiously each writes a love poem to his chosen lady. There is a great comic scene when each of the men in turn is caught by his fellows with his poem. The last to be exposed is Biron. While he is smugly and tauntingly berating the others for their weakness, a servant stumbles onto the scene with his love poem. The ladies, after another witty scene in which they tease the men, are amenable to marriage.

A number of the scenes are "skits" involving secondary characters who burlesque the prevalent styles of misusing the English language in the search for an elegant effect. There is a Spanish military braggart, Don Armado, who will not call anything without prettifying it. He writes with what he calls a "snow-white pen" and "ebon-coloured ink," and a woman to whom the villager Costard refers as a "wench" is to him "a child of our Grandmother Eve, a female." He talks of an appointment to take place "in the posteriors of this day, which the rude multitude call the afternoon." His pageboy, Moth, is an educated youngster with a talent for hairsplitting disputation of the kind then taught in schools. The rustic Costard confuses words, like "contempts" for "contents." Later Holofernes enters, a schoolteacher, who spices every other phrase with Latin to show his culture. He is also, in his own eyes, a literary critic who can prove other's verses to be lacking in "poetry, wit, and invention," while he himself writes atrocious lines. There is also, among the characters, Sir Nathaniel, a preachy curate.

With the character Biron, really the hero of the play, and with the King and the other two nobles, the word play moves to a much higher level. The love poem that each writes to his mistress is in the elegant courtly style of the time, using rhymed verse of the kind that was frequently sung and called a "canzonet." This is Biron's:

If love make me forsworn, how shall I swear to love?
Ah, never faith could hold, if not to beauty vowed!
Though to myself forsworn, to thee I'll faithful prove;
Those thoughts to me were oaks, to thee like osiers bowed.
Study his bias leaves, and makes his book thine eyes.
Where all those pleasures live that art would comprehend.
If knowledge be the mark, to know thee shall suffice;
Well learned is that tongue that well can thee commend.
All ignorant that soul that sees thee without wonder;
Which is to me some praise that I thy parts admire.
Thine eye Jove's lightning bears, thy voice his dreadful
thunder
Which, not to anger bent, is music and sweet fire.
Celestial as thou art, O, pardon love this wrong,
That sings heaven's praise with such an earthly tongue.

It is a sonnet, except for the Alexandrines, or six-beat lines, instead of the more customary five. It can roughly be paraphrased as follows: If I have broken my oath against love falling in love, why should I be believed when I swear that I am in love? But the only oath that can hold fire is one that is pledged to beauty. And so, if I have betrayed myself, I will be faithful to you. The determination that I thought was strong as an oak bent before you like a willow. The student leaves his books and instead studies your eyes. If his aim is knowledge, to know you is all he needs. Whoever knows enough to praise you is a learned person. Whoever is not amazed by you is an ignoramus. Then I deserve some credit for admiring you. Your eyes are like Jupiter's lightning, your voice is like thunder, but if you are not angry both are sweet to me. Although you are a heavenly person, pardon the uncouthness of my praising an angel with earthly words.

This rough paraphrase conveys the poem's witty argument, with its deliberate parody of scholastic logic. The qualities that make the lines poetic—images from nature like those of the oak, osier, and lightning; the neatly measured lines that regularly break in the same place and end each thought with the end of the line; the equally neat rhyme scheme; the hyperbole that depicts the lady as a celestial being whose eyes give off lightning—all these are elaborate artifices that merge with the wit of the argument to make the whole an airy display of virtuosity in words.

The poem is written with Shakespeare's finesse in language, but it conveys no feeling of any special qualities of personality on the part of either the lover or the beloved. In fact, it is written really to disguise those personalities. It does not convey any real feeling of being in love, for it is not meant to do this. Rather, the wooer is showing off his skill at poetry before his would-be mistress just as he might show off his skill at fencing or horsemanship. The poem is in the conventional mold of the courtly game of lovemaking or the ritual of seduction. The stylistic conventions or formalities are part of the test of skill to show how clever the wooer can be without breaking the rules. And these conventions or formalities are the hallmark of a certain caste or coterie; they show that the writer belongs to the educated gentry. The nature images do not really serve to evoke memories of nature; they are images that follow a poetic formula—the oak for strength, the osier or willow for pliancy, and so on.

Altogether different as poetry is Biron's soliloquy when he realizes that he has actually fallen in love; he, the once invincible master of the love-making game, the satirist of lovesick weaklings, has now fallen victim:

> And I, forsooth, in love! I, that have been love's whip;
> A very beadle to a humorous sigh;
> A critic, nay, a night-watch constable;
> A domineering pedant o'er the boy,
> Than whom no mortal so magnificent;
> This wimpled, whining, purblind, wayward boy;
> This Signior Junior, giant-dwarf, Dan Cupid;
> Regent of love-rhymes, lord of folded arms,
> Th' anointed sovereign of signs and groans,
> Liege of all loiterers and malcontents,
> Dread prince of plackets, king of codpieces,
> Sole imperator and great general
> Of trotting paritors:—O my little heart
> And I to be a corporal of his field,
> And wear his colours like a tumbler's hoop!
> What, I! I love! I sue! I seek a wife! . . . .
> And among three, to love the worst of all;

A whitely wanton with a velvet brow,
With two pitch-balls stuck in her face for eyes . . .

Real life now commands the poetry. A genuine human portrait, an internal conflict, emerges. The man feels the rapture of love; the boy Cupid, he says, is magnificent. Against this there is the hurt pride, the rueful knowledge that he himself will be the butt of some wiseacre's ridicule, the thought that he who saw himself as so superior to others is as vulnerable as they. This human and inner portrait is the meaning of the passage, and no transcription can convey it, for it is bound to the images. And these images come largely from ordinary English life as it is known to all the listeners, highborn or low, courtiers or farmers' sons. Because of the realism of the images, coming from a life shared by the poet and his listeners, they are rich in associations for the audience. And it is these associations and memories called up in the listeners' minds, along with the feeling tones they bring up, that the poem exercises its power.

Thus, Biron, describing his former state as a chastiser or "whip" of other lovers, uses images of the officious peacekeepers in common English life; the beadle or parish officer keeping order in a church, the night-watch constable prowling about for infractions of the law, the pedantic teacher reproving an irrepressible boy. Describing how his independent spirit has fallen into bondage to love, he indicates that he, a lord, has become like one of the ordinary folk. Cupid is his "general," and he, Biron, is a "corporal" in the field, a "tumbler" or mountebank. And since he is now talking of the real human relationship of love, there is the recognition of its physical side: "dread prince of plackets, king of codpieces, . . . general of trotting paritors" (officers used in cases of adultery). Something of a real portrait of his beloved emerges; no angel or goddess but a "whitely wanton" with black eyes like two "pitch-balls."

Thus Shakespeare can write elegant verse; he can write a sonnet in Alexandrines as well as a poem like this soliloquy, which appears to be plainer but cuts deeper. And it is to the latter kind of writing he turns. It is connected in his mind with honesty and truth—the recognition of a real world and the complexity of human feelings in it.

In the last act of *Love's Labour Lost,* when Biron is making love in person to Rosalind, he renounces "Taffeta phrases, silken terms precise,/Three-piled hyperboles, spruce affectation" and vows: "Henceforth my wooing mind shall be expressed/in russet yeas, and honest kersey noes." When the Princess hears of the death of her father, Biron says, "Honest plain words best pierce the ears of grief." Later, Rosalind makes the profound remark concerning jests, which could be expanded in meaning to embrace Shakespeare's own development in his writing:

> A jest's prosperity lies in the ear
> Of him that hears it, never in the tongue
> Of him that makes it.

It could describe Shakespeare's own turn to images taken from everyday life and experiences familiar to the London audience of apprentices and mechanics, as well as to the educated and aristocratic. And it is noteworthy that this play with its cast of a king, noblemen, princesses and their ladies ends with two rustic lyrics, with "russet yeas and honest kersey noes"—one on spring beginning, "When daisies pied and violets blue," and one on winter beginning, "When icicles hang by the wall."

Many of Shakespeare's sonnets date, according to scholars, from about the time of *Love's Labour Lost,* the early 1590's. They were intended for a more courtly audience than the theater. Yet there are indications in them of a determination, even though accompanied by humility and an apparent confession of lack of education and talent, to reject ornamental imagery and substitute "honest, plain words." An example is the 21st sonnet, which pledges how he will "truly write":

> So is it not with me as with that Muse
> Stirred by a painted beauty to his verse,
> Who heaven itself for ornament doth use
> And every fair with his fair doth rehearse,
> Making a complement of proud compare
> With sun and moon, with earth and sea's rich gems,
> With April's first-born flowers, and all things rare
> That heaven's air in this huge rondure hems.
> O, let me, true in love, but truly write,

And then believe me, my love is as fair
As any mother's child, though not so bright
As those gold candles fixed in heaven's air.
    Let them say more that like of hearsay well;
    I will not praise that purpose not to sell.

In the 78th sonnet he writes of rival lovers who are more
"learned" than he, and whose verse has been enhanced by the
beauties of his beloved; but he, with no such graces, writes only
plainly of her. He ends:

Yet be most proud of that which I compile,
Whose influence is thine and born of thee.
In others' works thou dost but mend the style,
And arts with thy sweet graces gracéd be;
    But thou art all my art, and dost advance
    As high as learning my rude ignorance.

In the 82nd sonnet he repeats the thought but is more sharply
critical of his learned rivals:

                        yet when they have devised
What strainéd touches rhetoric can lend,
Thou truly fair wert truly sympathized
In true plain words by thy true-telling friend;
    And their gross painting might be better used
    Where cheeks need blood; in thee it is abused.

This reaches a kind of climax in sonnet 130, which begins:

My mistress' eyes are nothing like the sun;
Coral is far more red than her lips' red.
If snow be white, why then her breasts are dun;
If hairs be wires, black wires grow on her head.

And it ends:

I grant I never saw a goddess go:
My mistress, when she walks, treads on the ground.
    And yet, by heaven, I think my love as rare
    As any she belied with false compare.

In the 143rd sonnet, he uses so homely an image that it almost
destroys the courtly tone that clings to these love poems. It is an
expanded image, developed in detail from real life:

> Lo, as a careful housewife runs to catch
> One of her feathered creatures broke away,
> Sets down her babe, and makes all swift dispatch
> In pursuit of the thing she would have stay;
> Whilst her neglected child holds her in chase,
> Cries to catch her whose busy care is bent
> To follow that which flies before her face,
> Not prizing her poor infant's discontent.
> So runn'st thou after that which flies from thee,
> Whilst I thy babe chase thee afar behind;
> And if thou catch thy hope, turn back to me,
> And play the mother's part, kiss me, be kind.
> > So will I pray that thou mayst have thy will,
> > If thou turn back and my loud crying still.

Shakespeare insists on truth to what is seen, felt and thought,
expressed in true language, and also insists that he himself is a
plain man of the farms and streets rather than of the court.
Whether he thought that this kind of writing was an improve-
ment of poetry is open to argument; all we are sure of is that he
felt it was necessary for him.

As he continued to write, he developed imagery taken from the
everyday life of the ordinary person—which was also his own life.
The true writer draws upon past experiences that evoke not so
much a simple emotion as a complex state of mind bearing on the
present situation—a combination of thought with inner feeling.
It is opposite to the theory of Ezra Pound's and T. S. Eliot's
"objective correlative," a way of "expressing emotion" that finds a
"set of subjects, a situation, a chain of events that shall be the
formula for that particular emotion." This, Eliot thinks, is "the
only way of expressing emotion in the form of art."[1]

As to Shakespeare's images, they are complex but not in the
sense that they give difficulties to the listener or reader; they are
complex because life as it is understood by the poet is not simple.
The images may evoke somewhat different emotional reactions
in different listeners, but they reflect living experience, and that
is all Shakespeare wants.

In Mercutio's "Queen Mab" speech in *Romeo and Juliet,* the playwright has the fairy queen disturb a sleeping soldier. She drums in his ear . . .

> at which he starts and wakes,
> And being thus frighted swears a prayer or two,
> And sleeps again.

A soldier or a commander or one who had not been to battle at all would each react differently to this image. But all could get what is fundamental: the impinging of the outer world upon the sleeping mind, the implication that the soldier, before going to sleep, had been thinking of battle, and that he realizes on awakening that the drumming in his ear was not a call to battle but perhaps an insect—after which he utters a prayer or two for his own safety and relapses into sleep.

Hamlet, in a bitter soliloquy, uses an image that suggests the London slums. People in the audience might have somewhat different attitudes to whores, but all are able to get the point of a woman somehow hurt and outside the law who can find relief only in a stream of abuse. Hamlet says:

> Must like a whore unpack my heart with words,
> And fall a-cursing like a very drab,
> A scullion!

Dying, he evokes death in the image of a policeman with whom there is no arguing:

> Had I but time—as this fell sergeant, Death,
> Is strict in his arrest.—. . .

In *King Lear,* the Earl of Gloucester, a kindly old man, has been battered and actually blinded by people he thought were close to him. His world has turned upside down and his ordeal utterly senseless. This is a recognizably tragic human experience, and Shakespeare invokes an "existentialist" image (about which a whole essay might be written):

> As flies to wanton boys are we to th' gods:
> They kill us for their sport.

In *Antony and Cleopatra,* Shakespeare uses a simple "kitchen" image as the first part of an extraordinarily complex image that evokes Antony's waning fortunes. It is of a plucked fowl:

> Caesar, 'tis his schoolmaster.
> An argument that he is plucked, when hither
> He sends so poor a pinion of his wing,
> Which had superfluous kings for messengers
> Not many moons gone by.

Such imagery speaks for a democratic character in Shakespeare's thought, although his plays deal with kings and noblemen, since he is writing of affairs of state. He himself, born a "nobody," in terms of social station, packed his mind with experiences that could come not only from the careful observation of ordinary life but also from empathy with it. He does not challenge the right of kings to rule nor the high station of the nobility, but he brings to their doings the perspective of one who has known the common people, identifies with them, and knows that kings and commoners have the same flesh and blood.

It was truth of this kind that led to such peaks in his writing as the following passage from *King Lear.* Lear had been robbed of his royal dignity and tormented with inhuman cruelty by those he most trusted. In the course of his ordeal, harsh truths about the world he once had ruled and about himself as a human being had forced their way into his mind. His conflicts and sufferings had driven him to madness but in the end they were also to transform him into a man with no illusions about himself. In this passage, waking from sleep, he finds himself being treated humanely in the camp of Cordelia, his one loving daughter, whom, he thought, he had driven away forever!

> Pray, do not mock me,
> I am a very foolish fond old man,
> Fourscore and upward, not an hour more nor less;
> And, to deal plainly,
> I fear I am not in my perfect mind.
> Methinks I should know you and know this man;
> Yet I am doubtful; for I am mainly ignorant
> What place this is, and all the skill I have

Remembers not these garments, nor I know not
Where I did lodge last night. Do not laugh at me;
For, as I am a man, I think this lady
To be my child Cordelia.

There is nothing here of what the learned people of the age might have thought of as poetry; not a single figure of speech, no rhyme, and even the blank-verse rhythms are broken, replaced by what can be called the "rhythms of thought." Yet it is so intensely moving as poetry, because in it the King lays himself psychologically naked. Inner and outer life are one; he has nothing to hide. Every word is truth and trembles with feeling.

Whether from such completely unadorned passages or such images as those in which Prince Hamlet likens death to a law-enforcement officer "strict in his arrest," anyone in Shakespeare's audience, no matter how mean his occupation, could feel that the playwright was at heart one of them and that his language was in a sense tuned to "their ears." And later generations also realized that this devotion to truth had made him one of the greatest poet-dramatists of all time.

3

THE POLITICS
OF LOVE

Romeo and Juliet

SHAKESPEARE'S dramatic form stems from the way in which he constructed plays to meet the challenge of his times. This can be illustrated by a study of *Romeo and Juliet,* his first tragic play (if we leave aside the student piece *Titus Adronicus*).

There are three aspects to the form of the plays: the artifices necessitated by production methods; the language; and the structural succession of scenes and the way in which they achieve unity.

The artifices of a work that seem natural to its own age often seem strange and false to a later one. This is notably true of Shakespeare's work and was responsible in part for the wholesale revision of the plays that took place in later generations— including those of the entire 19th century and of the early 20th. The feeling of strangeness was not due to the fact that later audiences had a superior or more educated taste, but that habits and customs had changed. The Elizabethan frame of reference in which he conceived his plays had disappeared with the generations that followed his death.

Medieval in character, Shakespeare's stage consisted of a curtainless platform on which most of the action took place; a backroom and balcony; very little scenery; minimal stage properties, and no lighting effects. It lent itself to a swift succession of short scenes without interruption, and demanded some evocation of scenic effects in the speeches of the characters. But it required no more artifice than the modern stage, on which a curtain rises to let the audience peer at an apparently private scene.

All art, indeed, has artifices. It is not meant to copy nature absolutely. It may appear to reproduce life, but its function is actually to depict it and speak about it. The artifices are merely the conventions demanded by the kind of structure that brings the work of art and the audience together. What is most important about this structure is not merely its physical character, but the degree of freedom of expression permitted within it by the times. When this freedom is considerable, it attracts creative minds, who turn the artifices into assets, accepting the limitations and reacting within these limitations as the audience does.

Shakespeare's thought flourished because his theater was an open door to a great, popular, thinking audience. Admission was cheap—as low as a penny. For a short while there was relative freedom of discussion of major issues, and the scope of the audience that cut across class lines contributed to this. And so, with no strain, the playwright absorbed the special artifices. He evokes the physical properties of a scene marvelously. Thus *Hamlet* begins:

> *Barnardo.* Who's there?
> *Francisco.* Nay, answer me. Stand and unfold yourself.
> *Barnardo.* Long live the King.
> *Francisco.* Barnardo?
> *Barnardo.* He.
> *Francisco.* You come most carefully upon your hour.
> *Barnardo.* 'Tis now struck twelve. Get thee to bed,
> Francisco.
> *Francisco.* For this relief much thanks: 'tis bitter cold,
> And I am sick at heart.

Thus, with utter naturalness, the audience is immediately brought to a sentry's platform on a cold night.

Shakespeare takes advantage of the possibility of relatively short scenes to create a social picture with contrasting groups of characters, each playing his independent role. Thus, to cite *Hamlet* again, the first scene centers about the sentries on watch, Marcellus, Horatio and the ghost of the dead King. The second scene goes to the court, with King Claudius, the Queen, their retinue and Hamlet. The third scene is in the privacy of the home of Polonius, and centers about Ophelia, who is shown in relation to Polonius and Laertes. Thus three widely different areas of life are quickly drawn upon; the mysterious past, with the dead King; the panoply of the present court, with the antagonism of Hamlet; and Ophelia's intimate family group.

But the artifices themselves are not so important as the opportunities these structures give the artist to dramatize his thoughts to the people. The framework of the door becomes an integral part of his thinking; its presence helps to explain why a minor art form flowered into the major means of artistic expression of its time. This was true in the Elizabethan era and in no other subsequent period in England. The nearest thing to it was the Abbey Theater in Dublin during the rising struggle for Irish independence. In the 19th century, an Englishman with Shakespeare's literary powers was more likely to have to turn to the novel, as Dickens did, since that was the literary form giving the freest access to an audience at the time.

In his use of language Shakespeare departs completely from the smooth elegance and homogeneity of style that is sometimes taken for "good form." He prefers rough contrasts; his polished passages of imagery and rhyme are followed by exalted blank verse, then by rustic or folk-style songs and the raucous prose of the streets. He used language as an evocation not only of personality but also of the various strands of society, which he sees as a unity of opposites. His mind is always fixed on the social picture. Thus even in the early tragedy *Romeo and Juliet,* Shakespeare deals primarily with the gentry, but the talk of the servants also becomes a commentary on their masters. The

Nurse, for example, with her earthy and lusty language, plays a major role. This is less a mechanical "mixture" of comedy with tragedy than it is a step to social realism.

In the play's many short scenes, moving from group to group, he creates a society in motion with an abundance of characters. Even a figure who appears in only a couple of scenes and then disappears is important, for he helps round out the composition against which the protagonists play out their roles and reveal their limitations. Society becomes a major presence in every play not merely as background but in an active role.

This role is most apparent in the third and major aspect of Shakespeare's form—the way in which the layout of the play, the succession of scenes, the fitting together of its various parts are determined by the artist's conceptions of life. In this crucial sense, content controls form. For what the work says is determined less by political or philosophical speeches (which could be part of a characterization) than by the internal and external life of the individuals, their relations to one another, and what happens to them. In Shakespeare, each scene, as it contributes to the telling of the story and to the development of the dramatic conflict, is also a step in the unfolding of character and of the playwright's own thought. What the protagonists do has results that often differ from their intentions, because it becomes part of the life of society which no one man's intentions can control.

This is particularly manifest in a unique feature of Shakespeare's tragic plays, their central turning point. In the first part of a mature Shakespeare tragedy, the wills, plans and desires of the protagonists dominate, and in the relationships between the characters the lineaments of a social picture emerge. Near the middle of the play, the desires of the main protagonists approach consummation. Thus, in *Romeo and Juliet,* the lovers are joined in marraige. Then comes the twist, the turning point, unexpected by the characters in the play—the duel which Romeo tries to stop and, in so doing, causes the death of his friend Mercutio. This in turn impels him to get revenge by killing Tybalt, which results in his banishment. This sequence of events is not merely a surprise development; it shows society, in the broader sense, with all the sweep of real life, asserting its presence and its power to exert influence beyond the will of the leading figures. From this point on, the social forces take command and determine the course of the drama, providing an adversary force against which the main protagonists rise to their full stature.

This approach to tragedy is not chosen by Shakespeare out of an abstract search for novelty. Like other aspects of his dramatic form, like the diversity of language that weaves comic elements into the fabric of tragedy, like the dependence on an abundance of characters and on popular traditions, his plays draw upon the richness of the world around him and the relation of the individual to that world. All this was not attainable in the ancient Greek period when tragedy had first risen to great heights.

Romeo and Juliet opens with a "Chorus" in sonnet form that announced the theme of the play as social and political in its connotations. Verona, it says, is periodically in a bloody turmoil, because of the feud between two old noble households and "Civil blood makes civil hands unclean." And it is the two "star-crossed lovers," children of these households whose taking of their own lives "Doth with their death bury their parents' strife." Thus it announces a political story in which love is the central element, but in which the sacrifice of the lovers will change the politics of the city-state.

As it turns out, both the political conflict and the struggle of the lovers are involved with the old feudalism against the new humanism. The feudal Montagues and Capulets, who uphold their family honor with their arms and armed retinues. What started the feud does not matter; it periodically disturbs the city and the citizens' need for peace. Machiavelli, in his *Florentine History,* published in 1531, spoke of the "animosities . . . which prevail naturally in every city between the nobles and the people, and which rise from the nobles wishing to rule according to their own ideas, while the people desire to live according to the laws."[1] In the Wars of the Roses, of which the young Shakespeare had written in the three parts of *Henry VI* and *Richard III,* it was strife among the noble families that was tearing England apart. The conflict between the feudal-minded insistence that parents owned their children and must dictate their marriages, and the demand for the right to love and marriage regardless of station was the struggle between the old and the new. When Juliet says the much-quoted, "What's in a name? That which we call a rose / By any other name would smell as sweet," she is announcing a radical doctrine for the time.

The first scene of the play presents the broad social picture, and also illustrates how sensitively Shakespeare uses the common people not merely for laughs. On to the scene first come servants of the Capulets, then of the Montagues. They squabble and there is a comic quality in the way they parody and imitate the passions of their masters, but if their caution and prudence arouse laughter, they also treat the masters with a touch of mockery. What are the noblemen really fighting about? Then the Montague nobleman Benvolio enters, who tries to make peace among the servants, as well as the hotheaded Tybalt of the Capulets, who has made the family feud the center of his life and has a lust to kill. The fight spreads, despite the efforts of an officer and some citizens to stop it; old Capulet and Montague enter and leap into the fray, scorning the restraint of their wives. The Prince of Verona enters in a rage; quells the fighting, and decrees death to any Montague and Capulet who "disturbs our streets again." He is the leading political voice in the play and he speaks with passion. He appears only three times, but on these three occasions helps to constitute the central framework of the action. He will appear very significantly at about the middle of the play when he sentences Romeo to banishment for killing Tybalt, and again in the final scene when he reconciles the two families over the graves of their beloved children.

Romeo comes on the scene after the brawlers have gone. He has heard about the fight, and it appears to him to resemble his personal problem. He is pursuing a woman, Rosaline, who is cold to him; his conflict with her seems as irreconcilable at that of the two families. He says:

> Here's much to do with hate, but more with love.
> Why, then, O brawling love! O loving hate!
> O anything, of nothing first create!
> O heavy lightness! serious vanity!
> Mis-shapen chaos of well-seeming forms!

Feather of lead, bright smoke, cold fire, sick health!
Still-waking sleep, that is not what it is!
This love feel I, that feel no love in this.

This clash between extremes appears to lay down a motif for the play. It is echoed by the Prince when he later banishes Romeo: "Mercy but murders, pardoning those that kill." And it is expressed by Juliet when she hears that Romeo has killed Tybalt and has been banished. "Beautiful tyrant! Fiend angelical! / Dove-feather raven! Wolfish-ravening lamb!" Romeo says, when he parts from Juliet to go into exile: "More light and light: more dark and dark our woes." And, at the end, the Prince says:

Capulet! Montague!
See, what a scourge is laid upon your hate,
That heaven finds means to kill your joys with love!

One side of the new force in the direction of the city's peace is established in the form of the love of two young people who come from hostile families. Love, however, turns to death, and, from this death, the hatred of the families sorrowfully turns to friendship.

Romeo is developed in the first scene and in two others—one with Benvolio and another with Benvolio and a nobleman friend of his, Mercutio. Between the latter two scenes, Shakespeare presents Juliet with her mother, Lady Capulet, and the Nurse. It is a nice opposition. On the one side, Shakespeare gives a detached, affectionate yet clear-eyed look at the class of young noblemen. On the other, he shows, with equal affection and detachment, a nobleman's family.

The young aristocrats live with swords always at their side and are well trained in using them. They seize each day with the awareness that death may be around the corner. Personal courage is the standard by which they live and die. Benvolio is the wiser and more philosophical of them and even shows some civic spirit. Mercutio is an active fighter, quick to take offence and press an argument. But his gay wit and laughter, his poetic imagination and dreams lift him far above Tybalt, whom Shakespeare presents as a one-track mind carrying family honor to the point of fanaticism and thinking only of feuds and killing.

Mercutio is depicted as a man of some human depth as, for example, in the "Queen Mab" speech.

In the scene with the fourteen-year-old Juliet, a leading part is played by a character with no social prestige, the Nurse. She could be called a comic character, with her earthy language and her frank remarks about sex. Yet she represents a necessary element in the tragic drama—not a temporary comic device. Like other such characters in the tragedies, she is a real human being, with whom the audience can empathize. Thus Shakespeare has her reminisce about her daughter Susan who has died.

In Shakespeare's tragedies, it is among the personages of a higher class that the struggle between the old and the new is fought out, for they are the relatively free and powerful people whose wills are strong threads in the social fabric. Peasants and servants could play no such role. It is impossible for Shakespeare, in the 16th and early 17th centuries, to think otherwise. But his common-people "clowns," as I have suggested, are not objects of derision. If they are not in favor of the new, neither are they for the old; they are out of conflict. The life they are forced to live is one of earthy practicality. Above them, their masters fight each other, and the commoners must protect themselves against being inadvertently hurt. This practicality is the touchstone against which they rub the more high-flown desires of their commanding masters. And the contrast between their narrow concern with practical matters and the visionary desires of the higher-ups makes for the comedy pointed up by Shakespeare. The desires of the masters were sometimes dross, sometimes gold. But even when they were gold, the laughter of the audience at the clowns was evoked through the playwright's art to include a recognition of their hard lives.

The Nurse, for example, has given her whole life to the Capulets as their servant, has suckled Juliet and acted as her childhood companion. Juliet respects her real mother of course, but when problems arise in which Juliet must combat her whole family and class, the Nurse is closer to her, and it is she who helps her with her secret marriage. As we later see, she cannot follow Juliet in her sacrificial love, but she is not expected to go that far and the audience still remains affectionate toward her.

Juliet's mother wants her to consider marriage to the Count of Paris, who is courting her, but Juliet is cold to the thought. Meanwhile the young gentlemen go masked and unbid to the ball Capulet is giving, because Benvolio wants to cure Romeo of his dejection by showing him more beautiful women than his idolized Rosaline. This works more successfully than Benvolio expects when Romeo and Juliet fall in love with one another. This emotion is on a different level from the love that Romeo thought he felt for Rosaline—and it is a reciprocated love, which blossoms very quickly. They meet again the night after the ball and are secretly married the next day. But Shakespeare creates his own time frame by the richness and density of the language in these sections. So thoroughly does he squeeze every drop of the progression of feeling and character out of them that the audience is not aware of undue haste.

The poetry of these love scenes seems to light up the stage brilliantly with such lines as:

> Lady, by yonder blessed moon I vow,
> That tips with silver all these fruit-tree tops.

Romeo's and Juliet's quite different characters begin to unfold in these love scenes, as in the first balcony scene, for example. He speaks in impetuous hyperbole and throws himself wholly into the moment. She is wiser and though she speaks with passion and intelligence and lays her heart bare to him, she is more thoughtful:

> *Juliet.* The orchard walls are high and hard to climb,
> And the place death, considering who thou art,
> If any of my kinsmen find thee here.
> *Romeo.* With love's light wings did I o'er-perch these walls,
> For stony limits cannot hold love out.
> And what love can do, that dares love attempt;
> Therefore thy kinsmen are no stop to me.
> *Juliet.* If they do see thee, they will murther thee.
> *Romeo.* Alack, there lies more peril in thine eye
> Than twenty of their swords. Look thou but sweet,

And I am proof against their enmity.

> *Juliet.*   I would not for the world they saw thee
> here.
> *Romeo.*   I have night's cloak to hide me from their
> eyes;

And but thou love me, let them find me here.
My life were better ended by their hate,
Than death prorogued, wanting of thy love. . . .

> *Juliet.*   My bounty is as boundless as the sea,

My love is as deep: The more I give to thee,
The more I have, for both are infinite.
I hear some noise within: dear love, adieu!

Romeo, who a moment before had been willing to die, now thinks he may be in a dream. But it is Juliet who comes back with a plan for a clandestine marriage.

Since Juliet is in combat with her family, she must turn to the Nurse for help. Two serio-comic scene develop the Nurse's personality. In one of them her bawdiness matches Mercutio's, as she looks for Romeo, whose face she does not know:

> *Nurse.*   My fan, Peter.
> *Mercuito.* Good Peter, to hide her face, for her fan's
> the fairer face!
> *Nurse.*   God ye good morrow, gentlemen.
> *Mercutio.* God ye good den, fair gentlewomen.*
> *Nurse.*   Is it good den?
> *Mercutio.* 'Tis no less, I tell ye, for the bawdy hand
> of the dial is now upon the prick of noon . . .
> (Mercutio leaves).
> *Nurse.*   I pray you, sir, what saucy merchant was
> this, that was so full of his ropery?
> *Romeo.*   A gentleman, Nurse, that loves to hear
> himself talk, and will speak more in a minute than he will
> stand to in a month.
> *Nurse.*   And a speak anything against me, I'll take
> him down, and a were lustier than he is, and twenty such
> Jacks; and if I cannot, I'll find those that shall. Scurvy knave! I
> am none of his flirt-gills. . . .

---

*"Good den" here means "good afternoon."

The second is when the Nurse returns to Juliet and teases her by holding back the news of her meeting with Romeo.

> *Nurse.* Your love says, like an honest gentleman, and a courteous, and a kind, and a handsome, and I warrant, a virtuous,—Where is your Mother?
>
> *Juliet.* Where is my mother? Why she is within.
> Where should she be? How oddly thou repliest!
> 'Your love says, like an honest gentleman,
> Where is your mother?
>
> *Nurse.* O God's lady dear!
> Are you so hot? Marry, come up, I trow,
> Is this the poultice for my aching bones?
> Henceforward do your messages yourself.

And when the Nurse finally tells of Romeo's plans for the marriage to take place in Friar Laurence's cell, she cannot resist ending with an earthy joke:

> I am the drudge and toil in your delight;
> But you shall bear the burden soon at night.

Romeo and Juliet are married, and the great scene takes place in which the happy Romeo is challenged to fight by Tybalt, who had taken offence at Romeo's appearance at the Capulet's ball. Romeo, brimful of peace and love, gently refuses. Mercutio, ashamed and angry for his friend, takes up the challenge, and when Romeo rushes between them to make peace, Mercutio is stabbed under Romeo's arm. Here we have the irony of the play—good intentions turning into their opposite. When Romeo hears that Mercutio has died, he fights Tybalt and kills him. The furious Prince declares Romeo banished; it will be death for him to be found in Verona.

This scene is the turning-point of the drama; the surprise turning which has its own logic and puts the drama on a new footing. It is a logical development from the hot tempers that have flared up in the play with the Renaissance gentry, so quick to fight. Romeo's sudden conversion to peace-making seems to them ridiculous and of no avail. And it puts the drama on a new footing because now society itself is the powerful protagonist; not simply the Prince but the peace of the city for which he speaks.

The awesome event hangs over the main protagonists, impelling them to hurried and desperate deeds. Juliet grows to her full stature in her conflict with adversity in a great series of scenes. There is the scene in which she hears from the Nurse of her kinsman Tybalt's death at Romeo's hands. At first horrified, she steels herself to stand with Romeo. As for Romeo, he is ready to kill himself, until Friar Laurence and the Nurse, bearing a message from Juliet, give him new hope. There is the unutterably beautiful scene of Romeo and Juliet parting in the morning, after their night together, magnificently lit up by brilliant imagery:

> Look, love, what envious streaks
> Do lace the severing clouds in yonder east.
> Night's candles are burnt out, and jocund day
> Stands tiptoe on the misty mountain tops.

The speeches are wonderfully orchestrated with images of bird songs that also announce the dawn. She pleads with him to stay with her, but he knows he must go. But when he yields and is ready to stay to meet his doom, it is she who makes him go.

A scene follows when Juliet must dissemble and fight against the parents she loves. The Capulets have been made more obdurate by the fighting in which Tybalt was killed. The mother is quite willing to have Romeo poisoned:

> I'll send to one in Mantua,
> Where that same banished runagate doth live,
> Shall give him such an unaccustomed dram
> That he shall soon keep Tybalt company.

The father has become harsh and abusive. Basically a gentle person, at the ball scene he had prever ed Tybalt from drawing his sword at the masked Romeo. But now he is unnerved and out of his deep concern he acts brutally with Juliet. She must be given quickly the security of marriage. What better husband can she want than the rich, young and handsome Count Paris, who so adores her? And so he says bitterly:

> And you be mine, I'll give you to my friend;
> And you be not, hang, beg, starve, die in the streets. . . .

Juliet, when her parents leave, appeals to the Nurse for help. But when the good-hearted yet practical Nurse, who had stood up for Juliet against Lady Capulet, now agrees that it were best for Juliet to give up Romeo for lost and marry the Count, Juliet feels completely alone. But she fights on, pretending to agree with the wedding, and goes to Friar Laurence for "confession."

The role of the Friar grows more important. In a way he is the counterpart of the Prince, concerned with the principle of ending the feud between the warring families. The Prince works through laws, decrees and punishments. The Friar attempts to work with the intimate relationships between people. He had married Romeo and Juliet in the hope that it would eventually reconcile the two families:

> For this alliance may so happy prove
> To turn your households' rancour to pure love.

Now he proposes a scheme that he himself says is desperate. Let Juliet the next night drink the potion he will give her. It will cause her to simulate death for 42 hours. Meanwhile he will get word to Romeo in Mantua, so that he will be in the tomb when she awakes and will take her to Mantua. In her great monologue, Juliet, all alone, afraid of the liquor, afraid of the Friar's possible dissembling, afraid of what she may see in the tomb when she wakes up, brings herself to drink the liquor. So she rises to her tragic height. In the lamentations that end the act, when her parents find her apparently lifeless body, it becomes plain how much her parents loved her.

The Friar's plan fails, for the messenger he sends misses Romeo. Hearing only of Juliet's death, Romeo buys poison from an apothecary who is forbidden to sell it but needs the money. Romeo says bitterly:

> There is thy gold, worse poison to man's souls
> Buying more murther in this loathsome world
> Than the poor compounds that thou mayst not sell. . . .

In Verona he sees Juliet lying in the tomb. Paris enters and forces a fight. Romeo cries, "Good gentle youth, tempt not a desp'rate man," but he has to kill Paris, and he lays the dead body beside Juliet, to be lit up by her beauty. He asks forgiveness of Tybalt, whose body is also lying in the tomb, and says that Tybalt's enemy will now join them in death, as he drinks the poison:

> O, here
> Will I set up my everlasting rest,
> And shake the yoke of inauspicious stars
> From this world-wearied flesh.

This suicide is in consonance with his personality; real life to him is made up of moments of ecstasy set off by darkness, of things turning into their opposites. When Rosaline earlier had renounced his love, he told Benvolio, "Do I leave dead?" Now he has lived ardently through a far greater, reciprocated love. Juliet is dead. There is no further worthwhile life that he can contemplate.

When Juliet awakens in the tomb, Friar Laurence is near. He says he will install her in a nunnery. But Romeo's body is beside her, and when the Friar is called away for a moment, she kills herself. It is characteristic of all Shakespeare's great female characters that despite their strength, heroism, defiance and wisdom, their lives are wholly bound to the men with whom they have found true love. That was the most advanced position of the time—the right to marry the man of one's choice and, once married, it was forever.

As for the failure of the Friar's plan because of a series of mishaps, that also has its logic. Hegel discusses such misfortunes in Greek literature. "As a rule, art will not represent such mischance as mere accident but rather as an obstruction and misfortune whose necessity simply consists in assuming precisely this particular form rather than another."[2]

In other words, such accidents are to be taken for a kind of law of life. It is fatuous for one man to think he can control the events of a complicated society. It is only in comedy, where the audience, like the stage characters, pretend for at least the duration of the play that the world can bend to fit their desires; that such an intricate scheme as that of the Friar would have worked. Nor has the Prince's plan of ending the family feud by decrees and ordinances worked; and, as the Prince says, having lost two kinsmen, Mercutio and Paris, "All are punished."

What does the play say? What is its content? The questions are legitimate if we are referring to the thought with which the emotional aspects of the play are integrally bound. The playwright's mind played a powerful part in the ordering of the play. It is, on the one hand, an exposition of the reality and happiness of humanist love between man and woman; a love motivated by genuine, self-effacing and reciprocal giving rather than by vanity or desire for conquest or possessiveness. Based on sexual attraction, it builds on this a far richer structure of interchange between two people, each of whom is able to develop through the other. It calls for marriage, not in any moralistic sense but because a loving pair must live as one in society. On the other hand, it says that even this most intimate relationship may depend for its fruition on outside forces, that the society in which this love was conceived is still not geared to permit it to flower freely. Neither the old order of great aristocratic households, structured around estate, title, proficiency with weapons, and the independent "honor" that links its members together even while it causes them to hate the members of another household; nor the new order, with its ordinances and laws to keep the peace, allows for the demands of the human heart.

In the name of the stature and beauty to which human beings can rise, growing greater by giving up their individualistic preoccupations, the play demands that the problems of love and marriage be solved. By making the lovers' dilemma so real and moving, Shakespeare made his audience feel that the fruition of their own lives was also involved. Thus he placed the problems of his protagonists on the agenda of society.

4

COMEDY
ECONOMICS
AND MORALITY

Early Comedies and
The Merchant of Venice

THE dual concept of tragedy and comedy rose among the ancient Greeks: tragedy dealt with heroic personages or the ruling class and with history, real or legendary; comedy, as in Aristophanes, for example, created deliberate fantasy outside the known laws of reality, and it could deal in this way with contemporary persons and issues and also include low-born people. This tradition continued as it passed through Roman hands and then through the Renaissance. Tragedy was historical and mythological, although its philosophy reflected that of the existing society, while comedy could be contemporary in its setting.

Shakespeare inherited the tradition in which simply to speak of the common people was to be comic. But he married this to a tradition more fundamental for him, the long English popular tradition that existed before there were theaters as such, for example, mystery plays based on the Bible and produced by the guilds on public platforms; miracle plays or those of religious instructions, often performed in the schools; as well as entertainments by bands of strolling players, including comedians and acrobats, often produced in the courtyards of inns, and public pageants. Drama, as it grew, was produced for the court and also for popular entertainment. The tradition that developed was a mixture of serious and comic material. Religious or historical plays could be serious in intent and yet include comic scenes of peasant life, as, for instance, the old mystery play of Noah in which he has to deal with a shrewish wife.

Shakespeare worked in this popular tradition, raising it to a level of realistic characterization and penetrating thought expressed in exalted poetry, while sometimes preserving its rowdy, everyday language. No longer was tragedy simply legendary and comedy contemporary but fantastic. His tragedies could have a contemporary ring, and could include common people who were not exclusively comic. His comedies could embody his most serious characterizations, and a comic style of writing may enter into almost any of his works. In fact, a tragedy like *Romeo and Juliet*, with Mercutio, the Nurse and the many servants, contains more comic writing than a comedy like *The Merchant of Venice*, in which the clown-servant, Launcelot Gobbo, plays a relatively minor role. Actually, by bringing together the nobility of thought and polish of the classic tradition with the more raucous popular tradition, he created a new level of realism. The real world and real-sounding people appear on his stage, and the comic style becomes one of his methods of realistic characterization.

After Shakespeare's death, in the middle and latter 17th century, a neo-classic movement arose in France and exerted an influence on England. It sought to "purify" literature after the classic model. As a result of its influence, Shakespeare's dramas were considered to abound in barbarisms, although his genius was recognized. When his achievements really began to be understood, starting in the 18th century, both the world and literary art had become so different that his full social impact could not be felt. The novel became the form in which a new level of realism as to man in society was being forged, and it was in this form rather than in the drama that Shakespeare's kind of grandeur, combined with lustiness, was being carried on.

Unlike the style of writing that directly reflects reality, whether inner or outer, the comic presents an "upside-down" reality, with clues as to how to set it straight. It is the audience that sets it straight, discovering the apparently unexpressed reality; its delight in this creative act into which it has been trapped by the author is the cause of its laughter.

To give an example, the Nurse in *Romeo and Juliet* is talking about Juliet's babyhood and quotes a quip of her husband's when the child Juliet fell on her face and bumped her head: "Fall'st upon thy face? Thou wilt fall backward when thy comest to age." This is on the surface absurd. But the audience, helped by "comest to age," grasps the unsaid reference to sexual maturity when she will willingly lie on her back. And it laughs at its own creative act, into which it had been led by the author.

Shakespeare's comic writing has many moods and colorations. It can be sharply satiric, aimed to hurt or expose, as when in *Romeo and Juliet* Tybalt asks of Mercutio, "What wouldst thou have to me?" and Mercutio answers, "Good king of cats, nothing but one of your nine lives." The unsaid communication, which the audience is led to share, is that there is something catlike and inhuman in his stalking of other people's lives in his lust for swordplay.

His humor can be bitterly ironic, as when the jester aims the point at himself. Mercutio, mortally wounded, says, "Ask for me to-morrow, and you shall find me a grave man." The audience realizes that he is not saying that he will give up his witticisms but that he will be dead. The jest may be unconscious, reflecting a simple person trying to sound learned, as when the constable Dogberry, in *Much Ado About Nothing,* says, "only get the learned writer to set down our excommunication," when he means "communication." Or, while unconscious, it can be more tender, as when Miranda in *The Tempest* exclaims: "O brave new world. / That has such people in't." The audience laughs, realizing that she is very inexperienced, and that among the people she is looking at there are some scoundrels. But it also realizes how lovely it is to be able to look upon people as Miranda does, and how good it would be if people did justify that adoration.

Comic writing becomes for Shakespeare a wonderfully supple tool. There are people who are conscious jesters, like Mercutio in the tragedy *Romeo and Juliet* and Falstaff in the historical dramas of *Henry IV*. The comic writing becomes a means for developing their personalities. There are unconscious comedians, like Bottom The Weaver in *A Midsummer's Night's Dream* and Dogberry in *Much Ado About Nothing,* floundering around in matters they are too unlettered to cope with. This was a favorite method in Shakespeare's time of presenting the common people. A couple of centuries were to elapse and a number of revolutions were to take place before the working man forced his way into literature as a tragic hero.

But Shakespeare takes the step of putting the common people in his tragedies and serious histories, and while sometimes he does it in a tone of affectionate ridicule, he can also take on great tenderness and understanding as with the soldiers in *Henry V* telling the disguised King how atrociously they suffer in a war. He is a master of the conscious, bitter jesting of the plain people when their "betters" are fools or beat them and the jest is the only form of defense they have, their only guarded counterattack. An example occurs in a very early Shakespeare play, *The Comedy of Errors*. It is modeled after the *Menaechmi* by the Roman Plautus. It deals with twins, named Antipholus, who have long been separated, wandering about a city not knowing of each other's presence, and it extracts the utmost possibility of laughter out of their serious or mock-tragic consternation at finding a familiar world suddenly turned upside down, while the audience knows that the contradictions arise from their mistaken identities. The humor lies precisely in their serious demeanor and their fury and bewilderment at the bizarre situations in which they find themselves. Each of the Antipholuses has a servant named Dromio, and these servants are also twins and are involved in the puzzlement. But they have often been baffled by the beatings they have received whenever their masters are angry or frustrated. When Dromio of Ephesus tries to explain to his master's wife and her sister that his master is apparently mad, the comic mask becomes a conscious defense:

> *Dromio.* But, sure, he is stark mad.
> When I desired him to come home to dinner,
> He asked me for a thousand marks in gold.

'Tis dinner-time,' quoth I: 'My gold!' quoth he.
'Your meat doth burn,' quoth I: 'My gold!' quoth he;
'Will you come home?' quoth I: 'My gold!' quoth he;
'Where is the thousand marks I gave thee, villain?'
'The pig,' quoth I, 'is burned': 'My gold!' quoth he.
'My mistress, sir,' quoth I: 'Hang up thy mistress! I know not
    thy mistress; out on thy mistress!'
    Luciana. Quoth who?
    Dromio.   Quoth my master. . . .
For, in conclusion, he did beat me there.
    Adriana. Go back again, thou slave, and fetch him
    home.
    Dromio. Go back again, and be new beaten home?
For God's sake, send some other messenger.
    Adriana. Back, slave, or I will break thy pate across.
    Dromio. And he will bless that cross with other beating:
Between you I shall have a holy head.

To Shakespeare, writing a comedy didn't mean concentrating on comic speech. For the difference between tragedy and comedy lies in the role played by society. In tragedy, society is a powerful force, asserting its independent presence; in comedy it yields to human desires. Thus one of Shakespeare's early comedies, *The Two Gentlemen of Verona,* spins a long, complicated tale of loves, rivalries, intrigues, adventures and treacheries, the kind of material also found in tragedy, but in the end all the good people are happy and the evildoers forgiven, all conflicts are erased and all problems solved. It soothes the audience with a picture of the kind of world that follows their yearnings, and while they know well that the real world moves quite differently, they find comfort and release for a while in playing with these dreams. There are clown-servants, notably a delightful simpleton, Launce, who talks to his dog Crab as to his best friend, but this has little to do with the plot.

The Taming of the Shrew has three plots, barely connected, each employing a different style of comic writing. The scenes with Christopher Sly, the tinker, make a buffoon of him, by transporting him into a world of culture quite foreign to him. Katherine and Petruchio are conscious jesters, and her taming is an extravagant farce in which a basically intelligent woman who asserts her independence by acting in a bizarre manner is cured by a wooer who acts deliberately in an even more bizarre and seemingly cruel fashion. The wooing of Bianca by three rivals using various stratagems is romantic comedy in which the personages take themselves seriously and everything comes out well in the end.

The masterpiece of these early comedies with interwoven plots is *A Midsummer Night's Dream,* which is set in ancient Greece but is actually thoroughly English. Shakespeare here weaves together three lines of plot, each with its own unique tone and style. King Oberon of the fairies endeavors to tame his frivolously independent Queen Titania. There is a mock-serious romantic plot of a quartet of young lovers of the gentry. Hermia defies her father, who wants her to marry one Demetrius, by running off with her true love Lysander. Demetrius pursues them, and Helena, who loves Demetrius, follows. In the forest at night the men are bewitched by the fairies' mistake into transferring their affections to Helena, and the intense seriousness of the four people in a situation which they think is tragic but which the audience knows is artificial and ludicrous, creates the comedy. The great line of plot depicts six village artisans who are rehearsing a drama on the theme of Pyramus and Thisbe, which they aim to present at the wedding ceremonies of their Duke, Theseus. The fairies have their fun with them, too. And Shakespeare has great fun with their attempts to master a learned tradition of drama and story that is utterly foreign to them. All three plots exist in the framework of the marriage between Theseus and Hippolyta.

The fairies are part of English folklore, and this is established through the great comic character among them, one Puck or Robin Goodfellow. This speech of Puck's, for example, is thoroughly English in its imagery:

> I jest to Oberon, and make him smile,
> While I a fat and bean-fed horse beguile,
> Neighing in likeness of a filly foal:
> And sometimes lurk I in a gossip's bowl,
> In very likeness of a roasted crab;
> And when she drinks, against her lips I bob

And on her withered dewlap pour the ale.

And there is Oberon's typical English landscape:

I know a bank where the wild thyme blows,
Where oxlips and the nodding violet grows;
Quite over-canopied with luscious woodbine,
With sweet musk-roses, and with eglantine.

The climax of the play is the clearing up of the lovers' confusion and the rustics' performance of "Pyramus and Thisbe" before Theseus, Hippolyta and the court. Shakespeare is wildly funny in creating an inept, rustic presentation of the play, badly written to begin with. Bottom, pretending to stab himself, declaims:

Thus die I, thus, thus, thus.
   Now am I dead,
   Now am I fled;
My soul is in the sky.
   Tongue, lose thy light;
   Moon take thy flight:
Now, die, die, die, die, die.

The artisans are kindly treated. Their ignorance is not their fault. Theseus says:

Out of this silence yet I picked a welcome;
And in the modesty of fearful duty
I read as much as from the rattling tongue
Of saucy and audacious eloquence.
Love, therefore, and tongue-tied simplicity
In least speak most, to my capacity.

The Merchant of Venice, which probably follows shortly after, in the middle 1590's, is as different from *A Mid-Summer Night's Dream* as two comedies by the same genius can be. It makes a significant stride forward in its serious treatment of politics, economics and social morality. The chief butt of ridicule in the play, the Jew Shylock, is given such humanly tragic qualities that the comic effect of the play is overcast.

There can be little doubt that Shakespeare meant Shylock to be scorned by the audience. After his downfall in the Fourth Act,

Shakespeare devotes an entire act to the laughter and happiness of the people whose peace of mind Shylock had threatened, opening this act with some of his most beautiful love poetry. But what Shakespeare analyzes most keenly in Shylock is the money-haunted mind, more than real or fancied Jewishness, and in this analysis he shows a sharp eye for the Puritans in his own England.

The play is set in a time practically contemporaneous with Shakespeare's own—which is unusual for him. The ships of Antonio, the "merchant of Venice," go, among other places, to Mexico, which was conquered by Spain by 1520. The setting in Venice is not inconsequential as are the settings of other Shakespeare's plays in lands outside of England. For Venice was still a great trading republic ruled by a merchant oligarchy. And while the play is concerned with love, the Jews, and music, its pervading theme is that of money and its effect on society, politics and the concepts of law, justice, psychology and human relations. This thought is also expressed by Romeo in one short speech, beginning, "There is thy gold, worse poison to men's souls." It is unfortunate that Shakespeare chose a Jew as the character who is obsessed with gold, for more than one reason, one because the play has been used to promote anti-Semitism, and another because the thesis is historically inaccurate. But the play does go much beyond this aspect in the critical questions it raises.

The first words of the play are Antonio's: "In sooth, I know not why I am so sad." Of all Shakespeare's major figures, he is the least a man of action, indeed, he is most disengaged from the currents of life around him. He owns a fleet of merchant ships but he doesn't sail them. He accepts the profits he makes when they arrive in home port, but he despises profits made by lending money at interest. He himself, when he lends money, does it gratis. He hates Jews simply because they are not Christians and also because they are, as he sees it, actively engaged in the money market, where money exists simply to multiply itself. He is a bachelor and has no interest whatever in women. His one deep emotional attachment is to a young nobleman, Bassanio. He is not depicted as a homosexual and has little to do with his own class of merchants and traders, although it is for their interests that the very government of Venice exists. He adores the class of nobles, like Bassanio and Lorenzo, who would not be caught dead trying to make a living through trade or any other commercial occupation. When their estates are dissipated and they are short of money, as is the case with Bassanio, their only recourse is to marry for money. These are Antonio's friends, and it is they whom he is eager to assist. When he is in danger, he meekly submits. When Shylock demands the payment of his bond, the "pound of flesh," and calls on the law, Antonio's thought is, "The Duke cannot deny the course of law," and his one hope is that when he loses his life, "Pray God, Bassanio come / To see me pay his debt, and then I care not!" In the court scene, he says, "I am a tainted wether of the flock, / Meetest for death." A clue to what he signifies in the play is provided when Bassanio says that Antonio is:

> one in whom
> The ancient Roman honor more appears
> Than any that draw breath in Italy.

The intimation is that Antonio's detachment is due to Italy's decadence. And what the play makes clear is that this decadence, and particularly that of Venice, lies in its money-grubbing mentality, which pervades the dignitaries themselves.

The very opening of the play offers a keen insight into the commercial mind. Antonio is accompanied by two Venetian gossips, and one of them, Salerio, suggests to Antonio that his sadness is caused by his business worries:

> Your mind is tossing on the ocean
> . . . My wind, cooling my broth,
> Would blow me to an ague, when I thought
> What harm a wind too great might do at sea.
> I should not see the sandy hour-glass run,
> But I should think of shallows and of flats,
> And see my wealthy Andrew docked in sand
> Vailing her high top lower than her ribs
> To kiss her burial. Should I go to church
> And see the holy edifice of stone
> And not bethink me straight of dangerous rocks,
> Which touching but my gentle vessel's side

> Would scatter all her spices on the stream,
> Enrobe the roaring waters with my silks. . . .

This portrayal is a remarkable insight into a mind so obsessed with financial ventures that if its possessor blows on his soup he immediately thinks of the winds that might wreck his ship; if he sees the sand in an hour-glass he thinks of sands on which his ship might run aground; if he sees a stone church he thinks of rocks that could split his ship.

Antonio disclaims any such worries; his fortune is not bound up in any one venture. Then the gossips leave as they see "better company" approaching. These are the young noblemen, Bassanio and Lorenzo, and their friend Gratiano. Not only in Italy but in Shakespeare's England there were men of this kind—of aristocratic family—who knew nothing about money except how to spend it. Where it came from, least of all that it was wrested from the backs of the peasantry, did not concern them. They sold or mortgaged their land to sharper business minds, and when it was all gone, they were in trouble. As late as the 19th century, there were many such in Russia, and they figure in the novels of Dostoievsky and Tolstoi. Shakespeare devotes considerable attention to this "old order" of noblemen whose knowledge is limited to landholdings, fighting and love-making. And for all his admiration for their bravery and good looks, and his detestation of the new order of hard-headed business dealers who were replacing them, he realistically shows the old order being pushed off the stage of history. But in this comedy he is out to show them in their most genial aspect. Antonio's role is to save Bassanio, and we soon learn that he has already loaned Bassanio large sums of money for an attempt to win a bride. It failed but now there is another such prospect, and more money is needed. "In Belmont is a lady richly left; / And she is fair. . . ."

Bassanio had met her and feels that she likes him. But she is beseiged by "renowned suitors" and he needs the means "To hold a rival place with one of them."

Antonio is most willing, but his wealth is all in his ships now at sea; he has no commodity at home to pledge, and so he bids Bassanio find someone who will lend Antonio the money.

We then meet Portia with her confidante Nerissa at Belmont,

and gold or money is pushed to the background in a scene of merry jesting at the expense of noblemen of different nations, including the English. But the subject of gold arises here, too, in the wooing of Portia. Shakespeare makes use of old and familiar folk tales of mysterious "ordeals" set before the suitors. Portia's father, a "virtuous" man, now dead, has declared in his will that the man who wins Portia must choose the right casket among three he is offered. They are of gold, silver and lead. It is one of Shakespeare's foibles that when he uses ready-made stories he sometimes brings old legends into a setting in which they may be quite discordant. But he skillfully smooths over the edges when he intimates from the start that for all the casket hocus-pocus, the union of Portia with Bassanio will be one of true love. And the effect of this gentle laughing scene is to intensify the effect on the audience of the next scene, in which, from the first words, money is thrust harshly upon the mind. "Three thousand ducats: well."

Shylock, who now enters the play, is considering Bassanio's request for a loan to Antonio. And in this great scene, the first of three spaced-out confrontations of Shylock with Antonio, Shakespeare's dramatic-poetic art is at its grandly mature. Antonio accepts the loan from Shylock free of interest but on the bond of a "pound of flesh," and the lines of the drama to come are set. It approaches the tragic, as has often been said; it is intensely serious in tone, with a human life at stake. Yet this remarkable scene moves without a hint of strain, although Shakespeare delves into problems of economic morality and embarks on the "humanization" of Shylock—which does not at all mean that he goes over to Shylock's side.

To Shakespeare "humanization" is a process whereby he demonstrates that all evildoers are not inhuman monsters. They are people whose mentality, emotions and even wounds he must examine and reveal. They are members of the human brotherhood and what drives them to do evil is as important as the evil itself. The playwright has by now also achieved the maturity of fitting the poetry to the character, in sound and imagery, while keeping it poetry in its inwardness and revelation of the human condition. Thus Shylock, at first obsequious, later cries harshly to Antonio:

What should I say to you? Should I not say
"Hath a dog money? Is it possible
A cur can lend three thousand ducats? or
Shall I bend low and in a bondsman's key
With bated breath and whispering humbleness,
Say this:
Fair sir, you spit on me on Wednesday last;
You spurned me such a day; another time
You called me dog; and for these courtesies
I'll lend you thus much moneys?

Shakespeare has evidently given the life of Jews some study. He refers to dietary laws and the synagogue, (Shylock says: I will not eat with you, drink with you, nor pray with you.") And he makes clear in the speech above quoted that Shylock has turned sour but also that oppression has made him so.

The issue of economics and morality here is, of course, historically false in terms of Jew versus Christian, but the play does reflect some aspects of the rise of early capitalism within the feudal world. The views of Catholic, Calvinist and Puritan morality reflecting economics were very much alive in the mind of Elizabethan audiences.

To the medieval Church, the Jews had been the most dangerous "unbelievers," for the Jewish Bible was, of course, the Christian Old Testament, and the Jews' interpretation of it was non-Christian. To convert a Jew to Christianity was a victory. When the Crusades intensified the hatred of "unbelievers," myths were propagated about Jews as haters of Christians, "killers of Christ," who committed ritual murders of Christian children. To the kings, the landed nobility and the church of the Middle Ages it was useful at times to protect the Jews, and at others to permit them to be persecuted, plundered and murdered. The Jews could not own land; they were barred from the guilds and prohibited from most occupations. If many lived in poverty, there were some who, forced into money handling, could become fiscal agents and tax collectors for the potentates, as well as moneylenders. Periodically the wrath of the exploited peasantry could be channeled against them.

To the landed aristocracy, money was taken as the nobleman's

right. Spending money for commodities meant the encourage-
ment of trade and manufacturing. And as both trade and
manufacturing such as the great cloth industry rose to even
larger proportions, great sums of ready money were needed and
so were moneylenders. The feudal wars also demanded money,
and since church doctrine forbade usury—which at that time
meant any charge simply for lending money over a period of
time—this could officially be left to the Jews. They could,
morever, be robbed with impunity, looted and killed, with the
righteous conviction that they were enemies of Christendom and
agents of Satan. And when their monetary usefulness seemed to
be ended, they could be expelled from a land in wrath. Thus the
Jews were expelled from England in 1290 by Edward I, after three
frightful massacres at Lynn, Lincoln and York. They were not to
be allowed to live in England again until the reign of Cromwell in
the mid-17th century.

If forbidden in theory, moneylending of course became a
widespread Christian practice in Europe. The Papacy became, as
G. G. Coulton writes, "the greatest business organization in
Europe" in the 13th century, and Coulton quotes the monk and
chronicler, Matthew Paris: "The whole world knoweth that usury
is held in detestation in the Old and New Testament, and is
forbidden by God. Yet now the lord Pope's merchants or
money-changers practise their usury publicly in London, to the
disgust of the Jews."[1] By the 15th and 16th centuries, the great
international banking houses were Christian, the German Fuggers and Welsers, for example, and the Italian Medici and
Buonsigniori. But the myth persisted of the Jew as the moneylender.

In *The Merchant of Venice,* as we have seen, Bassanio shares
the mentality of the old aristocracy fallen on evil days. With his
estates gone, he can only marry for money, and even to array
himself for this enterprise he must borrow. Even Antonio, the
merchant who supports and lives for his upper-class friends, must
go to a moneylender when he needs money. That this had to be
Shylock, the Jew, in a great mercantile city like Venice, is hardly
credible, but this was part of the story that Shakespeare wanted to
write.

The pledge of a "pound of flesh" also has an old history, not connected with Jews. It was part of a tale that Shakespeare found and in his play turns into a piece of Jewish trickery. Nonetheless, if Shakespeare has no impulse to defend or protect the Jews, he nevertheless does not create a Jewish monster, as Marlowe had done in *The Jew of Malta,* and he does raise some cogent questions. Officially there were no Jews in his England, yet Calvinism and its English offshoot Puritanism were approving business practices as part of their doctrine. To Calvin, writes Tawney, "capital and credit are indispensable; the financier is not a pariah, but a useful member of society; and lending at interest, provided that the rate is reasonable and that loans are freely made to the poor is not *per se* more extortionate than any other of the economic transactions without which human affairs cannot be carried on." And in filling out the character of Shylock, Shakespeare draws on the money-mindedness of English Puritans. In the great scene of the loan at the end of Act One, Shakespeare presents the classic arguments of merchant and moneylender. The merchant claims that he earns his profits because of the risks he takes; the moneylender claims that the interest he gets is compensation for his thrift.

Of course, both arguments are, as Marx has shown, fallacious. The only reward people generally earn for "perils" is that of getting out of them with a whole skin. Soldiers and sailors are not rewarded for perils. And the only reward people get for thrift is having the money instead of spending it. Only productive human labor creates values, transforming the materials of nature into things of use. Neither merchant nor moneylender creates them. But in the network of economic relations of rising capitalism in the feudal world the merchant's profit appears to be "natural," while the moneylender's is "unnatural."

Shakespeare shows this as a real conflict between merchants and moneylenders. Antonio has no compunctions about accepting the profits from the trading voyages of his ships, even if he puts these profits at the service of his friends. But he is fierce against moneylenders and, from Shakespeare's account, he appears to have made many attacks upon them, especially the Jews. Shylock says, "He rails . . . On me, my bargains, and my well-won thrift / Which he calls interest." And Shylock appears to be aware of the risks of merchantry. "But ships are but boards, sailors but men; there be land-rats and water-rats, water-thieves and land-thieves, I mean pirates; and then there is the peril of waters, winds and rocks."

Of course, despite these perils, the merchants of Venice had built up considerable affluence. But here the playwright is against the moneylender's profession. What is important, however, is not the correctness of Shakespeare's economics but that he reveals that calculation is part of the mental life of those engaged in moneylending. And so Shylock, now that Antonio has been forced to ask him for a loan, can rail at Antonio; then pretend to be agreeable and give him the money gratis to revenge himself, provided he "merrily" agrees to give up a pound of his flesh if he doesn't return the money in the agreed three months. Antonio is confident he can do this since his ships are due back in two months.

With the elopement of Lorenzo and Shylock's daughter Jessica in the second act of the play, the confrontation becomes not simply Shylock against Antonio but Shylock against the whole Christian community. There are three scenes in Belmont, telling of how the Princes of Morocco and Aragon both fail in their suit for Portia by choosing the wrong casket. The act also deals with Jessica's elopement. As she steals away from the house, dressed as a boy, to join Lorenzo and his friends, she takes with her as many jewels and as much money as she can lay her hands on. When she appears at the window, she says: "I will make fast the doors, and gild myself / With some more ducats, and be with you straight." Gratiano's comment on this is, "Now, by my hood, a Gentile, and no Jew." To the gentry, it is apparently a good Christian deed to rob a Jew.

Early in the act there is a scene in which the clown, as often happens in Shakespeare's plays, presents a parody of the thinking of the gentry. He, Launcelot Gobbo, is Shylock's bondservant. But since a Jew "is the very devil incarnate," one can run away from his service with easy mind. Shakespeare's attack in this act is actually upon Shylock's response to this action as that of a Puritan who detests the gay, frivolous entertainment of the young aristocrats, as he does their music—"the vile squealing of the wry-necked fife." As he leaves the house for the evening, he tells Jessica, "Let not the sound of shallow foppery enter / My sober house." Referring to Launcelot, he says, "Drones hive not with me."

Max Weber, in his *The Protestant Ethic and the Spirit of Capitalism,* quotes the *Christian Directory* of Richard Baxter, a Puritan theologian and moralist of 17th century England: "Keep up a high esteem of time and be every day more careful that you lose none of your time, than you are that you lose none of your gold and silver. And if vain recreation, dressings, feastings, idle talk, unprofitable company, or sleep be any of them temptations to rob you of any of your time, accordingly heighten your watchfulness."[3]

A Puritan attack upon the theater in 1597, in the form of a letter from the Lord Mayor and Aldermen of London to the Privy Council, claimed that the theaters "maintain idleness in such persons as have no vocation, and draw apprentices and other servants from their ordinary works.[4] The virtues were frugality, thrift, and industry. To waste time and money seemed sinful. And indeed, historically, in the struggle of the middle class against the landed nobility for some share in state power, their great strength was their money, which also could miraculously multiply itself. Shakespeare's concern is with the dessicating effect of obsession with money upon the mind and the sensibilities. Later in the play he makes an eloquent tribute to music:

> The man that hath no music in himself
> Nor is not moved with concord of sweet sounds,
> Is fit for treasons, stratagems and spoils . . .

And the climax of Act II is the scene recounted by Solanio of Shylock's consternation at his double loss, as he is jeered at by the children of Venice as he goes about the streets crying, "My daughter! O my ducats! O my daughter!" ·

Shakespeare's audiences undoubtedly found the juxtaposition of "ducats" and "daughter" howlingly funny. But far beyond the Jew-baiting impact of this scene is the grotesquerie of the conflict between money values and human values. A little more than two centuries later, Balzac would provide a perfect picture of this in Eugénie Grandet's father, who lives like a frugal peasant even though he has made himself one of the richest men in France; keeps his gold sealed in kegs at home; and at the loss of a few gold coins renounces his daughter and drives his wife almost to her death.

The high point of Shakespeare's humanization of Shylock comes at the beginning of Act III, when Shylock's desolation at his loss turns into a furious desire for revenge against Antonio. "Let him look to his bond." Challenged about this, he makes the great speech, "Hath not a Jew eyes? Hath not a Jew hands, organs, dimensions, affections, passions? . . . . If you prick us, do we not bleed? If you tickle us, do we not laugh? If you poison us, do we not die? And if you wrong us, shall we not revenge?" Significantly Shakespeare has him add that he is only following Christian example, "The villainy you teach me, I will execute." He hears of his daughter throwing about his money and jewels in Genoa, even giving away a fine ring for a monkey, and speaks the touching line, "Thou torturest me, Tubal. It was my turquoise. I had it of Leah when I was a bachelor." And he finds no sympathy in the Christian community, "no sighs but o' my breathing; no tears but o' my shedding."

In Belmont, Bassanio wins Portia by selecting the leaden casket, making a speech which again denounces gold and silver:

> Thus ornament is but the gilded shore
> To a most dangerous sea. . . .
>   Therefore, thou gaudy gold,
> Hard food for Midas, I will none of thee;
> Nor none of thee, thou pale and common drudge
> 'Tween man and man.

That he needed gold to make his appearance in Belmont, and that for all his love for Portia it was her fortune that attracted him to her is not in his mind now nor is it part of Shakespeare's thinking here: the accent in the Belmont scenes is on the ectasy of love and marriage, with Gratiano also wooing and winning Portia's companion Nerissa. And then the two lines of plot are again firmly linked together, as the letter arrives from Antonio in

Venice telling of how his ships have miscarried and the Jew is
demanding his bond. Bassanio leaves for Venice; Portia makes
her own plans to defend Antonio in Venice, dressed as a male
lawyer; and there is a clownish parody of the economic motifs of
the play. Launcelot Gobbo, jesting with Jessica, laments that
"this making of Christians will raise the price of hogs," and she
repeats this to her husband, "in converting Jews to Christians,
you raise the price of pork."

Shakespeare is not and could not have been a realist in the 19th
century literary sense—one who makes his outer world conform
as closely as possible to an existing society (either in his own time
or in history), and who consciously creates the mentality characteristic of that society. In terms of general artistic history,
Shakespeare—along with the Renaissance and Elizabethan
age—represents an immense step forward in the secularization of
art. In other words, he begins to examine real life, outer and
inner, without using the prism of the supernatural. His realism is
shown in that whatever the tale, old play, or historical episode he
chooses to turn into one of his dramas, he rethinks it in terms of
the social problems and conflicts of his own time and creates an
interior world that is linked with them. So, in *The Merchant of
Venice,* Shakespeare's social-realistic thought and political interests are seen in the fact that despite the focus of the plot on the
crafty attempt of a Jewish money-lender to kill a Christian
merchant and friend of the aristocracy, the play repeatedly goes
beyond the theme of Jew versus Christian. If the Jew is not
exculpated, he is humanized, and the Christian society is criticized for its worship of money. Shylock cries to the Christian
world of Venice, "The villainy you teach me" is what he is
carrying on. And the theme of Jew versus Christian is roughly
elbowed aside by the much greater, truer and more political
theme of the nature of the merchant state itself, its exaltation of
property values and the sacredness of contract against human
values.

The point is made as the climactic courtroom scene in Act IV
approaches. Antonio meekly agrees that the Duke of Venice
must enforce the law which brings Antonio's doom:

> For the commodity that strangers have
> With us in Venice, if it be denied,
> Will much impeach the justice of the state;
> Since that the trade and profit of the city
> Consisteth of all nations.

The bourgeois state must uphold bourgeois contracts. The law, on the one hand, knows no race, religion or nation; on the other, it knows no humanity—only property or trade and profit. It is a principle that has had an interesting future since Elizabethan times. In the United States, it was used to justify slavery and to uphold the Fugitive Slave Laws. The argument was that however human feelings were lacerated by slavery, the slave was "property" and property was sacred. It served to uphold the abysmal contracts made between imperialist governments or corporations and various Latin American and Asian governments through force, bribery or political chicanery. Whatever the immense resources that were drained away, whatever the enormous fortunes that were made by the imperialist powers from these resources, the contract remained sacred beyond the power of the exploited country to renounce or change it. Any threats of such change justified an invasion by army, navy or marines. Thomas Paine wrote sardonically in *The Rights of Man* of "men who can consign over the rights of posterity forever, on the authority of a moldy parchment," and on such a basis the United States still holds the fortress at Guantanamo Bay in Cuba.

Shylock in court demands that Venice enforce its own laws:

> You have among you many a purchased slave,
> Which, like your asses and your dogs and mules,
> You use in abject and in slavish parts,
> Because you bought them. Shall I say to you,
> Let them be free, marry them to your heirs?
> Why sweat they under burthens? Let their beds
> Be made as soft as yours, and let their palates
> Be seasoned with such viands? You will answer
> 'The slaves are ours': so do I answer you:

And Portia says in her sweet speech on mercy that she is appealing "to mitigate the justice" of Shylock's plea.

Then Portia discloses the loophole that brings destruction upon Shylock. This, too, plays a part in subsequent history. For what it really says is that Shylock cannot get the law to act in his behalf. However bestial it is to kill a man, Shylock is upheld in this by the laws of Venice. But since he is a Jew, somehow the loophole will be found. And this is what is to happen much later in the development of capitalist society. When property rights are threatened in the lives of the dispossessed, the exploited, or of an oppressed people like the Black people in the United States, in the attempt to make the law operate in their favor, a loophole generally turns up.

In the play, Portia declares that Shylock is entitled to his pound of Antonio's flesh, but not to a drop of blood. There is general relief; Antonio is saved. And then the torrents of wrath and of the law break upon the Jew. He is willing to accept repayment of his loan, but again Portia upholds the law. He has renounced an offer of payment and is bound by this. Furthermore, he has conspired against the life of a Venetian, for which he can be condemned to death. Mercifully he will be spared; but half his wealth must go to the state and the other half to Antonio. Then Antonio becomes "merciful." He doesn't want half of Shylock's estate but only the use of it and that it be willed to Lorenzo, who has stolen his daughter. And Shylock must become a Christian. Shylock's exit is not without dignity:

> I pray you, give me leave to go from hence.
> I am not well. Send the deed after me,
> And I will sign it.

The dramatic effect of the play comes when Shylock points his knife at Antonio's breast, and no mitigating logic can erase this impact. The life of a pleasant man is threatened, and he is saved. But the plot reveals in distorted form, to be sure, something of the actual treatment of the Jew in medieval times. The Jew, who could at times be useful to society, could also be robbed not only with impunity but with a lofty sense of righteousness. Thus, in the play, Shylock the moneylender is needed to provide a stake for Bassanio's marriage venture. But having done this, not only does he not get his money back, he also loses half his estate and must will away the other half. And all this is done to him with a virtuous air of having defeated a villain. The "right" people come out of it all very profitably.

This is not what Shakespeare intended as the impact of the play, for the entire last act is given over to the raptures of the six lovers and to the praise of love and music, spiced by laughter. Antonio even learns that his ships have arrived safely. Yet Shakespeare's realism has contributed enough so that much later Heine could write of a woman weeping after the fourth act, exclaiming "the poor man is wronged." The play also shows how Shakespeare's political thought enters into its very structure. It is interesting to compare *The Merchant of Venice* in this respect to two later comedies of the age.

Ben Jonson's *Volpone,* or *The Fox,* produced in 1605, is also set in Venice, and in its opening speech there is a diatribe against gold:

> Riches, the dumb god, that giv'st all men tongues,
> Thou canst do nought, and yet mak'st men do all things;
> The price of souls. . . . Thou art virtue, fame,
> Honour and all things else. Who can get thee,
> He shall be noble, valiant, honest, wise—

The point is made by showing all the main characters avid for money. Yet they are not typical of Venetian or any other society, in the sense that Shakespeare's characters are recognizable as human beings who reveal the pressure and mental shaping of real social forces and historical movements. Jonson's characters are all atypical; they are not even typical lawbreakers. Volpone is a shady trickster and swindler; his servant Mosca is another shrewd liar and conniver; the lawyer Voltore, the merchant Corvino and the old man Corbaccio think of nothing but how to induce Volpone, who pretends he is dying, to leave them his wealth as they give him munificent gifts. One lends Volpone his wife; another disinherits his son. Even their "humours," or the peculiar traits or warps that Jonson gives to each, serve the opposite role to Shakespeare's—the humanization of people. The effect of Jonson's comedy is to induce the audience to feel very superior to all of them. The Venetian senate is simply a dull and ordinary court of justice, which assigns the proper penalties when all the villainies are unveiled before it. The play puts money-grubbing in a ridiculous light making the characters all ridiculous from the start.

Philip Massinger's *A New Way to Pay Old Debts,* which appeared in 1633, contrasts the good and gentle people who possess estates to a hateful, obsessive swindler who tries to ruin them and gain their possessions. The extortioner, Sir Giles Overreach, employs a corrupt justice of the peace in his crooked operations. In the end he is exposed, goes mad and is sent to Bedlam. The effect of the comedy is to present a changing society in which social forces, new and old, are in conflict, as if it were a static situation in which the good and innocent people are simply ranged against the wicked. The aim of the play is to give the gentry, who are afflicted with real problems, the happy illusion that all is well; their virtues will be rewarded and their enemies destroyed.

Both of these comedies about money-grubbing are extremely well written—Jonson's brilliantly so. They move more smoothly than Shakespeare's play. It is possible that Ben Jonson, who admired Shakespeare, regarded himself as the superior writer, or at least as one in command of the more artistic techniques. Yet both comedies mentioned are on a far lower level of art than *The Merchant of Venice.* The crucial difference lies in Shakespeare's grasp of social reality and its political expression, along with his ability to make this an organic part of his dramatic conflict and structure. From this, spring other qualities such as the humanization of his characters without in any way softening their social or even moral behavior and the splendid variety of their language styles.

As we see from *The Merchant of Venice,* if we focus on the money-obsessed mentality that both Shylock and the commercial republic of Venice represent in the play, Shakespeare was very aware of the conflict between new and old in his time. He doesn't allow his sympathies in the play to alter the movement of history. His nobleman heroes are triumphant in the end, so far as their private life is concerned, but the republic of Venice remains devoted to trade and money. And while he immerses himself in the life of his time, he is by no means enamored of everything that represents the new. As it happened, the money-dominated mentality achieved tremendous power after his death. Yet today, when the grip of the state and its destruction of human values are so glaringly evident, the Shakespearean criticism has a new cogency. The question today is not "My ducats, my daughter," but "my profits, regardless of what human slaughter they spring from." On the other hand, a radical change is possible in which the human values that Shakespeare upheld can be realized by people on a scale undreamed of by him.

5

ENGLISH HISTORY AND THE COMMON PEOPLE

King John
Richard II
Henry IV. Parts 1 and 2
Henry V

SHAKESPEARE'S English historical plays of the later 1590's, *King John, Richard II,* the two parts of *Henry IV,* and *Henry V,* are not accurate history. A disciplined devotion to ascertainable facts was unknown then, although such histories were being written as Holinshed's *Chronicles of England, Scotland and Ireland.* However, while using Holinshed and sharing his confusion of fact with myth and rumor, Shakespeare departs from him when he pleases, leaving out figures and changing the time scheme. But he does mean the plays as history, and his characterizations of famous men are not whimsical but offered as serious views of the English past.

Shakespeare's historical plays can be compared to the modern historical novel, but they differ in one crucial respect. Where the modern serious historical novel is often an attempt to think back to the mind of the past, with the realization that the human mind also has a history, in Shakespeare's time there was no such history. People of the past were considered pretty much the same as those of one's own day except for some superficial historical coloring. His great achievement, which provided a basis for the later approach to history, was the grasp of the truth that there was such a thing as society with its own organic life, and that even the individual's private wishes, desires and resentments were shaped by it.

The characterizations in these historical plays are taken from the clashing personalities of Shakespeare's own England. What they present as having been fought out in the past are his views of the English nation. These are, first, that there must be loyalty to the king as a strong force to insure internal peace and to curb the ambitions and pride of the warring old-line nobles; second, that this power must embrace a concern for the welfare and happiness of the common people, the "nobodies" who cannot rule the nation but who suffer, are poor, and die in its wars.

The weakest play of the five is *King John*. It was based on an existing two-part play on the same subject. There is no independent English nation in the play; the English king and armies swarm over France as if they were in their own land; the French support a claimant to the throne; the nobles in both camps are related to one another; and the legate of the Pope demands subservience from both French and English kings. The time of the events is in the early 1200's, hardly 150 years after the Norman Conquest. But Shakespeare's view is not so much that this was an "old" England, when things were different, as that it was a "wrong" England. He builds up a patriotic character precisely to express this, that of Philip Faulconbridge, the Bastard, and he is the most human and memorable figure in the play.

The emphasis Shakespeare placed on the Bastard is the most attractive feature of the play and yet highlights its dramatic weakness in that he is not decisively involved in its great events. The play is a succession of fierce and cruel episodes, including battles; King John's plan to burn out the eyes of a young legitimate heir, Prince Arthur; Arthur's violent death, and the poisoning of John. Shakespeare gives the Bastard a richly racy language which at times reaches a tone of high comedy. Most of the first act has this comic quality, with the Bastard at first arguing for the rights to his supposed father's estate against his younger brother, then willingly renouncing these rights when he delightedly discovers that he is really the illegitimate son of the dead Richard Coeur-de-Lion. He would rather be a penniless bastard son of this esteemed King than have an estate. And so when King John, who is Richard's brother, and Elinor, his mother, confirm his illegitimate lineage, he says:

> Brother, take you my land, I'll take my chance,
> Your face hath got five hundred pounds a year,
> You sell your face for fivepence and 'tis dear.
> Madam, I'll follow you unto the death.

And when Elinor answers jokingly, "Nay, I would have you go before me thither," he says, "Our country manners give our betters way."

The phrase "country manners" is the clue to his racy speech. For he is a country boy, not accustomed to the refinements of the court. And while his illegitimacy prevents him from ever having hopes for the throne, he acts throughout the play as its conscience. Loyally he follows King John for unity even when he feels John may be in the wrong; and when John, taking the advice of a clever citizen of a besieged town, proposes marriage between his niece and the son of the French king, the Bastard makes his long and bitter monologue denouncing "That smooth-faced gentleman, tickling Commodity,/ . . . This bawd, this broker, this all-changing word." By "Commodity" he means convenience, seeking advantage at the expense of principle: "kings break faith upon Commodity."

When the Bastard comes upon the dead body of King Arthur, who had a legitimate claim to the throne of England, he voices another criticism:

> How easy doest thou take all England up!
> From forth this morsel of dead royalty,
> The life, the right, the truth of all this realm
> Is fled to heaven; and England now is left
> To tug and scramble and to part by th' teeth
> The unowed interest of proud-swelling state.
> Now for the bare-picked bone of majesty
> Doth dogged war bristle his angry crest
> And snarleth in the gentle eyes of peace.

But with Arthur dead, the Bastard supports John against the French invasion, for John is the legitimate king. He denounces the English nobles who have joined the French against John:

> You bloody Neroes, ripping up the womb
> Of your dear mother England, blush for shame.

The Bastard fights courageously. And when at the end King John dies, and his son, Prince Henry, takes the throne, the Bastard pledges allegiance and makes the final speech of the play:

> This England never did, nor ever shall
> Lie at the proud foot of a conqueror
> But when it first did help to wound itself.
> Now these her princes are come home again,
> Come the three corners of the world in arms,
> And we shall shock them. Nought shall make us rue,
> If England to itself do rest but true.

There are anachronisms in the play, like the mention of "cannons" and "cannon-fire," which did not exist in the 1200's. And, in general, Shakespeare did not understand the period he is writing about. It was a high point of a feudalism that had long preceded the establishment of the nation. But the Bastard is a genuine Shakespearean figure. He makes one think of John of Gaunt in *Richard II,* a nobleman who loves England and is heartbroken at the King's evil deeds but will not rise against him, saying, "God's is the quarrel . . . I may never lift / An angry arm against his minister." We also have the case of King Henry V, who is pleased that he can be mistaken for a farmer.

On a much higher level is *Richard II,* the opening play of a tetralogy that includes the two parts of *Henry IV* and *Henry V.* Shakespeare sees this as a tetralogy, for in each of the three later plays he has references to the preceding one. Yet each is independently built about its own theme. And *Richard II* is organized like Shakespeare's great tragic dramas, with a central turning point, followed by the kind of revelation of the inner life of a king that inspires his greatest poetry.

Richard is not a good king; he is greedy, selfish and wasteful. But he sees himself not as a mere man among men but rather as the Lord's anointed. Around him Shakespeare constructs a great society of strong noblemen, many of whom feel wronged. But it is not England's welfare with which most of them are concerned but rather with their own personal advantage. Their rebellion enables a shrewd and ruthless nobleman, Henry Bolingbroke, who also has been wronged, to seize the throne. But he must step over dead bodies in order to do this, and when he deposes Richard he lets loose the hounds of war over the land.

In the first part of the play Shakespeare appears to damn Richard for his selfish and unreasonable attack upon the nobles. The turning point is Richard's realization that his world has turned against him, that he is no longer supreme, that he must take orders. This to him is the destruction of his reason for living. Nevertheless, faced with this brutal world, he reveals his humanity. And the cunning Bolingbroke, moving to take power, inevitably brings about civil war.

The point of the play, although it stresses Richard's conviction of his own sacredness, which a world turned evil now denies, is that it rests its case against the nobility not on Richard's arrogance but on the peace and welfare of England. Bad as Richard is, it says, what his enemies do is far worse. They lead the nation towards disunity and war. The last part of the play is a magnificent contrapuntal interweaving of the mentality of Richard as he faces the brutality of a world, whose harshness he never before knew, against the forces of history unleashed by the nobles, which were stronger than any one of them.

The early part of the play deals with Richard's assault upon the nobility. A conflict takes place in his presence between Henry Bolingbroke, Duke of Hereford, and Thomas Mowbray, Duke of Norfolk. Henry accuses Mowbray of treachery and of killing the Duke of Gloucester. Mowbray calls Henry a liar. The King is strangely uninterested in the rights and wrongs of the argument, and the play reveals later that it was really he who instigated the murder of Gloucester. Now he simply wants to quell the argument, while insisting on his own supremacy. When a gage is thrown, he says, "Give me his gage: lions make leopards tame," and when the antagonists refuse to make peace, "We were born not to sue, but to command." A combat to the death is set for the two dukes at Coventry. But when it is about to start, the King forbids it and banishes both of them, Mowbray for life, and Bolingbroke for six years. It is plain that he wants to get rid of them, and he makes them swear not to communicate with each other in exile. His real hatred of Bolingbroke is due to the popularity Bolingbroke courts among the common people, whom the King despises. He describes Bolingbroke thus:

> How he did seem to dive into their hearts
> With humble and familiar courtesy,
> What reverence he did throw away on slaves,
> Wooing poor craftsmen with the craft of smiles . . .
> Off goes his bonnet to an oyster-wench.

This section also introduces John of Gaunt, who is the Duke of Lancaster and Bolingbroke's father. A stalwart figure, he hates the King for his murders but will not seek revenge, for the King is "God's substitute, / His deputy anointed." Only heaven can take revenge, "for I may never lift / an angry arm against His minister." The King decides to pursue his war in Ireland and, having spent his money liberally, has to raise more by sending agents to demand "large sums of gold" from the rich. Hearing that John of Gaunt is grievously ill, he hopes that John will die quickly. He, the King, will plunder the estate. "The lining of his coffers shall make coats / to deck our soldiers for these Irish wars." It is the dying John of Gaunt who expresses his love of country in flaming words:

> This royal throne of kings, this sceptered isle,
> This earth of majesty, this seat of Mars,
> This other Eden, demi-paradise;
> This fortress built by Nature for herself
> Against infection and the hand of war;
> This happy breed of men, this little world,
> This precious stone set in the silver sea.

And it is he who denounced the state to which King Richard brought it, "this dear, dear land, / Dear for her reputation through the world, / is now leased out . . . / Like to a tenement or pelting farm."

The King twits the dying nobleman, who tells him furiously, "Landlord of England art thou now, / Not King: / Thy state of law is bondslave to the law." John of Gaunt dies, and the King seizes "His plate, his goods and his lands." This also, he knows, robs John of Gaunt's son, the banished Henry Bolingbroke. The King leaves for Ireland.

Revolt rises among the nobles. The Earl of Northumberland informs the Lords Ross and Willoughby that Bolingbroke is sailing back to England with eight ships and 3,000 men of war, and they rush off to join him. Others follow; Bolingbroke lands, executes two agents of the King, and explains to those who question his actions that all he wants is his dead father's estate, of which he has been robbed.

Richard returns from Ireland, and the great scene, Act III, Scene 2, in which he moves from happiness to despair, is the turning point of the play. From this point on, Bolingbroke, with power in his hands, moves step by step to achieve the throne, while Richard sinks to his doom. And it is Richard who now dominates the play with his self-searching, expressed in wonderful poetry. At the opening of the scene, he is joyful:

>   I weep for you
> To stand upon my kingdom once again.
> Dear earth, I do salute thee with my hand,
> Though rebels wound thee with their horses' hoofs.

Told of Bolingbroke's strength, Richard is confident of his sacred right:

> The breath of worldly men cannot depose
> The deputy elected by the Lord.
> For every man that Bolingbroke hath pressed
> To lift shrewd steel against our golden crown,
> God for his Richard hath in heavenly pay
> A glorious angel: then if angels fight,
> Weak men must fall, for heaven still guards the sight.

He can believe that God will support him with angels, as long as he also has some real fighting men. And when he learns that Henry is strong in soldiers while he himself is militarily bankrupt, his mood changes to abject misery. The vulnerability of a King is to him the tragedy of the whole world:

> Of comfort no man speak.
> Let's talk of graves, of worms and epitaphs,
> Make dust our paper and with rainy eyes
> Write sorrow on the bosom of the earth. . . .
> For God's sake, let us sit upon the ground
> And tell sad stories of the death of kings!
> How some have been deposed, some slain in war,
> Some haunted by the ghosts they have deposed,
> Some poisoned by their wives, some sleeping killed,
> All murthered; for within the hollow crown
> That rounds the mortal temples of a king
> Keeps Death his court, and there the antic sits,
> Scoffing his state and grinning at his pomp,
> Allowing him a breath, a little scene,
> To monarchize, be feared and kill with looks,
> Infusing him with self and vain conceit,
> As if this flesh which walls about our life
> Were brass impregnable, and honoured thus
> Comes at the last and with a little pin
> Bores through his castle wall, and farewell king!

Henry Bolingbroke cannot seize the crown directly. It must be offered to him and approved by the commons. Richard must be accused of misdeeds. But the power is already in Bolingbroke's hands, and both he and Richard know this. Richard will not permit him the hypocrisy of pretended innocence. When Henry tells him, "My gracious lord, I come but for mine own," Richard answers, "Your own is yours, and I am yours, and all." But Richard will admit to no crime; he is the elect of God; no man can hold him spiritually to account. The world, however, has become a harsh and evil place. He tells Henry, "For we must do what force will have us do." He will also call this harsh reality "necessity." He tells the Queen, "I am sworn brother, sweet, / To grim Necessity, and he and I / Will keep a league till death." He sees himself as Jesus Christ, who also was treated in the world like a criminal; his enemies are Judases.

A lowly gardener, working for the Queen, states Richard's mistake: "O, what a pity is it / That he had not so trimmed and dressed his land / As we this garden."

Meanwhile Henry executes those noblemen who are sup-

porters of Richard and who stand in his way. And there are
reiterated cries of war coming over the land. So when Henry first
demands of Richard that he repeal his banishment, Henry says,
"If not, I'll use the advantage of my power / And lay the summer's
dust with showers of blood / Raised from the wounds of slaughtered Englishmen," Richard says, "He is come to open / The
purple testament of bleeding war." When Richard yields the
crown to Henry, the Bishop of Carlisle says, "If you crown him,
let me prophesy, / The blood of English shall manure the
ground." And later he says, "the children yet unborn / Shall feel
this day as sharp to them as thorn." Richard bitterly tells the Earl
of Northumberland, who has helped Henry, that he has endangered himself. "He shall think that thou, which knowest the
way / To plant unrightful kings, will know again, / Being ne'er so
little urged, another way / To pluck him headlong from the
usurped throne."

With the opening of Act IV, Henry is not yet King, but he has
taken command of state affairs. He has arranged before Parliament a great trial of various nobles, some of whom will be
selected for execution. And he has prepared a list of Richard's
alleged crimes. Richard sends word that he has declared Henry
his heir and, as such, Henry takes over the throne. But there are
protests. Richard must appear in person. He is sent for, and the
scene becomes Richard's. He laments his misfortunes and says,
"With my own hands I give away my crown," thus preserving his
dignity. His deposition is his own will. "I," he says, "with my own
tongue deny my sacred state, / With mine own breath release all
duteous oaths." He is asked to confess a list of crimes to make his
deposition seem more worthy before Parliament, and he refuses,
challenging the powerful Earl of Northumberland. "If thy of-
fenses were on record, / Would it not shame thee in so far a troop
/ To read a lecture of them?" He calls his accusers Pilates,
delivering him to his "sour cross." He is helpless before Henry's
power. "Good King, great King, and yet not so greatly good." He
wants only to be away from the sight of Henry. He is led to the
Tower, insisting that he is a "true king" who has fallen.

A touching scene of parting between Richard and his wife
further adds to the pathos; it is in sharp contrast to a scene with

the family of the Duke of York. York has become a loyal supporter of Henry, and tells of Henry's high standing with the common people and their scorn of Richard. He discovers that his own son has joined a conspiracy of nobles to kill Henry and rushes to inform on him. Henry pardons the son on the plea of his mother but is furious at the other conspirators: "Destruction shall dog them at the heels."

So Henry's reign is established by killing some opponents and pardoning others; and the last to be killed is Richard. Henry intimates that a true friend would rid him of "this living fear," which hint is taken by one ambitious person. In his prison cell Richard again speaks at length, criticizing himself at last, in that he had no ear "for the concord of my state and time." He is grateful for a gift, "a sigh of love . . . in this all-hating world." And when the assassins break in, he fights and kills two of them before he is himself killed. Henry is not grateful and abuses the murderer with this sophistry: "They love not poison that do poison need." He will wash out the stain in the Holy Land. For, as he says, my soul is full of woe, / That blood should sprinkle me to make me grow."

Richard II is an anointed King, feeling he is God's choice, and the world revolves about him. But he is a bad king, who wastes the country. Perhaps the best thing to have done would be, as John of Gaunt advises, to have left him alone, to wait, he might change, or be followed by a better King. But can the nobility be so patient? As Shakespeare interprets it, they cannot. And in the second half of the play, in contrast to the great lyrical outpouring of Richard as he awakens to brutal necessity, the playwright shows the lamentable character of those who helped depose him, the great nobles, each fighting for his own possessions, and Henry Bolingbroke who, not essentially of murderous intent, must seize and hold the throne over a litter of corpses. Henry courts the commoners, but does he really care for their welfare? Perhaps a group of thieves have chosen Richard only for him to be chastised for rising above the others, and, by so doing, have made him the most human person of the lot. Who in the play really cares for the common people? There was the dying John of Gaunt, who said that the English people were being destroyed by

Englishmen; that the land, "Hath made a shameful conquest of itself." Possibly his son Bolingbroke represents something of a new spirit in his courting of the commoners. But what Shakespeare shows as a new thought in the mind of Henry IV is not any feeling for the nation but the fact that he is always troubled by his crime.

There is one passage in Richard II in which Henry's older son is mentioned as "unthrifty," a plague to his father, and one who prefers the "stews" of London to the court. And as Prince Hal, the Prince of Wales, he will play a major role in the two parts of *Henry IV*. And afterwards, as King Henry V, in the play of that name, he will express a new personality.

One of the qualities of Shakespeare's mind is the affectionate understanding he gives to representatives of the old order. He links morality to politics, and he realistically shows that the rise of the nation has brought a new aspect of social morality. And from this standpoint, he presents a critique of the old order, in that it disdains the nation and the common people. His criticism is also historical. He shows the representatives of the old order being elbowed off the stage of history. But in their defeat, which is inevitable, he still lingers on their more human qualities. In this way he had developed the character of Richard II more fully than that of the man who supplanted him. And while the main plot of the first part of *Henry IV*, which guides its action, is the opposition between Henry IV and his son Prince Hal, with its amicable solution, the content of the play is filled in with two great and opposite portrayals of the old order: Sir John Falstaff, and Hotspur, or Henry Percy, son of the Earl of Northumberland. Hotspur had also figured as an unimportant character in Richard II.

Hotspur is the model feudal warrior. He is proud, strong, fearless, honest, with not a cunning or treacherous thought. He fiercely defends his honor, which, however, does not include any devotion to the nation. He would willingly divide the land in three, sharing it with Scotland and Wales. In the first scene, King Henry wishes Hotspur were his own son. Prince Hal later speaks of him laughingly:

. . . the Hotspur of the north, he that kills me some six or seven dozen of Scots at a breakfast, washes his hands, and says to his wife 'Fie upon this quiet life! I want work.' 'O my sweet Harry,' says she, 'how many hast thou killed today?' 'Give my roan horse a drench,' says he; and answers 'Some fourteen,' an hour after; 'a trifle, a trifle.'

But Hal, after killing Hotspur, says, "This earth that bears thee dead / Bears not alive so stout a gentleman."

Falstaff shares with Hotspur the feudal nobleman's aversion to work or trade of any kind, and he is high enough in rank to associate with the King and other great noblemen. For the battle of Shrewsbury, which ends the play, he has to press into arms a troop of villagers and lead them. But he lives in squalor, associates with thieves and whores, is a glutton, swills and has become grossly fat. Always in need of money, he has no compunction about robbing merchants. Called to impress troops, he purposely picks good householders or bachelors on the verge of getting married, who are sure to buy themselves off, and thus he raises 300 pounds. He is left with 150 scarecrows and says: "there's not a shirt and a half in all my company." He has no standards of honor, avoids all danger and prizes only a whole skin.

Shakespeare gives Falstaff a vocabulary made up of the slang of London with its imagery of the common man's city; of taverns and alleys, garbage, oysters and stinking fish, and the muck of the streets. But it has wit and a classical poetry stood on its head, as it were, "We that take purses go by the moon and the seven stars and not by Phoebus, he 'that wandering knight so fair.'" He has had a classical education, which he deliberately misuses, and his wit has the shock quality of flouting conventions. He says to Prince Hal, "I prithee, sweet wag, shall there be gallows standing in England when thou art king? And resolution thus fubbed as it is with the rusty curb of old father antic the law?" He is cynical. "I would to God thou and I knew where a commodity of good names were to be bought." He explains his purse-taking, "Why, Hal, 'tis my vocation,. 'Tis no sin for a man to labor in his vocation." A typical comparison he makes is, "as good a deed as drink." He laughs at virtue. "Well, God be thanked for these rebels, they offend none but the virtuous." He laughs at himself:

> I was as virtuously given as a gentleman need to be; vigorous enough, swore little, diced not above seven hours a week, went to a bawdy-house not above once in a quarter—of an hour—paid money that I borrowed, three or four times. . . .

The secret of Falstaff's appeal is that in his laughter he defies all of official society. He declares war on all conventions, and he gleefully capsizes the moral concepts of the time. He is an outlet for all the resentments people have felt against social strictures (and who in class society has not felt them at times?). It is safe to laugh with him because it is all comic pretense, a dream of a kind of freedom impossible in real life. And at the same time, in the frankness and unconventionality, he becomes a test for the honesty of those who live by conventions. There is nothing, for example, admirable about his frank contempt for all forms of honor except his frankness. But how it does expose those who pretend to live by honor yet compromise with it! He is a knight who in his decline has become a kind of 16th century anarchist.

The marvel of the play is the balance Shakespeare achieves between the Falstaffian laughter and the serious business without allowing one to overwhelm the other. The reason is that Falstaff, with all his ebullient wit, is as real as any of the serious characters, as real as Hotspur. And so, with all the comedy of the Falstaff scenes, in the alternation between these scenes and those of the noblemen's plots against Henry IV, there is the presentation of two real sides of England—the court and the tavern. Thus it is no shock to find a touch of grim popular reality even in Falstaff's talk at the battle of Shrewsbury, "God keep lead out of me! I need no more weight than mine own bowels. I have led my ragamuffins where they are peppered. There's not three of my hundred and fifty left alive; and they are for the town's end, to beg during life." The voice is Falstaff's, but few, if any, playwrights at that period would have given thought to the tragic fate of common soldiers slaughtered and, if wounded in battle, afterwards forced to beggary.

The sharp contrasts of the two levels of life do not preclude meaningful links between the two—the comic Falstaff scenes serving as a commentary on the serious ones. The play opens with a link of this kind. King Henry laments the "riot and dishonor" of his son Harry; and the next scene opens with the Prince and Falsftaff in a London apartment exchanging a flood of lusty street language. Then there are scenes that alternately show the growing rebellion of the great noblemen—like the Archbishop of York, the Earls of Worcester and Northumberland, and Hotspur, the latter's son—and the trick played by Prince Hal and Poins on Falstaff in getting him to rob some merchants at night, and then robbing Falstaff himself. In the rebellion scenes, it is Hotspur who is filled out as a character, as he is shown in a curt farewell to his wife before he rides off eagerly to meet the other conspirators: "this is no world / to play with mammets and to tilt with lips. / We must have bloody noses and cracked crowns." And Hotspur is also proud before the other conspirators, to the point of contempt for their idiosyncrasies. He is hot for battle. Their bitterness is against the authority that King Henry exerts against them. They see him as no more royal than they, and they put all the blame on him for seizing the crown and then having Richard murdered. They ignore their own share in the rebellion against Richard. It was intended by them as a setback to the independent power of the great nobles, and they plan to divide the country. The Falstaff-Prince Hal scenes are packed with a lusty vitality and reflect an England that cares little for noblemen's pretensions. And another significant link appears between the two contrasting lines of the story. For when the Prince is summoned to the court, he and Falstaff act out a hilarious burlesque of his projected meeting with the King, his father—Falstaff first acting the King and Prince Hal his son, and then the two reversing their parts. Two scenes later comes the real confrontation between the King and Prince Hal.

This scene, the second of Act III, is the turning-point of the play. The King makes clear that his courting of the common people was a way of improving his public image. "I", he says, "dressed myself in such humility / That I did pluck allegiance from men's mouths." He says this while Richard was King. Fulsome in his praise of Hotspur, who opposes him, he calls his own son, "my nearest and dearest enemy." Prince Hal vows to end his "intemperance," and to take up arms against Hotspur. The two are reconciled, and from this point on the play moves towards the battle of Shrewsbury.

Falstaff is as always the rebel—in comic speech. When Prince Hal reports that he and his father are now friends, Falstaff says, "Rob me the exchequer the first thing thou doest, and do it with unwashed hands too." When the Prince says that he has procured for Falstaff "a charge of foot," Falstaff complains, "Where shall I find one that can steal well?" But he takes the commission and turns it, as we have seen, to a profit of his own of some 300 pounds. There is another significant commentary in the Falstaff scenes about the doings on the high level of national politics. Falstaff, on the verge of battle, makes his famous soliloquy, disavowing any allegiance to honor:

> . . . Can honour set to a leg? No. Or an arm? No. Or take away the grief of a wound? No. Honour hath no skill in surgery, then? No. What is honour? A word. What is in that word honour? What is that honour? Air. A trim reckoning! Who hath it? He that died o' Wednesday? Doth he feel it? No. Doth he hear it? No. 'Tis insensible, then? Yea, to the dead. But will it not live with the living? No. Why? Detraction will not suffer it. Therefore, I'll none of it. . . .

And in the very next scene the rebel leaders, who are divided and weakened but are seemingly the soul of honor, commit a truly dishonorable act. They keep from Hotspur the fact that the King has made an offer to be friends if the rebels lay down their arms. They are afraid that the King, for all his professions of friendship, will not forgive them. A "hare-brained Hotspur" might be excused because of his youth, but not they. They tell Hotspur, instead, that the King is unrelenting in his fierceness to them.

And so the battle takes place. The King, always cunning, has other noblemen dress in his clothes, and three of them are killed. When he himself is in mortal danger, Prince Hal saves his life and, in the end, the Prince kills Hotspur. Meanwhile Falstaff saves his own life by simulating death. The Prince speaks an eulogy over what appears to be his dead body:

What, old acquaintance! Could not all this flesh
Keep in a little life? Poor Jack, farewell!
I could have better spared a better man.
O, I should have a heavy miss of thee,
If I were much in love with vanity!
Death hath not struck so far a deer to-day,
Though many dearer, in this bloody fray.

But when he leaves, Falstaff rises, gives the dead body of
Hotspur another wound and carries the body off, claiming that
he has killed Hotspur and asking an earldom or dukedom for his
reward. The Prince says:

For my part, if a lie may do thee grace,
I'll gild it with the happiest terms I have.

Of the captured rebel leaders, the King has some executed and
judiciously spares others. He is always the careful politician. And
the play ends as the army marches off to demolish the other
rebels who were not at Shrewsbury.

The keynote of *King Henry IV, Part One,* is rebellion. The
chronological history it tells is of the revolt of a group of strong
old-line noblemen against Henry IV, exposing the insecurity of
Henry's reign. His rule was bound to be a bloody one, despite his
intentions, because of the brutal way in which he had seized the
crown. The weakness of the rebels, Shakespeare points out, is
their disunity and self-centredness, which is part of their old-line
character. And to some small extent, Henry IV touches on the
new order in his courting of the commons. But Shakespeare has
enlarged the picture with a study of various kinds of rebellion that
raise questions concerning the old order. There is Hotspur, who
is of the old order but rises above it because of his unselfish valor,
almost like that of a shining knight. His limitations, the play
points out, are a lack of imagination, national spirit, and humanity. There is Falstaff, who, with a rousing humor, defies the
conventions of not only his own class but of all society. And there
is Prince Hal, who abandons the court for the rough-and-tumble
of taverns, but knows that he cannot continue to live such a life.
Hotspur is killed as much by his own unreliable allies as by Prince
Hal. Falstaff comes up against harsh reality, although he man-

ages to squirm past its dangers. And Prince Hal becomes a warrior to defend his father.

In *Henry IV, Part Two,* Prince Hal becomes Henry V and cuts his ties with Falstaff; "I know thee not, old man." This has aroused shudders among many critics. Hazlitt wrote: "The truth is that we could never forget the Prince's treatment of Falstaff, though perhaps Shakespeare knew what was best, according to the history, the nature of the times and the man. We speak only as dramatic criticis. . . . Falstaff is the better man of the two."[1] E. E. Chambers writes, "The treatment of Jack Falstaff remains a stain even upon 'the mirror of all Christian kings.'" But Shakespeare is not writing a comic fantasy. He is dealing with people in a real society, and in Part Two more than in Part One, he has to indicate not only that Henry V cannot live according to Falstaff's standards and remain a good king, but also that Falstaff's way of life, for all his lusty humor, has its seamy side in actual life. Falstaff retains his lovable wit, which is his defense against adversity, and if the focus of *Henry IV, Part Two,* more than of Part One, is on Falstaff's combat with official society, this society also has its dishonor. Henry IV's reign is troubled not only by continued revolts of the old-line noblemen but by his own conscience, and his rule is bolstered by brutal deception.

Prince Hal is found in Falstaff's society only in the early part of the play, and even that part suggests a coming cleavage. To make up for the loss of the Prince's company, there are a number of additions to Falstaff's circle, including a page boy given by the Prince to Falstaff, the blustering soldier Pistol, a loose gentlewoman Doll Tearsheet, and a local Justice of the Peace, Shallow.

In his first appearance, Falstaff is berated by the Lord Chief Justice but evades responsibility for his misdeeds, pleading his service at Shrewsbury. But he is approaching sixty, feels his age, has infirmities, and needs money. He says, "A good wit will make use of anything. I will turn diseases to commodity." He beats off a demand by the inn hostess for the money she loaned him, is twitted by Prince Hal, courts Doll Tearsheet, and jokes with lively imagination, but the laughter has an edge of desperation for, from the beginning, he is defending himself against attacks.

Meanwhile the revolt of the noblemen continues against King Henry IV and gains religious support by involving the Archbishop of York. The demand to enlist men for the coming battles devolves upon Falstaff, and there is a fantastic place of comedy at the end of the second act, in which he has to say farewell in the midst of a love scene with Doll Tearsheet and the blubbering inn hostess. It is a sardonic travesty on the parting of a nobleman from his woman before a battle.

The play depicts both Falstaff's war against society and the war of the noblemen against Henry IV, and Act Three dramatizes these contrasting themes. In one, the King is afflicted by conscience and cannot sleep. He recalls the prophecy of the deposed King Richard that war would be unleashed upon the land. Those who were false to Richard would also be false to his successor. In the other, Falstaff, with Shallow and his servants, is pressing men into arms. It is a great comic scene, in which two very healthy men bribe themselves out of service, and which ends with a soliloquy by Falstaff on Justice Shallow's pretensions to friendship with the nobility. The scene is bitter comedy, for within it lies the cruel truth about how the peasantry were pressed into wars that concerned their masters but not the peasants themselves. There can be no doubt that Shakespeare meant to convey this reality, for in the next play, *Henry V*, he was to write the deeply moving speech of a villager on what it means to be torn away from home to die in battle.

The play turns on the end of the revolt, the death of Henry IV and the ascension of Prince Hal to the throne. The Earl of Westmoreland and Prince John of Lancaster, acting for the King, meet the leaders of the rebels and tell them of their willingness to redress their list of grievances, if they will lay down their arms. Then when the rebel troops are disbanded, with great joy among them, Westmoreland and Lancaster arrest the rebel noblemen for execution as traitors. The King's agents have cunningly kept their troops intact. Under the shadow of this monstrous duplicity, Falstaff performs his own little duplicity, claiming a dashing victory over a rebel nobleman who has merely looked for someone to whom to surrender. And then he speaks a paean to the virtues of drink.

The coming of peace finds the King tormented, unhappy and on the edge of death. He is still wildly suspicious of those close to him, and when Prince Hal, mistaking the quietness of his father's sleep for death, takes away the crown, the King wakes to accuse him of being a ruffian. But the two are then reconciled, and the King confesses to him of the "bypaths and indirect crook'd ways" by which he got the crown. He tells Hal when he becomes King, "to busy giddy minds / With foreign quarrels" and so get the past to be forgotten. He then dies.

Hal, as Henry V, meets a group of noblemen, including his brothers and the Lord Chief Justice, all afraid that his reign will be madcap and vindictive. But he promises them love, even for the Lord Chief Justice who once committed him to jail. And around this scene there are two great Falstaff scenes. In one he laughs at the silly Justice Shallow, promising to entertain Prince Hal with stories about him. But, as we later learn, he also borrows a thousand pounds from Shallow, on the basis of his status with the Prince. And in the second scene, when the news comes that the Prince is now King, his joy is unbounded:

> Saddle my horses, Master Robert Shallow, choose what office thou wilt in the land, 'tis thine. . . . Master Shallow, my Lord Shallow,—be what thou wilt: I am fortune's steward! Get on thy boots: we'll ride all night. . . . I know the young King is sick for me. Let us take any man's horses: the laws of England are at my commandment. Blessed are they that have been my friends; and woe to my Lord Chief Justice!

In London, the inn hostess and Doll Tearsheet are being dragged off to prison, but are confident that Falstaff will free them. And Falstaff awaits the King's procession, confident that he will be a new power behind the throne. It is at this point that the King comes and says, "I know thee not, old man." He warns Falstaff never to come near him. He then tempers his harshness: "For competence of life I will allow you, / That lack of means enforce you not to evils." But Falstaff is still in the hands of the Lord Chief Justice.

There is logic to Falstaff's discomfiture. For him to have become a power behind the throne, or to have had any influence in the running of the state, would have made the country a shambles. Yet nobody feels happy at it. This is the dilemma of the play. For Shakespeare, as a responsible historian and thinker, cannot permit the state to become a shambles. Yet, in creating Falstaff, he let loose a great peal of laughter at it.

Henry V closes the tetralogy. Each of the four plays is an entity in its own right, yet there is an all-over higher unity in that they move in succession from the presentation of a King who thinks he is one of the elite of God and feels no responsibility whatsoever to the nation, to a King who feels he could be mistaken for a farmer and recognizes a sense of responsibility to the nation and common people.

The thought that Henry V might be taken for a farmer is not in Holinshed's *Chronicles* but is Shakespeare's own, expressed in an earnest but comically worded speech made by Henry when courting Katherine, Princess of France. And this is an indication of the "democratic" tendencies of the play. For the events dealing with the nobility, the reasons for the war with France, the war itself, and the battle of Agincourt—all come from Holinshed. And they are recreated by Shakespeare in grand and splendid blank verse, including, as in no other play, five Prologues or Choruses, one to each act. Together with speeches in the same narrative or descriptive historical vein, these choruses indicate how sumptuous and great an epic-historical poem Shakespeare might have written, had he been so minded. But his intention was quite different. He invents comical elements, mostly in prose, not simply to lighten the tone but to deal with the common man. And with this the play takes on a quite different and broader political attitude than that of the official histories of the time. It is Shakespeare's own politics; a concept of the nation as resting on the common people, with a ruler who recognizes this.

The first act and practically all of the second act of *Henry V* are in an epic-historical vein, leaning on Holinshed. They tell of a bill suggested by the Commons to deprive the Church of donated lands and use the money to support among other things a hundred almshouses. The Archbishop of Canterbury and Bishop of Ely plot against the bill and offer to support an expedition by Henry to France. We learn something of the devious reasoning aimed to show Henry to be a legitimate inheritor of French lands, and also of his willingness to take on a war if the Bishops give him just reasons. We learn as well an insulting message from the Dauphin of France. Embarking at Southampton, Henry discovers a plot against his life by two noblemen and a knight in the pay of France, and has the traitors executed. There also are some scenes of the Falstaff community, without Falstaff. The characters are Bardolph and Pistol from the earlier plays, the inn hostess, whom Pistol has now married, and a Corporal Nym. The news comes of Falstaff's death, heartbroken at his repudiation by Henry V. With all the lusty language of these scenes, their effect is of bitter comedy. For the three men are windbags and thieves, particularly loathsome when they are parasites on others who are risking their lives. In going off to the war, Pistol cries: "For I shall sutler be / Unto the camp, and profits will accrue." Later he says, "Let us to France, like horse-leeches, my boys, / To suck, to suck, the very blood to suck!" In France, as it later turns out, Bardolph and Nym are hung as thieves, and Pistol is cudgelled.

There are early exploits of the English in France, and then for the latter part of Act Three and all of Act Four, the play expands on the battle of Agincourt and takes on a new dimension. For Shakespeare's purpose is not to recount the course of the battle in any detail, but to develop the differences between the French and English armies, which he shows as the difference between two stages of history.

The French (Shakespeare shows them as aristocrats of the old order) are concerned with their horses and armor and coming exploits on the field, contemptuous not only of the English whom they vastly outnumber, but of their own common soldiers "and our superfluous lackeys and our peasants." After their defeat, the French envoy asks the English King for permission to examine the dead and bury the noblemen among them:

> For many of the princes—woe the while!—
> Are drowned and soaked in mercenary blood;
> So do our vulgar drench their peasant limbs
> In blood of princes.

Among the English, Shakespeare's accent is on the common soldiers and Henry's closeness to them, as well as on relaxing the chauvinistic antagonisms that arise among the Welsh, Irish and Scots. Of Henry, the Chorus preceding Act Four says:

For forth he goes and visits all his host,
Bids them good morrow with a modest smile,
And calls them brothers, friends and countrymen.

And the play shows him doing this. The Chorus appears to appologize for what the audience will see. Yet there is a hint that by listening to the "mockeries," it might be helped to learn some truths:

Behold, as may unworthiness define,
A little touch of Harry in the night.
And so our scene must to the battle fly;
Where—O for pity!—we shall much disgrace
With four or five most vile and ragged foils,
Right ill-disposed in brawl ridiculous,
The name of Agincourt. Yet sit and see,
Minding true things by what their mock'ries be.

What follows is perhaps the most extraordinary scene in the entire play. Shakespeare cannot use the "Falstaff company" for the purpose of displaying the common soldier, since, on the eve of battle, their thievery is especially despicable. And so he invents others who come on the stage. Henry asks to be left alone in the night and makes himself unrecognizable as the King. The braggart Pistol enters, defames Welshmen, and then leaves. A Captain Fluellen appears, who speaks in windy fashion in a Welsh dialect and walks off, while Henry says, "There is much care and valour in this Welshman." Then three ordinary soldiers appear, of whom two, John Bates and Michael Williams, speak at length. They tell of the King who has led them to these dire straits, and Henry tells them, "I think the King is but a man, as I am . . . . all his senses have but human conditions. His ceremonies laid by, in his nakedness he appears but a man; and though his affections are higher mounted than ours, yet, when they stoop, they stoop with the like wing." It is a distinct contrast to the grandiosity felt by Richard II. Bates wishes he were back in London, even in the Thames with the water up to his neck. As for leaving the King, Bates says, "Then I would he were here alone; so should he be sure to be ransomed, and many a poor men's lives saved." Henry explains that the King's cause is just and his quarrel honorable. But Williams is doubtful, and says:

> But if the cause be not good, then the King himself hath a heavy reckoning to make when all those legs and arms and heads, chopped off in a battle, shall join together at the latter day and cry all 'We died at such a place'; some swearing, some crying for a surgeon, some upon their wives left poor behind them, some upon the debts they owe, some upon their children rawly left. I am afeard that few die well that die in a battle, for how can they charitably dispose of anything when blood is their argument? Now, if these men do not die well, it will be a black matter for the King that led them to it, who to disobey were against all proportion of subjection.

The reference is to the Day of Judgment, when souls will rise and reclothe themselves in their bodies. The King answers, but evades the fundamental issue. He takes the words "not die well" in battle to mean doing some sinful thing, and says that each man's sins are on his own conscience. But the incisive picture remains, as sharp and realistic as a Goya etching in *The Disasters of the War* (done more than two centuries later) of the suffering and neglected peasants dying in battle. The listener is forced to recognize that they too are human beings who have wives, children and money troubles, and suffer pain.

The unrecognizable King becomes nettled as Williams expressed doubt of the King's honesty in saying he would not be ransomed, and game-cock Williams turns it into a quarrel. They exchange gloves and promise to meet after the battle, if they are still alive. And after the battle, King Henry pretends anger at Williams but fills his glove with gold coins.

There are scenes involving the Welsh Captain Fluellen, the Irishman Captain Macmorris, and the Scottish Captain Jamy, in which Shakespeare insists that they do not laugh at each other's idiosyncracies but make peace among themselves, as valiant people in a common cause. And the battle of Agincourt is portrayed, with Henry's glorious victory against almost impossible odds. During its course, Henry, angry that the French seem to have rallied, gives orders for his men to kill their French prisoners, and the French plunder the English pile of luggage, killing the boys set to guard it. The emphasis is on the brutality of war, and Henry's appreciation of the fellowship of his men. He says:

> But we in it shall be remembered,
> We few, we happy few, we band of brothers;
> For he today that sheds his blood with me
> Shall be my brother; be he ne'er so vile,
> This day shall gentle his condition. . . .

Pistol is cudgelled for his cowardice by Fluellen. He goes off vowing to continue his thievery in England and to claim that his cudgel wounds are battle scars.

Shakespeare does not dramatize King Henry's rousing welcome when he returns to London, but covers it in the Chorus preceding Act Five. The play ends with Henry's courtship of the French Princess Katherine. He has no pretty ways with words. From his way of speaking, he tells her, "thou wouldst find me such a plain king that thou wouldst think I had sold my farm to buy a crown." He cannot dance elegantly, spin poetry, or play music, but he is strong, he says, can ride a horse well and win battles; "take me, take a soldier; take a soldier, take a king."

So Shakespeare has begun his tetralogy with a portrait of a King who is wrapped up in himself, regards himself as one of God's elite and is crushed by reality or "necessity" and has ended with a portrait of a King who welcomes this "necessity" and grows with it. He has spent his young manhood in the taverns, and while he later renounces them, he sees himself as companion to the common soldier while having preoccupations that they cannot share. Yet the play makes the commoners in the audience share in these preoccupations.

This portrait of a people's King is forced upon the chronicle of history. Yet that is what makes it Shakespeare's play. By not feeling bound, he has opened up a new facet of history which only our own age is beginning to explore—the place and activity of the common people. They are not, to Shakespeare, a conscious political force. But they are a presence that must be recognized. And his genius is that if he has risen above them, in that he is educated and a skilled servant of the aristocracy, he can still see with the people's eyes and give voice to the questions in their minds.

Shakespeare was not a political democrat; his political demands could be satisfied only by modern communism. The term democracy has changed in meaning with the changes of society. The ancient Greeks who gave the term circulation were slave-owners, and their democracy meant the right of the freeborn people of a city, not the slaves, to choose their leaders. In Shakespeare's England, the burden of productive labor rested on the backs of the peasantry and the village and city "mechanics." The thought that this largely unlettered mass could be entrusted with the responsibilities of government was unthinkable to him. But neither did he think the old-line nobility were fit to run the state. The nearest to a democratic political movement in his England was that of the Puritan tradesman class, whose democracy consisted of the conviction that people with commercial property or money should share governmental responsibilities with the landed families. Shakespeare felt aversion to this class, which he regarded as inhumanly money-driven. What remained to him was the king or individual ruler, seemingly independent of class. But consistently in his plays he demands of these rulers that they pay attention to the common people's life, needs and welfare, as not only a humane act but as an imperative precept for rule.

The English history plays of the late 1590's open up Shakespeare's greatest period. And in the tragedies and comedies he will write between 1599 and 1606 he will explore in all the ramifications possible the political issues he raises.

6

THE TRAGIC AND COMIC JESTER

Julius Caesar
Hamlet
As You Like It

JULIUS CAESAR and *Hamlet* were probably written close to one another, *Julius Caesar* in about 1599–1600, and *Hamlet* in about 1600–1601. One is a tragedy of almost crystalline clarity, and the other is Shakespearean tragedy at its most complex. Yet both follow the basic pattern of tragedy which Shakespeare had worked out in *Romeo and Juliet*. Taking full advantage of the Elizabethan open stage, he builds the play through a series of contrasting scenes that weave a broad social fabric. There is a central point to which the previous scenes lead and, surprisingly, this is also the turning point of the drama. From this point on the social forces assert themselves strongly, and it is against these that the main protagonists reveal their full psychological depth, while the play is being carried to its conclusion. Every step in the drama is guided by Shakespeare's thinking, in which political considerations play a foremost role.

In *Julius Caesar* it is English, not Roman, politics, and its social-psychological patterns that Shakespeare draws upon. This does not mean that he intends that the play be a masquerade with

English personages hiding under Roman costumes. It means simply that English politics is what he knows and it provides him with the social material that will bring the events to life. Thus, the assassination of a Roman emperor, with its reasons and consequences, becomes his commentary on the issues in England. It is likely that he thought politics in Rome were much the same as those of England in his time. For his story and many of its details, he follows *Plutarch's Lives* of Caesar, Antony and Brutus, but he is not primarily interested in providing a chronicle of Roman affairs. He simplifies Plutarch and speeds up the time scheme. In this respect he differs from Ben Jonson, who filled the published version of his Roman play *Sejanus* (written about 1603) with footnotes referring to Tacitus, Suetonius and other Roman historians, in order to establish his play as authentic history. But Jonson raises no political questions and shows no awareness of historical conflicting forces. And these are precisely what concern Shakespeare.

The first scene of the play begins to create the social fabric. The mechanics and artisans of Rome have called a holiday to attend the festive ceremonies for the victorious general Julius Caesar. Two tribunes, Marullus and Flavius, depicted as officials who despise the commoners, berate them: "You blocks, you stones, you worse than senseless things!" The tribunes send the mechanics home to assemble with "all the poor men of your sort" and weep at Caesar's victory over Pompey. And the tribunes go on to tear the decorations that honor Caesar from the images in the city. We learn in the next scene that they are "put to silence" for this.

Within this framework, Scene Two presents the principal personages. Caesar appears with his devoted following, including Mark Antony, and reveals his suspicions and fears along with his determination to show himself to the public as a fearless man. For the main part of the scene, Brutus and Cassius are alone. It is a wonderfully written scene, with a density of psychological change so that the audience feels these few minutes as a much longer time. Cassius tries to probe Brutus's feelings about Caesar and to win him to lead a conspiracy against Caesar's life. A key word in the scene, and indeed of the entire play, is "honour," as when Cassius says, "Honour is the subject of my story." It becomes clear that the two men are patricians or noblemen of Rome. Cassius's honor is of a special, narrow kind. He is an old-line nobleman, proud of his name and military prowess, and will have no man above him. Fiercely he resents Caesar, who:

> doth bestride the narrow world
> Like a Colossus, and so we petty men
> Walk under his huge legs and peep about
> To find ourselves dishonourable graves.

But to preserve this personal honor, he must be crafty with others. Thus he must win Brutus to the conspiracy, for Brutus has the image of a truly unselfish public image and his participation will give the killing of Caesar the appearance of a public duty. Cassius says in his soliloquy at the end of the scene:

> Well, Brutus, thou art noble; yet, I see,
> Thy honourable metal may be wrought
> From that it is disposed. . . .
> If I were Brutus and he were Cassius,
> He should not humour me.

Brutus combines Cassius's kind of honor with an absolute public honesty that Cassius lacks. He is devoted to the "general good," and it is for this reason that he is troubled about the possibility of Caesar's making himself a king. He doesn't want to reveal his inner debate until he settles it. Yet he is shaken by Cassius's thoughts. A friend of theirs appears, Casca, who comes from the ceremonies. He speaks with a typical old-line nobleman's disdain for the common people:

> The rabblement hooted and clapped their chopped hands and threw up their sweaty nightcaps and uttered such a deal of stinking breath because Caesar refused the crown, that it had almost choked Caesar, for he swounded and fell down at it. . . . I durst not laugh, for fear of opening my lips and receiving the bad air.

Casca will join the conspiracy against Caesar, and it becomes clear that his conspiracy is neither a matter of private spite by Cassius nor a struggle for democratic liberties by the downtrodden against a tyrant. It is a struggle of noblemen against one of their own class who would court the commons and make himself a king, depriving other members of the nobility of their independence. Shakespeare could not be expected to have fathomed the intricacies of the actual Roman republic in Caesar's time. It had become a mighty slaveholding power, dominating with its military strength all the lands about the Mediterranean and extorting fabulous wealth as tribute. This wealth went to the great landowners, politicians and generals, and could also be used to calm the common people of the city with bread and circuses. The government of the elected consuls and the nobleman-senators was a shell within which the struggles for power were going on. Rome was endangered by its own armies, which were loyal mainly to their own generals and the spoils they won in battle. Shakespeare relates the situation to the pattern of the struggle of the great noblemen in England against a powerful monarch. In *Julius Caesar,* as in the English histories, he rests the success of the political leaders on their ability to command the affections of the common people. So Cassius needs Brutus, for at least Brutus holds the confidence of the common people, and the great second scene of Act I ends with his planning to make his appeal to Brutus so that the plot may appear to have public following. He plans to have little anonymous notes "in several hands" thrown into Brutus's window, "all tending to the great opinion / That Rome holds of his name, wherein obscurely / Caesar's ambition shall be glanced at."

There are touches of the supernatural; signs, omens, a terrible storm, apparitions, warning dreams, a soothsayer who tells Caesar to "Beware the Ides of March"—all of which Shakespeare takes from Plutarch but he does not allow them to influence the action fundamentally. The emphasis is now on Brutus, who is further humanized with a show of his tender relations with his servant Lucius, his close relationship with his wife Portia. He engages in a monologue of internal conflict, or "insurrection," as he calls it, in which he determines that Caesar must be killed not for anything he has done but for what he is capable of doing. As Brutus joins the conspiracy he also takes leadership of it, which brings his personality into conflict with that of Cassius. He meets the conspirators and is annoyed at their muffled faces. A secret conspiracy is not to his liking, "Sham'st thou to show thy dang'rous brow by night, / When evils are most free?" He rejects the demand of Cassius that they all swear an oath. Are they not all honest men? "What need we any spur but our own cause / To prick us to redress?" He then rejects Cassius's suggestion that they also kill Mark Antony. This has been cited by many commentators as the "blunder" made by Brutus, the impractical idealist, but such is not altogether the case. It is a matter of the principles on which he joined the conspiracy. He says:

> Our cause will seem too bloody, Caius Cassius . . .
> Let us be sacrificers, but not butchers, Caius. . . .
> Let's carve him as a dish fit for the gods,
> Not hew him as a carcass fit for hounds. . . .
>   This shall make
> Our purpose necessary and not envious;
> Which so appearing to the common eyes,
> We shall be called purgers, not murderers,

The people, to him, must feel liberated, not intimidated. Again the thought of the public is in his mind, the "common eyes." And if his decision not to kill Antony turns out unfortunately, it is because the conspiracy itself was not truly principled and for the common welfare.

The next scene shows Caesar being affably taken to his appointment with the senate by the conspirators, and also reveals further the elements in his personality that Shakespeare wants to emphasize—his fears and suspicions and, on the other hand, his desire to show the public his unshakeable firmness.

Caesar is killed in the first scene of Act III, but this is not yet the central climax and turning point of Shakespeare's play. Skillfully he keeps up the tension after the killing, devoting the latter half of the scene to the confrontation of the conspirators by Mark Antony and to the development of Antony in depth. There is no conflict in Antony's passionate devotion to Caesar, now dead. The assassins to him are simply "butchers." He is afraid they will kill him, too. But he is also a crafty politician, seeking power. And so he is humble before the conspirators, not hiding his affection for the dead man but offering his friendship to the killers and asking to be allowed to speak some funeral words in the Forum, over the body. Again Brutus makes what is called a "blunder." He agrees to this, despite Cassius's warning. But this agreement follows the principles by which Brutus joined the conspiracy. Everything they do must appear to be fair. Caesar must have "all true rites and ceremonies." He, Brutus, will speak first, giving the reason for the killing. Antony must explain that he speaks by their permission and must promise not to blame them. In a soliloquy, Antony prophesizes civil war and destruction. Caesar's spirit will "cry 'Havoc,' and let slip the dogs of war."

The turning point of the play is the next scene, the second of Act III, which takes place in the Forum. It opens, as does the first scene, with the plebeians. They demand of Brutus an explanation of the murder, and he gives his logically worded and dispassionate answer. But it rests mainly on his esteem for himself, which he is certain the people share. He, Brutus, is a man of "honour." He loved Caesar, but he loved Rome more. Caesar was "ambitious." Brutus has rescued the Romans from being turned into "slaves," a slavery which in fact they had not felt. Whoever is offended by his act must be one "so vile that will not love his country." He introduced Antony who has entered with Caesar's body, and departs.

Brutus, for all his genuine honor, remains the nobleman-patrician. He has no awareness that in a land where there has been bitterness between rich and poor—Shakespeare has shown this—"love of country" means something different to each side. When Antony speaks, he is well aware of this, and his speech is a masterpiece of demagogy, while given warmth by his genuine affection for Caesar. He plays on two motifs: the claim that Caesar was "ambitious," and the claim of the conspirators that they are "honorable men. He appears to keep to the letter of his agreement and to praise the killers. "For Brutus is an honourable man; / So are they all, all honourable men." But the word "honourable"—a key word of the play—takes on an increasing tone of sarcasm in its repetition in his context. He craftily gears the speech to the poor. Caesar has taken many captives, and their ransoms filled the "general coffers." Caesar loved the poor. "When the poor have cried, Caesar hath wept: / Ambition should be made of sterner stuff." Amid this, his incessant harping on the claim of the killers that they are "honourable men" has, as he intends, precisely the opposite effect on his listeners. When he says, "if I were disposed to stir / your hearts to mutiny and rage, / I should do Brutus wrong and Cassius wrong," he is precisely inspiring them to mutiny and rage, making them think this is their own independent thought.

At this point, Antony mentions Caesar's will and claims he must not read it, for if he did, "they would go and kiss dead Caesar's wounds." This, of course, is better than reading it. And when the crowd demands that he read it, and he says, "I fear I wrong the honourable men / whose daggers have stabbed Caesar," the cry comes that they were "traitors," and then that they were "villains, murderers." He still doesn't read the will, but having put in their mind the thought of a wonderful legacy to the common people, he swells on the piteous spectacle of the dead body of the mighty Caesar, stabbed by those he thought were his best friends and, for the first time, he uses the word "traitors." The crowd is now ready to tear the conspirators apart. Antony pretends to try to calm them. Undoubtedly, he says, the conspirators had some private "griefs" against Caesar and can explain them reasonably. He, Antony, is only a "plain, blunt man." Brutus is an orator; he, Antony, isn't. If he only had the powers of Brutus, he would stir up even "the stones of Rome to rise and mutiny." He then reads part of the will, claiming that Caesar left to each Roman citizen 75 drachmas and left his land in Rome to be used by the citizens for public walks.

At this point the crowd runs off to burn the houses of the conspirators, and Antony, alone, says, with satisfaction, "Now let it work. Mischief, thou art afoot." A servant enters, telling Antony that Octavius, Caesar's heir, has come to Rome, and that Brutus and Cassius have ridden "like madmen" out of Rome. Antony says, "Belike they had some notice of the people, / How I had moved them." In Plutarch nothing so dramatic happens. But Shakespeare has combined clues taken from Plutarch and created magnificent theater that simultaneously captures the essence of the situation as he saw it—the poverty of the people. And from this point on, Plutarch is considerably simplified and the play is freed to focus on Brutus and Cassius in adversity.

That the people are a force in history does not mean that their leaders are necessarily honest. Here they have been incited by a demagogue. There is a short scene showing the unreasonableness of a crowd on a rampage. Cinna, the poet, who has had nothing to do with the events, is torn to pieces, because his name is like that of one of the conspirators. But the scene immediately following, the first Act IV, shows the far greater, colder and more calculating cruelty of the gentry. Antony, Octavius, and the wealthy general Lepidus are making a list of eminent Romans they plan to kill in order to consolidate their grip on Rome. Their victims will number 70 to 100 people, as we are later told. And Antony is planning to get rid of Lepidus when he is no longer useful. They also reduce the legacies in Caesar's will.

From this point on, the emphasis of the play is on the truly honorable man Brutus, who no longer has the people behind him. He appears to make a further series of blunders, but these are blunders only to a man who aims to be practical at all costs. To Brutus they are matters of principle; he must stand by principle, else why did he kill Caesar? He has a bitter quarrel with Cassius, who has an "itching palm" and also supports a follower who takes bribes. Brutus cries, "Did not great Julius bleed for justice' sake?" He has asked Cassius for money and is denied. "By heaven, I had rather coin my heart, / And drop my blood for drachmas, than to wring / From the hard hands of peasants their vile trash." The fiery Cassius will not be reproved, and they are at the point of a total break when Brutus relents; "Sheathe your dagger . . . . a dishonour shall be humour." He has spoken, he adds, out of "ill-temper." He also has had many griefs. Portia has killed herself.

Another situation arises. Octavius and Antony have landed with their troops at Philippi. The crafty Cassius wants to remain at Sardis and let the enemy waste himself looking for them. Brutus insists on marching to Philippi. His reasons sound mostly philosophical:

> There is a tide in the affairs of men
> Which, taken at the flood, leads on to fortune;
> Omitted, all the voyage of their life
> Is bound in shallows and in miseries.

But what this means is that a drawn-out life of crafty maneu-
vering is not for him. Let one battle decide the issue. The killing
of Caesar preys on his mind. Then, at night, Caesar's ghost
appears to Brutus, telling him it is "thy evil spirit." When it
vanishes, Brutus says, "I would hold more talk with thee."

The battle is fought. Cassius, mistaking its course, is in despair
and kills himself. Brutus, fighting on alone, is defeated, and kills
himself. When about to die, he says:

> I shall have glory by this losing day,
> More than Octavius and Mark Antony
> By this vile conquest shall attain unto.

Antony speaks over Brutus's dead body:

> This was the noblest Roman of them all.
> All the conspirators, save only he,
> Did what they did in envy of great Caesar.
> He, only, in a general honest thought
> And common good to all, made one of them.

Brutus is honorable in defeat. But it was a wrong cause, for
Shakespeare shows that he mistook the thinking of the poor and
hungry to be the same as that of his own class. They wanted a
strong monarch to protect them against the patricians, who
despised them.

In *Hamlet,* the people are also a political factor. There are
references to Julius Caesar in the play. Horatio remarks in the
first act that ghosts did walk the streets "a little ere the mightiest
Julius fell." Polonius, in Act II, recalls that in his youth, "I did
enact Julius Caesar. I was killed i' the Capital. Brutus killed me."
Hamlet, standing over Ophelia's grave, philosophizes, "Imperious Caesar, dead and turned to clay, / Might stop a hole to keep
the wind away." Whether or not there references indicate that
Shakespeare had in mind the earlier play, in *Hamlet* he does
carry further a central theme of *Julius Caesar*—that of a philoso-
pher-hero who feels morally compelled to kill a ruler. Both
Brutus and Hamlet are philosophers who are concerned with the
values of life in the face of death, disdaining the pomp and drives
for power that move other men, and possessed of a high social

morality. They are well liked by the common people; and an important element in both plays is how the killing will be accepted by the common people.

In *Hamlet,* the political situation is somewhat different from that in *Julius Caesar,* and the working out of the drama is far more complex. Brutus is one of a band of conspirators who find no obstacles to the physical killing of Caesar. What follows, however, is that the people turn away from them, and Brutus is haunted to the end of the play about whether the killing of Caesar was morally justified. Hamlet, on the other hand, is alone. He early resolves any doubts he has had about the villainy of King Claudius, who, unlike Caesar, is an actual villain. But Hamlet finds that killing the King, especially in a way that would appear to be morally justified, is a difficult task.

And *Hamlet* is on a far higher level than *Julius Caesar* in its psychological complexity. Mark Antony says of Brutus at the end, "His life was gentle, and the elements / so mixed in him that Nature might stand up / And say to all the world 'This was a man!'" *Hamlet* has many personages in whom the elements are so mixed, that not only are they prey to inner conflicts but they must hide what disturbs them and show a different face to the world. Ophelia is in conflict between her love for Hamlet and her devotion to her family, who insist she must not show her love. The conflict ends in her madness and death. King Claudius has secretly murdered his brother and married his widow to gain the throne and must show a noble face to the public while he remains terrified at the thought that his secret life may become known. The Queen is torn between the sensual life she is living with her second husband and her guilt over her unfaithfulness, with which her son so cruelly taunts her. Rosencrantz and Guildenstern must enact the part of friends of Hamlet while attempting to spy on his secret thoughts. Polonius enacts the role of a spy and is killed in the act of espionage. And, more complex than any of them, there is Hamlet, who is truly gentle and not only forced by his conscience to engage in a public life, which he detests, but even to the killing of a king. He is also impelled, as part of his strategy, to enact the role of one who has gone mad.

In this role Shakespeare has performed the remarkable feat of not only indicating that Hamlet is a philosopher but of having him think and talk as if he were. All this is recreated in language of the utmost richness, splendor and variety—exalted poetry that expresses the most subtle play of interior thought, and prose that is at times scarcely less beautiful and witty.

The fact that so many personages in the play must, as Shakespeare writes it, act a part to disguise their interior life, is repeated on a different level by the presence in the play of a troupe of actors who have come to entertain the court; and along with this diversion there was intensive discussion of the role of dramatic art, not only in representing outer reality but also in penetrating its depths. This is no simple or abstract interpolation, but an integral part of the drama. For a central element in Hamlet's attempt to find out the truth of whether the King killed his father is the purpose of this play within the play, and it is acted according to his special directions.

Thus *Hamlet* is a extraordinary drama, in which the personages on the stage enacted by actors are themselves people acting a part. And woven into this picture, combining real life with the false face characters must show to the world, is Shakespeare's own statement of the aethetics of dramaturgy, stressing its relation to both real life and outer appearances.

Out of this rich fabric, one element has unfortunately been selected for stress and distortion by critical commentary. It is Hamlet's delay in killing King Claudius, after the ghost of his father has told him how Claudius murdered him. This delayed action is made into a personal trait of character instead of one called for by social morality, and it causes critics to identify more closely with Hamlet than with any other Shakespeare character. They read into his character their own outlook.

Thus Goethe wrote in Part I, Book IV, Chapter 13, of *Wilhelm Meister:*

> Shakespeare wished to describe the effects of a great action laid upon a soul which was unequal to it. In this sense I find the play to have been thoroughly worked out. Here it is an oak tree planted in a costly vase which should only have born pleasing flowers in its bosom, but the roots expand and the vase is shattered.

Coleridge is harsher:

> The Ghost of the murdered father is introduced, to assure the
> son that he was put to death by his own brother. What is the effect
> upon the son?—instant action and pursuit of revenge? No: endless
> reasoning and hesitating—constant urging and solicitation of the
> mind to act, and as constant an escape from action; ceaseless
> reproaches of himself for sloth and negligence, while the whole
> energy of his resolution evaporates in these reproaches. This, too,
> not from cowardice, for he is drawn as one of the bravest of his
> time—not from want of forethought or slowness of apprehension,
> for he sees through the souls of all who surround him, but merely
> from an aversion to action, which prevails among such as have a
> world to themselves.[1]

There may be some self-projection in these images of Hamlet.
Engels wrote of Goethe:

> Thus Goethe is now colossal, now petty; now a defiant, ironical,
> world-scorning genius, now a calculated, complacent, narrow
> philistine . . . . at the time when Napoleon was cleaning out the
> vast Augean stables of Germany, he could manage with a cer-
> emonial seriousness the most trivial affairs and minute details of
> one of the most trivial little German courts.[2]

As for Coleridge, who abandoned the politically radical sentiments of his youth to become a conservative he is thus described
by Southey in a letter to Wordsworth:

> His mind is in a perpetual St. Vitus dance—eternal activity
> without action. At times he feels mortified that he should have
> done so little, but this feeling never produces any exertion. 'I will
> begin tomorrow,' he says.

Such judgments as Goethe's and Coleridge's, with all their
sensitivity, ignore the social context that was very real to Shakespeare and his audience.

For the act about which Hamlet is accused of being so dilatory
is an awesome one to anyone who was living in an age of kings. It
is that of killing a king and taking over the kingship. This, as
Shakespeare has shown in his English histories and in the slaying
of Julius Caesar, not quite a king, sends shock and disruption

through the country. And this is also said in *Hamlet,* in Act III, Scene 3, Rosencrantz speaks to the king of "majesty." The phrasing is that of a sycophant, but the thought, freed from rhetoric, has general truth:

> O, 'tis a massy wheel
> Fixed on the summit of the highest mount,
> To whose huge spokes ten thousand lesser things
> Are mortised and adjoined; which, when it falls,
> Each small annexment, petty consequence,
> Attends the boist'rous ruin. Never alone
> Did the king sigh, but with a general groan.

What is Hamlet, a man proud of his integrity, to say to the councilors, let alone the public, when he kills the King and prepares to ascend the throne? That the ghost of his father had said that he had been poisoned by his brother, who is now King? Hamlet himself thinks that the ghost might have been an apparition of the devil.

What takes place from the outset is a veiled duel between two antagonists. On one side is the murderous King, who has all the power and machinery of the state behind him, but must appear to be a just monarch. On the other side is Hamlet, who is alone but is liked by the people. Each must maneuver. The King uses espionage, at which not only he but also his councilor Polonius is adept, to try to pry into Hamlet's mind.

Hamlet defends himself by pretending madness. Then he uses the device of a play within the play—the weapon of art, with its ability to cut beneath surface appearances. It may shake the King so that his guilt becomes manifest to the court. So the weapons are prepared; set in motion; and then complications occur that have not been foreseen.

Again the motifs of the first part of the play concern the inner reality of people in contrast to their appearances, involving the use of subterfuge, espionage, and art.

The first scene with its sentinels watching all night outside the castle at Elsinore with Horatio, whom they have called upon to speak to the ghost of the dead king if it comes again, evokes a feeling of general unrest. The ghost appears and is recognized by

Horatio, but does not speak. The atmosphere is beautifully created from Francisco's "'tis bitter cold, / And I am sick at heart, to Horatio's "But look, the morn in russet mantle clad, / Walks o'er the dew of yon high eastward hill."

With the second scene we are in court. King Claudius, having married the widow of his recently dead brother, acts like a reasonable and capable king. He sends ambassadors to Norway to stop the threatened foray of young Fortinbras, gives leave to Polonius's son Laertes to return to France, then addresses himself kindly to Hamlet, "my cousin Hamlet, and my son." Hamlet's muttered interjection, "A little more than kin, and less than kind," is a shock, with its first sign of enmity. The Queen pleads with Hamlet to leave off mourning for his father, and Hamlet's answering speech is the next sign of a reality hidden under deceptive appearances; "But I have that within which passes show: / These but the trappings and the suits of woe." The King continues his affable speech, asking Hamlet to end his mourning. But there is a hint of an iron hand. He does not want Hamlet to go back to the University at Wittenberg. And there is also the suggestion of espionage, the hint that a watch is being kept on Hamlet. He asks him "to remain / Here in the cheer and comfort of our eye." Hamlet continues his hostility to the King, for only when the Queen adds her pleading does he yield, saying, "I shall in all my best obey you, madam." The King's "Why, 'tis a loving and a fair reply" may be sarcastic, but he appears imperturbable. Hamlet, then left alone, reveals what has shaken him to the depths. A world in which he had happiness has collapsed and has been replaced by an unreliable reality. His father, a most noble King, has suddenly died, and his mother, who had seemed to dote on her husband, has shown so little respect for him or such beastly sensuality as to marry his puny brother. Incestuous longings—and in less than two months! There appears no way out from this unbearable reality but to kill himself, which is prohibited by the Everlasting.

Then Hamlet's mood changes as the sentinels appear, looking for him, and he sees Horatio for the first time. Horatio, a fellow student from Wittenberg to whom he can speak frankly, addresses him as "your poor servant" and Hamlet brushes this aside for "my good friend." Hamlet talks openly about the offensive speed of his mother's marriage. Then Horatio and Marcellus tell him of the ghost that resembles his father; Hamlet sheds his depression and becomes excited. He promises to join them that night. The feeling of a world incomprehensibly running down is changed to a suspicion of foul play which can be unearthed. "Foul deeds will rise, / Though all the world o'erwhelm them, to men's eyes."

A scene follows in Polonius's house where Laertes is saying farewell to his sister Ophelia. A sweet maiden, she is familiar, like most women of the Elizabethan age, with the facts of sexual life. Laertes warns her not to take Hamlet's professions of love seriously, for a prince can take advantage of a young lady. She accepts this good-humoredly and suggests that Laertes also behave himself in Paris. Polonious enters to give Laertes sensible and practical parting advice. Then when his son leaves, Polonius questions his daughter about Hamlet's professions of love and demands that she be cold to his advances. Polonius will later believe that the coldness he forced on Ophelia was the cause of Hamlet's apparent madness. Actually, and ironically, it is the first stage of the conflict between her love for Hamlet and the ties to her family which will later help to unhinge her own mind.

That night the ghost unfolds the bloodcurdling story to Hamlet to how he was killed by Claudius by poison poured into his ear while he was sleeping. Then Claudius did "seduce" or win to his "shameful lust" the will of the queen. The dead King, having been killed with no opportunity to confess his sins, was "cut off even in the blossoms of my sin, / . . . No reck'ning made, but sent to my account / With all my imperfections on my head." This will later prevent Hamlet from killing the King when he finds him praying. As for the Queen, Hamlet must not harm her, "Leave her to heaven, / And to those thorns that in her bosom lodge."

But Hamlet must revenge the murder. Again the theme of appearance and reality comes up. Hamlet exclaims, "That one may smile, and smile, and be a villain." Horatio and the sentry Marcellus burst in on him. He cannot divulge to them what the ghost has told him, for it is a problem he must bear alone. He speaks what one of them calls "wild and whirling words" and demands that they swear never to tell what has happened that night. Already the thought has entered his mind of pretending madness, or assuming an "antic disposition" as a defensive shield while he ponders over the means for revenge. And he makes them promise that when he puts on this antic disposition they must never act as if they knew about it or hint at previous knowledge of it. And as the scene ends, he cries: "The time is out of joint, O cursed spite, / That ever I was born to set it right!" A great burden has been laid on him alone. Significantly, it is not merely the murder of his father but also the age of which this was a part that he must combat.

Supernatural figures, like the ghost that Shakespeare takes over from older stories or plays he reworks, are accepted by him but not in the form of a decisive influence in human affairs. And so while the ghost seems a real one to the playwright, it also is a reflection of the suspicions that already were in Hamlet's mind. He cries, "O my prophetic soul! My uncle!" when the ghost is telling him of the murder. And later he will test the truth of the ghost's story with his experiment of the play within the play.

The first scene of Act II, Polonius sends a servant to spy on his son's behavior in France, giving him expert instructions in how to gather information. Meanwhile Hamlet has been acting strangely, and in the second scene two of Hamlet's old friends, Rosencrantz and Guildenstern, arrive, sent for by the King to penetrate Hamlet's unusual behavior and to draw him out and discover what is in his mind. Polonius then comes in with his own spying scheme. Hamlet has been sending Ophelia love letters, and she, under orders by her father, has rebuffed him. This, says, Polonious has affected Hamlet's mind. And so he decides to let his daughter meet Hamlet, while he and the King watch the meeting from behind a curtain.

By now a troupe of players, whom Hamlet knows from earlier days, has been sent for. Hamlet starts a literary speech (and has the first player finish it) from a purported play based on Virgil's *Aeneid,* in which Aeneas tells Dido of the fall of Troy. Probably written by Shakespeare himself, it satirizes the imitation classical style of the period, with its lofty wordiness and pious comments on the action. But the player so enters into the role that tears are in his eyes.

Hamlet tells Polonius to put the players up well, for "they are the abstract and brief chronicles of the time. After your death you were better have a bad epitaph than their ill report while you live."

Shakespeare is here commenting on the contemporary meaning of drama, even if it is based on ancient subjects. When Hamlet is alone with the first player, he asks if the troupe could enact the next night a play called the *Murder of Gonzago,* with some added "dozen or sixteen lines" that Hamlet would write. The player agrees.

There have been critics who theorize that Hamlet is really mad. So John Dover Wilson writes, "We are driven, therefore, to conclude with Loening, Bradley, Clutton-Brock and other critics that Shakespeare meant us to imagine Hamlet suffering from some kind of mental disorder throughout the play."[4]

Hamlet, however, is not a living person whom Shakespeare is trying to describe but the playwright's own creation. And Shakespeare is very clear about the difference between real madness and assumed madness. He portrays both. Real madness, as he demonstrates with Ophelia, and later with King Lear and Lady Macbeth, cannot be imitated. It springs from a profound psychological conflict in which people are unable to reconcile their cherished beliefs with the realities thrust upon them by a harsh world. In an assumed madness, a person consciously acts the part of someone entirely different from himself. So Edgar in King Lear makes himself appear to have gone mad by imitating a poor beggar, Tom O' Bedlam. Malvolio in *Twelfth Night* appears to be mad because he has been tricked into imitating a kind of courtier entirely unlike his own known personality. And Hamlet makes himself appear to be mentally deranged by assuming an "antic disposition," playing the role of a lowly court clown under whose protective nonsense there are usually acute observations. Shakespeare leaves no doubt about the real madness of Ophelia later in the play. And Hamlet, not being mad, can turn his "antic disposition" on and off at will. So, in this second scene of Act II, he plays the "antic" with Polonius, who observes, "How pregnant sometimes his replies are! A happiness that often madness hits on." But he turns it off when Rosencrantz and Guildenstern appear, for he regards them as old friends. He asks why they have been sent to "prison," for Denmark is a prison. When they tell him that his own ambition makes it so, he answers with the wonderful poetic-philosophical line, "O God, I could be bounded in a nutshell and count myself a king of infinite space, were it not that I have bad dreams." But he has felt their probing and begs them to tell him, in the name of their old friendship, whether they were sent for. Their embarrassment gives them away, and when they confess to having been sent for, he tells them he knows the reason; it is to investigate his sudden turn of mind. He turns antic again with Polonius when he enters and drops it when the players enter, for they, too, are old friends and he needs them. And the scene ends with Hamlet's great and perfectly rational soliloquy, beginning, "Now I am alone."

In this soliloquy Hamlet berates himself for his inaction about his father's murder, while even an actor can work up tears of emotion when declaiming the passions of a fictitious character like Hecuba of Troy. "What's Hecuba to him, or he to Hecuba / That he should weep for her?" Can he, Hamlet, be a coward for wasting his bitterness in a lonely outpouring of words?

But there is a solution in the play that will be acted the next night. It will act out what the ghost told him about the murder. He has heard that guilty people have been so struck by a play that cunningly recreates their secret actions that "they have proclaimed their malefactions." And the ghost itself might have been the devil, working on his own "weakness and melancholy." Hamlet wants surer grounds than a ghost's story. "The play's the thing / Wherein I'll catch the conscience of the King."

So Hamlet's social conscience speaks. In Denmark's court and indeed in all the world of courts and courtiers, Hamlet is a prince of a rare kind. He is not a casual killer; he must have firm grounds for killing the King. He has a sense of social morality. The irony is that when on the following evening Hamlet does kill a man who he thinks is the King, it turns out to be Polonius. An aspect of life that he cannot control has taken charge of the proceedings. This is the turning point of the play.

The third act opens with espionage in high gear. Rosencrantz and Guildenstern have reported to the King on their spying efforts, and the King is meeting with Polonius to set up their own espionage operation. They plan to listen in when Hamlet meets Ophelia, according to their arrangement. While Polonius is busily directing her in how to behave, Hamlet enters, speaking the most famous of all soliloquies. Again he thinks of death, "to be or not to be," with death as a possible welcome end to the overwhelming oppressions of life. He proceeds to name these "whips and scorns of time" with a keen sense of prevalent social evils:

> Th' oppressor's wrong, the proud man's contumely,
> The pangs of despised love, the law's delay,
> The insolence of office, and the spurns
> That patient merit of the unworthy takes . . .

But, he asks himself, in trying to end these evils with death, who knows what more dread things may occur after death? Then come the lines:

> Thus conscience does make cowards of us all,
> And thus the native hue of resolution
> Is sicklied o'er with the pale cast of thought,
> And enterprises of great pith and moment
> With this regard their currents turn awry
> And lose the name of action.

In other words, Hamlet's hesitancy is due not to simple aversion to action, around which Coleridge builds his case, but to the profound thought of how little certain a man can be of the results of his action. It is this "conscience" that holds him back.

Hamlet speaks tenderly to Ophelia, "Nymph, in thy orisons, / Be all my sins remembered." But there is special significance in the word "sins." For he wants Ophelia to believe that he deceived her when he said he loved her, that he is not worthy of her, that he is a sinner. "Get thee to a nunnery," he cries. "Why wouldst thou be a breeder of sinners?" She should be sheltered from a world of evil-doers. He himself has "more offences at my beck than I have thoughts to put them in . . . . We are arrant knaves all: Believe none of us. Go thy ways to a nunnery." It is his fiercest outburst against a corrupt world, where even those who would set its evils right must corrupt themselves. He appears to suspect that her father is listening. "Where's your father?" When she answers, "At home, my lord," he gets more bitter and begins to talk more wildly becomes more antic. But his closing words are still, "To a nunnery, go."

There are some critics who construe the word "nunnery" as meaning a brothel, following the Elizabethan slang use of the term, but this is as if Hamlet had suddenly become Falstaff. There is no reason to bring in the slang connotation of the word when nowhere else in the scene does Hamlet use any colloquial speech.

Ophelia's speech when he leaves is as much as picture of her own mind as of Hamlet's, whose madness she laments:

> The expectancy and rose of the fair state,
> The glass of fashion and the mould of form . . .
> And I, of ladies most deject and wretched,
> That sucked the honey of his music vows,
> Now see that noble and most sovereign reason,
> Like sweet bells jangled, out of tune and harsh . . . .

She has been brought up with mirrors, gardens, honey and music. She is no Juliet, no Desdemona, to defy her father. And the loss of Hamlet is destroying her.

Now the two eavesdroppers, the King and Polonius, enter. The King is certain from what he has heard that Hamlet is not mad, but rather has some secret thoughts that spell danger. He must be gotten rid of. He will be sent to England. Polonius still clings to his theory and sets up another espionage scheme. The Queen will question Hamlet, and he, Polonius, will be listening.

While the troupers' play is being prepared, there is another discussion of aesthetics, with Hamlet demanding more natural gestures and affirming his bent toward realism, to study "nature" and to show "the very age and body of the time his form and pressure." There is a touching dialogue with Horatio, in which Hamlet again shows his social morality. He calls Horatio a "just" man and this, he says, is not flattery. Horatio is poor, and what profit is there in flattering him?

> Why should the poor be flattered?
> No, let the candied tongue lick absurd pomp,
> And crook the pregnant hinges of the knee . . .
>   . . . And blest are those
> Whose blood and judgment are so well co-meddled
> That they are not a pipe for Fortune's finger
> To sound what stop she please.

He asks Horatio to watch his uncle carefully, when the play is on, especially in the scene that is to depict the tale his father's ghost had told him of the way in which he was killed.

Then the court gathers to watch the play. Hamlet is "antic" with the King, with Polonius, and then with Ophelia, with whom his wild joking takes on a sexual coloration. Perhaps he still wants her to regard him as a sinner.

The play is preceded by a "dumb-show" presenting the action to come in pantomime. Critics have wondered why the King is not immediately offended at seeing this, but this is easily answered. He doesn't know that the play he is seeing was especially selected by Hamlet, let alone that Hamlet has made some additions to it. Stories of a man murdering a husband to steal his wife were not uncommon, especially in the stories from Italy which were often used as plots for plays in England. And, most important, the King knows he must keep a tight rein on himself and not show any disturbance at what he sees. Then the first scene, in which the Player Queen swears eternal fidelity to the Player King, even should he die, is not especially close to the events in Elsinore, although Hamlet thinks it might disturb the conscience of his mother. Hearing that Hamlet is familiar with the play, the King does get suspicious, and asks him if there is any offence in it. Hamlet replies, "No, no, they do but jest, poison in jest. No offence i' the world." But in the middle of the next scene, when the murderer pours his poison in the sleeping Player King's ear, with a speech that describes the poison's effect in terms very similar to those used in the Ghost's story, the King loses his control and rises, wounded in mind, and stops the performance. There can be little doubt that this speech was the "added" one written by Hamlet, who now is triumphant at the success of his ruse. Rosencrantz and Guildenstern enter to tell him that the King is enraged and the Queen wants to speak with him. Hamlet is merciless to them in his "antic disposition." When they again ask him what is disturbing his mind, he gets bitter and contemptuous, asks Guildenstern to play upon a recorder, and when he says he cannot, demands to know why Guildenstern thinks it easier to play on him, Hamlet, than on a pipe. Polonius enters, repeating the Queen's request for an audience. Then Hamlet, in a soliloquy, speaks of his readiness now to do the most fearsome deeds. His doubts and conflicts are over. "Now could I drink hot blood / And do such bitter business as the day / would quake to look on."

The King speaks frankly to Rosencrantz and Guildenstern about how dangerous Hamlet has become to him, of the "hazard so near to us as does hourly grow / Out of his lungs," and tells them that Hamlet will go with them to England, with a "commission" that the King will write. Then, alone, the King reveals how afflicted his conscience has become by the play's picture of the murder he himself has performed. He kneels and tries to pray for forgiveness. Hamlet comes behind him, and thinks that now he can dispatch the King. What holds him back, however, is the thought that to kill the King while he is cleansing his soul through prayer would send him to heaven, while Hamlet's own father was murdered with no chance to atone for his sins. And so Hamlet postpones his revenge. This is frequently cited as another example of Hamlet's intellectualist clutching at excuses to avoid action, but the reasons Hamlet gives are perfectly cogent in the light of the kind of religious beliefs Shakespeare has attributed to him, and the father'ghost's fury at his having been "Cut off even in the blossoms of my sin . . . / sent to my account / With all my imperfections on my head."

A scene then ensues between Hamlet and his mother, who chides him as she had promised the King she would do. Hamlet answers her bitterly and threatens to call for others who can confirm her authority over him. When he prevents her from leaving, she thinks he is about to kill her and cries for help. Polonius, listening behind the arras, echoes the cry, and Hamlet runs his sword through the arras, killing him, in the belief that he is the King. Hamlet discovers that it is Polonius he has killed. "I took thee for thy better," he says. He pities the old man and is regretful but stern. Polonius has intruded into the midst of tragic happenings and has paid the penalty for his foolishness.

Hamlet then turns back to his mother and berates her for having married so sorry a specimen as the King after having been married to a man like his father, and he accuses her of having acted like a flighty young girl. He breaks through her outer shell, and she is aghast at seeing herself as her son sees her, "stewed in corruption." Furthermore, he cries, her present choice is a "murtherer," a "villain," a "slave," a "cutpurse of the empire," a thief who stole the kingship. Just as he has won her over, the Ghost enters, seen only by Hamlet. When he speaks to the Ghost, who wants to "whet" Hamlet's "blunted purpose," and she sees nothing, she again thinks Hamlet is mad. But he denies this. He is rational and can prove it by his pulse. He again demands that she confess her corruption, and that from now on she withdraw from the King's embraces. She is completely humble before him. He "repents" having killed Polonius. But heaven has pleased itself to "punish" him, Hamlet, in this way, and to have used him to punish Polonius. So he must be heaven's "scourge and minister," and he says the words so significant for the real conflict in his mind, "I must be cruel, only to be kind."

A humanist-philosopher who wants only to be "kind"—that is to treat people as kin to him—has to make himself "cruel"—cruel to Ophelia, in driving her from him to save her from the savagery that reality forces on him; cruel to his mother to win her from her dissipations; cruel to the King, in the name of justice. Hamlet asks one more thing of his mother: that she do not divulge to the King that he, Hamlet, is not really mad but "mad in craft." He knows he is being sent to England with sealed letters and a "mandate" carried by Rosencrantz and Guildenstern, whom he "will trust" as if they were "adders fanged." But he can cope with them, and he will destroy them. For justice, he must act the part of a "knave." (They "marshal me to knavery.")

And so the drama has reached its surpise and turning point. Men make plans, but they turn out differently. Hamlet's accidental killing of Polonius, when he thought he was killing the King, has created new difficulties and complications. The King is now watchful and closely attended, while Hamlet becomes more vulnerable now, for he must take care that the "whisper o'er the world's diameter . . . may miss our name." The duel has reached a new phase. After guarded stratagems, there has been a fierce lunge, which missed its mark, and now the two antagonists are involved to the death. The King is determined to kill Hamlet, but he must be circumspect, for "He's loved of the distracted multitude," as the King tells his attendants. Hamlet enters, attended, and is philosophically "antic," with remarks like "a man may fish with the worm that has eat of a king, and eat of the fish that hath fed of that worm." The King tells Hamlet that the ship for England is ready to sail, and then, alone, speaks of the sealed letters he has written to England ordering that Hamlet be killed.

Again Hamlet portrays his new state of mind—forcing himself to be cruel—for justice. This is the short scene in which, while on the way to the port, he meets Fortinbras' troops and learns that they are advancing to Poland for a battle in which perhaps 20,000 men will die, with the prize a worthless piece of land. This speech does not have quite the antiwar implications it would have today, when there is a world-wide peace movement and a realistic vision of an end to all wars. To Shakespeare's contemporaries and to Hamlet, it is a humanist question raised in a world that seems steeped in corruption. And the point to him is that if respected leaders dare death and danger over a "quarrel in a straw," why should he have any qualms about what he must do who has a father murdered, and a mother "stained." And so he proclaims, "O, from this time forth, / My thoughts be bloody, or be nothing worth!"

The next scene depicts Ophelia's madness, and Shakespeare, as always, is quite clear (and at the same time movingly poetic) as to what is haunting her mind: the death of her old, dear father at Hamlet's hands and her frustrated love for him repressed by the fears her father had instilled in her of maidens who were wrongly treated by men. So she pathetically sings of her father:

> He is dead and gone, lady,
> He is dead and gone;
> At his head a grass-green turf,
> At his heels a stone . . .

and at her fantasies about Hamlet:

> Quoth she, before you tumbled me,
> You promised me to wed.

In the midst of this, Laertes, armed, breaks in, followed by armed Danes, leading a rebellion with cries of "Laertes shall be king." It is a sign not so much of the desire to make Laertes king as of the unpopularity of the present King, Claudius, and the fears and hatred he seems to have engendered in the people. There is no serious move to make Laertes king. He himself is only angry at his father's death, the circumstances of which the King has kept s ret. It is easy for the King to mollify him and promise to disclose the truth.

In a short scene, Horatio hears that Hamlet is back, and then the talk between the King and Laertes continues. The King puts all the blame for Polonius's death on Hamlet, who he says also wants to murder him. But he cannot charge Hamlet with this publicly because of "the great love the general gender bear him." Then the startling news comes to the King of Hamlet's return, and Claudius moves to the attack again, using Laertes as his tool. The plan of a fencing display is concocted, with Hamlet and Laertes taking part. Laertes will stealthily use an unbuttoned foil; he will also anoint it with a deadly poison, and the King will furthermore prepare poisoned wine for Hamlet to drink. Act IV ends with the news of Ophelia's drowning.

Act V begins with the scene at Ophelia's grave, and in contrast to Hamlet's assumed "antic disposition, Shakespeare provides two genuine 'antics' or clowns—the two gravediggers. They have the sharp legalistic or argumentative wit that so often characterizes Shakespeare's 'common-people' clowns, and they have a keen sense of class injustice; 'Will you ha' the truth an't? If this had not been a gentlewoman, she should have been buried out o' Christian burial." "The more pity that great folk should have countenance in this world to drown or hang themselves more than their even-Christian [fellow-Christian]." And the relation between them and Hamlet, who enters with Horatio, is an odd one. Hamlet has a strong sense of class or caste difference; "the age is grown so picked that the toe of the peasant comes so near the heel of the courtier, he galls his kibe [chilblain.]"

Yet in the banter between Hamlet and the grave-digger, who does not recognize him, one scores as many points as the other. It is as if underneath the class differences, there was also a fundamental kinship in humanity. This is shown by death, which levels all differences.

The thought was nothing new for the times; it had been expressed militantly in popular interpretations of Christianity during the late Middle Ages, which showed potentates and commoners alike naked before Judgment after death. John Ball, the 14th century communist or Lollard preacher, inspired the popular rhyme, "When Adam delved and Eve span, who was then the gentleman?" And there is a hint of this in the gravedigger's: "There is no ancient gentlemen but gard'ners, ditchers and gravemakers. They uphold Adam's profession . . . . The Scripture says that Adam digged: could he dig without arms?" (This, in context, is also a satiric thrust at the gentleman's coat of arms.) Hamlet certainly cannot accept the gravedigger as an equal. Yet when he picks up the skull of Yorick, he speaks with the warmest affection of one who was also a clown, his father's jester.

When the burial procession approaches with the body of Ophelia, Hamlet learns that it is she who has died. He matches Laertes' laments in her grave by leaping into it himself, and when Laertes attacks him and they are parted, Hamlet cries out the poignant:

> I loved Ophelia. Forty thousand brothers
> Could not with all their quantity of love,
> Make up my sum.

Then, just as Hamlet has hardly caught his breath on his return to Elsinore, the King proceeds to attack first. Hamlet is recounting to Horatio how he stole from Rosencrantz and Guildenstern the sealed mandate that directed England to kill him and substituted their names for his own and then was parted from the ship. As Hamlet tells Horatio of his determination to kill the King, he is still very much aware of problems of "conscience," morality. Of Rosencrantz and Guildenstern, he says, "Why, man, they did make love to their employment, / They are not near my conscience." Of the King, he says:

He that hath killed my king, and whored my mother;
Popped in between th' election and my hopes;
Thrown out his angle for my proper life,
And with such coz'nage – is't not perfect conscience,
To quit him with this arm? And is't not to be damned,
To let this canker of our nature come
In further evil?

The words "my hopes" are the first mention by Hamlet in the play of any ambitions on his part to be king. And even here they are little stressed, but only one of a list of charges in the case he builds against the King. And his reason for killing the King is not simply to revenge his father's murder and his mother's seduction but in a more social connotation to prevent this agent of evil from doing more evil. The time, he knows, is short, for the report must soon come from England of how Rosencrantz and Guildenstern had been faithfully executed. But suddenly a courtier, Osric, enters, with the challenge to a mock duel, on which, he says, the King has wagered that Hamlet will win. Osric becomes a butt for sharp joking at the expense of rich courtiers and fops: "Dost know this water-fly? . . . 'Tis a vice to know him. He hath much land and fertile. Let a beast be lord of beasts, and his crib shall stand at the king's mess." Osric is turned into a genuine fool, unlike the peasant gravedigger.

The duel then takes place and Hamlet is wounded by the poisoned foil. But before he dies, he wounds Laertes with the same foil and kills the King. The Queen drinks the poisoned wine meant for Hamlet. And on the stage littered with corpses steps Fortinbras, who is in line for the throne.

The story of Shakespeare's *Hamlet* then is that of a prince who is a humanist philosopher, who despises the court society about him for its inequalities, injustices, oppressions and murders. The killing of his father prevents his withdrawal from this society into a life of the mind. He must now engage himself in an active role because of the demands of his humanism, which includes a compelling social morality. He must war against a king. He is alone in this and faces the entire mechanism of the state, with its courtiers, councillors, armed defenders, and its network of espionage. He has the affections of the common people, the "general gender." He cannot call on them, but his social morality demands that he justify his actions to the public. And while this "general gender" does not play an active role, it is a strong force in that the king must take cognizance of it in his dealings with his opponent. The King also must try to keep his own name clean and his crimes a secret.

Since the struggle takes place in an active society moved by its own forces, the actions of the antagonists bring results and repercussions unplanned and unsuspected by them. Hamlet achieves his goal; he removes a murderer and evildoer from the throne. In the process, he himself dies. And others are caught up in the conflict and become its victims: Polonius, an old councillor whose duty as he sees it is to serve faithfully whoever represents the state; Laertes, his son, whose mind is limited by women, horses, swordplay and family honor; Ophelia, a sweet maiden humbly obedient to her father and whose love for Hamlet is thwarted; Rosencrantz and Guildenstern, the servile toadies of the King; and the Queen, Hamlet's mother, whose weakness has led her to be entrapped by her first husband's murderer.

The play gives no assurance that the corruption of monarchy and court society can be ended. What is vital and significant is that it raises a critical question of this society; that Hamlet does not withdraw into his mind but engages actively to remedy a social evil; that although he must harden himself in the struggle, and take on some of the ugly practices of this society, he never loses his social morality nor his conscience. And so it is a historic achievement that the challenges and questions so universal in Shakespeare's time be made public. Hamlet's dying demand of Horatio is to "tell my story," which will reveal "things standing thus unknown." And confirming Shakespeare's acuteness in the political realm, the corruptions germane to absolute monarchy were soon to come onto the stage of history.

The discussion of the aesthetics of acting, theater and poetry, touched off by the troupe of players in the play within the play has wider implications than would at first appear. The personages in the drama are engaged in acting, and art, Shakespeare seems to say, can imbue acting with a kind of truth to nature that cuts below surface appearances.

Hamlet, speaking of the First Player's declamation, says:

> What's Hecuba to him, or he to Hecuba
> That he should weep for her? What would he do
> Had he the motive and the cue for passion
> That I have.

Here he is not simply referring to the fact that Hecuba is a figure in an ancient legend, while he, Hamlet, is a living person. His implication is that the emotional effect upon the hearers of such a declamation as that about Hecuba was due less to the honest evocation of her feelings than to the declamatory rhetoric of the poet's and the actor's skills, such as forcing tears to his eyes, getting a break in his voice at the right moment, and so on. For Hamlet's purpose he wants a different kind of art; a kind of play and playing so cunningly contrived,

> That guilty creatures, sitting at a play,
> Have by the very cunning of the scene
> Been struck so to the soul that presently
> They have proclaimed their malefactions;

And this, as he later puts it in his speech to the players, demands a kind of truth to nature that avoids overemotional voice and gestures but seeks a kind of modest yet deeper insight into underlying forces, or typicality. Its "end" is "to hold, as 'twere, the mirror up to nature; to show virtue her own features, to show scorn her own image, and reveal the very age and body of the time, his form and pressure."

It could be surmised that Shakespeare saw his own society as one where people in public view also acted parts or wore masks, so to speak; that truth was hard to find, and that the realism of his plays could show this age its "form and pressure."

It could also be that Shakespeare ironically thought of himself as, in a sense, a "court jester," who told the age some realistic truths about itself under the guise of entertainment. For technically he was one of the Lord Chamberlain's "servants," his company belonged to the Lord Chamberlain. Yet in this world where the new was rising within the old, he was actually a bourgeois enterpreneur, since he was a full shareholder in the company, which depended for its success not on the Chamberlain but on people of all classes who paid admission. He might have had some friends among the nobility, but there was a strong caste difference—he still had to call himself their "servant." And a play could be thought of as a "jest." In *Hamlet,* while the play of the murder of Gonzago is being acted, and the King becomes suspicious, Hamlet answers, "'Tis a knavish piece of work; but what of that? Your Majesty, and we that have free souls, it touches us not."

In the radiant comedy *As You Like It,* there is a good deal of aesthetic discussion about the role of the jester. The play is attributed to the end of the 1590's, about a year before *Hamlet,* and it can also throw more light on the "jest" in *Hamlet.*

As You Like It is a kind of counterpart to *Hamlet,* although it is at the same time its opposite, like one's right and left hand or the opposite sides of a coin. Shakespeare's new form of comedy is as much a unique development for his age as his form of tragedy. In neither does he seek the stylistic homogeneity that Ben Jonson, for example, aimed at, both in "classical" tragedies and in comedies of "humours," styles that would be far more influential than Shakespeare's in English drama of the late 17th and early 18th centuries. Shakespeare's art received the spark it needed from Italian and French Renaissance literature, even from the Roman classics, but what this accomplished was to raise to a higher artistic level his own approach, which was founded in the English popular dramatic tradition. "Mixed styles" were part of this tradition, and what appeared to be "comic" was actually the only way that part of the real life of the common people could break its way into serious art.

Thus, in the Wakefield mystery plays of the 15th century, in the play of Noah, not only does God speak solemnly but there also is a down-to-earth altercation between Noah and his obstinate wife. *The Second Shepherd's Play* laments the shepherds' poverty and has them deal with a swindler and sheep-stealer before going to Bethlehem to adore the infant Jesus. And on a far grander scale, in Shakespeare's tragedies, there are comic scenes and even clowns, while the comedies involve characters and dramatic events that could be the themes for tragedies. The seeds of his popular sympathies, fertilized by currents of art from abroad, flowered into rich human sympathies, cutting across class lines. Shakespeare achieves his unity not through a homogeneous style or a learned rhetoric, but through the force of the thought driving the course of the play and profiting from the contrasts that parallel the clashing currents of social life. And he intensifies this realism with delight in giving the varied characters a varied language that is characteristic of both their voices and their mentalities.

The difference between Shakespeare's mature tragedies and comedies is essentially this: In the tragedies, the main personages fight to realize their hopes and ambitions—not against the dictates of gods or of a supernatural "fate," or even against their antagonists—but against the operations of a society with its own laws of movement that they find they cannot control. The effect of the tragedy is neither despair nor a paean to individualism, but a light thrown on the workings of a society that is also man-made. The possibility is raised that if enough light continues to be shed on society, people will be better able to gauge the farflung results of their actions and find better ways to realize or even change their hopes.

In comedy, such dramatic action may become the framework of the play, the outline of the plot. But "necessity" or the obstinate force of nature and society, disappears. Obstacles are overcome; the good people emerge happy, wounds are healed and evil-doers defeated. Within this framework there is the full expression of affection of people for one another and of uproarious joy in life. The effect is that the world has become a place where people can truly live like human beings, and if, after the end of the play the audience is restored to harsh reality, the hope remains that perhaps the world can be brought closer to human desires.

At the opening of *As You Like It,* the audience learns that a Duke has been robbed of his rule by his brother Frederick and driven to live with some of his followers as an outlaw in the Forest of Arden. A nobleman, Oliver, is persecuting his younger brother Orlando, denying him even what money his father willed to him. He hates Orlando because, Oliver says, "he is so much in the heart of the world, and especially of my own people," and he wants to kill him. Then Frederick persecutes Rosalind, daughter of the exiled Duke, who has remained to become the bosom friend of his own daughter Celia. Rosalind runs off to Arden Forest to find her father, accompanied by Celia, and so does Orlando.

But all this is framework, and the evildoers are all rendered harmless. The outlaws live in their caves in the forest of Arden almost like gentlemen at a country estate. At the end, Oliver is saved by his brother Orlando from the attack of a lion and the experience transforms his character. Frederick meets a "holy man," is impressed by his teachings and restores his exiled brother to his Dukedom. There are four couples and four marriages. The burden of the play is its display of wit, affection, song and laughter.

Here Shakespeare has created an extraordinary assemblage of wits, each different in character. The two gentlewomen are keen in word-play; Rosalind, who bravely tries to hide her gender under a man's clothing, and Celia, who always tries to find the sunny side in adversity. There are Jaques, a courtier turned melancholy philosopher, who always sees the bones under the skin. He is called "Monsieur Melancholy," and says, of melancholy, "I do love it better than laughing." Rosalind says to hims in jest, "I fear you have sold your own land to see others." And Jaques answers seriously, "Yes, I have gained my experience." He hates not simply individual people but human society and ends in complete withdrawal from social life. There is the nobleman attendant Amiens, who sings with others some of Shakespeare's most beautiful rustic songs: "Under the Greenwood Tree," "It Was a Lover and his Lass," and "Blow, Blow, Thou Winter Wind." There are the rustics themselves, Phebe, Audrey, Silvius, William, whose lovemaking is a kind of counterpoint to that of the gentle folk. And there is the great court jester Touchstone, whose brilliant flaying of courtier fopperies reaches a high point in his classic speech about how to quarrel "by the book"; he enumerates and illustrates the "Retort Courteous," the "Quip Modest," the "Reply Churlish," the "Reproof Valiant," the "Countercheck Quarrelsome," the "Lie with Circumstance," and the "Lie Direct." Even the "Lie Direct" can be softened, he says, with an "If," adding "Your If is the only peacemaker: much virtue in If."

Foreshadowings of Hamlet are seen in this play not only in sentiments but even in similar wording. Thus the Duke exiled in Arden says of the "churlish chiding of the winter's wind" that "This is no flattery: these are counsellors / That feelingly persuade me what I am." This is like what Hamlet tells Horatio: "Nay, do not think I flatter; / For what advancement may I hope from thee . . . / Why should the poor be flattered?"

In Arden, Orlando tells his old servant Adam:

> Thou are not for the fashion of these times,
> When none will sweat but for promotion,
> And having that do choke their service up
> Even with the having.

This is like the continuation of Hamlet's speech above:

> No, let the candied tongue lick absurd pomp,
> And crook the pregnant hinges of the knee
> Where thrift may follow fawning.

Touchstone tells Audrey: "Honesty coupled to beauty is to have honey a sauce to sugar." And Hamlet tells Ophelia, "If you be honest and fair, your honesty should admit no discourse to your beauty." Touchstone's lacerations of courtiers are like Hamlet's twitting of Osric. And there are discussions of poetry in *As You Like It,* with examples, as in *Hamlet.* Like the player's declamation in *Hamlet* about Pyrrhus and Hecuba, in that it is obviously written with an expert hand and a fine command of language, deliberately overdone, are the verses in praise of Rosalind that Orlando pins to the trees in Arden—verses with galloping four-beat lines and overstrained rhyming, which arouse such witty comment. Rosalind says, "I was never so be-rhymed since Pythagoras's time that I was an Irish rat," referring to the legend of rats being rhymed to death in Ireland.

A notable explanation of the uses of comedy are the discussions of Touchstone, the "wise fool," whose eyes are keen behind the comic mask. When Celia tells Touchstone that the mighty Duke Frederick might whip him, he answers, "The more pity,

that fools may not speak wisely what wise men do foolishly." The
Duke in Arden says of Touchstone, "He used his folly like a
stalking-horse and under the presentation of that he shoots his
wit." Most important are Jaques' remarks in admiration of
Touchstone. Jaques wishes that he too were a fool:

> I must have liberty
> Withal, as large a charter as the wind,
> To blow on whom I please; for so fools have:
> And they that are most galléd with my folly,
> They most m⸱ ⸱t laugh . . . .
> Invest me in my motley: give me leave
> To speak my mind, and I will through and through
> Cleanse the foul body of the' infected world,
> If they will patiently receive my medicine.

To use "folly" in order to "cleanse the foul body of the' infected
world" could be a thought leading to Hamlet's description of
"playing" that is aimed "to hold, as 'twere, the mirror up to
nature, scorn her own image, and the very age and body of the
time his form and pressure."

> I have heard
> That guilty creatures sitting at a play,
> Have been by the very cunning of the scene
> Been struck so to the soul that presently
> They have proclaimed their malefactions;
> For murther, though it have no tongue, will speak
> With most miraculous organ.

It could be that Shakespeare thought of himself, in a way, as
such a "jester," and what were his plays, not only the comedies
but also the tragedies, but "jests" of this kind? The murderers did
not really murder, the murdered did not really die, the actor who
played Hamlet rose from his bier to go out and eat his supper.
And so this "aesthetics" discussion in *As You Like It* could be the
prelude to the aesthetic discussion in *Hamlet* and then to the
plays of social-political criticism that Shakespeare would write in
the first six or seven years of the 17th century; in the bitter
comedies *Troilus and Cressida* and *Measure for Measure,* and the
tragedies *Othello, King Lear, Macbeth and Antony and Cleopatra.*

7

COMEDY
SWEET AND BITTER

*Much Ado About
Nothing
Twelfth Night
Merry Wives of Windsor
All's Well That
Ends Well
Troilus and Cressida
Measure for Measure*

The relative social fluidity of England in Shakespeare's time, with the aristocracy held in check by the monarch (the handsome Earl of Essex led an uprising against Queen Elizabeth in 1601 and was executed), and the Crown encouraging and profiting from the growth of trade as well as piracy, made it possible for Shakespeare to write openly of the weaknesses of the aristocracy. He himself, to be sure, made money as a businessman-artist, for he built up a sizeable investment in his company (although it belonged officially to the Lord Chamberlain) and it yielded a profitable return. But since the business of formula-manufactured art or pseudo-art was still some centuries in the future, his work was popular but not dictated by a commercial mentality.

His criticism of the aristocracy could not be achieved through a direct portrayal of the England of his time. Such documentary realism did not exist until after the upheavals in England from 1648 to 1688, when a new England came into being and many of the institutions of the past were wiped out. By then the bourgeoisie had taken part in a revolution; it had gained a position of strength in the state, consolidated itself as a class, and openly become an exploiter of labor. In this period, a new documentary realism would permit bourgeois and aristocrat to lash at each other's weaknesses, but both lived on the backs of the proletariat. The wide-ranging critique of society that Shakespeare expressed, even while avoiding the direct representation of the England of his day, was hardly possible within official society. In the advanced capitalist countries it could arise only in the latter part of the 19th century, when a class-conscious proletariat was emerging.

Shakespeare could, however, express his dislike of the money-controlled mentality—despite the fact that on at least one occasion he is known to have loaned money at interest; and he could also make clowns and fools of his aristocrats and raise questions as to the running of the state. Such motifs are apparent in the seven comedies produced in the last years of the 16th century and in the opening of the 17th. *As You Like It* has already already been discussed. There are two other radiantly merry and poetic comedies: *Much Ado About Nothing* and *Twelfth Night.* Shakespeare's method in these three comic masterpieces is to use a flimsy melodramatic plot as a framework for bringing together a group of fanciful persons from different strata of society, whose witty interplay with one another makes up the comedy; a development, airy and perfectly handled, of the method initiated in *Midsummer Night's Dream.* We also have *All's Well That Ends Well* and *Merry Wives of Windsor,* in which there is abundant plot but less emphasis on significant characters. After these, two masterpieces of a new order appear, one of them *The Merchant of Venice,* in which the plot is very serious, and the intensity of social criticism includes tragic elements that almost burst through the confines of comedy.

Much Ado About Nothing has a melodramatic plot involving the love of the young nobleman Claudio for Hero, daughter of the Governor of Messina, and the machinations of the evil Don John that almost destroy their projected marriage. Within this framework, Shakespeare gives us the virtuoso verbal dueling of the noblewoman Beatrice, who appears to despise all men, and the young nobleman Benedick, who appears to despise all women. Shakespeare devotes his supreme mastery of language to their verbal rapier-thrusts. Then each is tricked into imagining that the disdain the other expresses really hides an overwhelming love, and they discover they actually do love one another. There is a climactic scene with an inspired comic twist, for just as they are at the high point of admitting their rapturous love, he says, "Come, bid me do anything for thee," and she answers, "Kill Claudio." This strikes like a bolt of lightning at a picnic. Claudio is the young nobleman, Benedick's best friend, who has just broken his engagement to Hero, Beatrice's best friend, because he has been tricked into thinking he saw her at an assignation with someone else. Obediently Benedick goes off to challenge his friend to a duel.

Then the melodramatic plot is settle by another layer of comedy, that of the rustic constable Dogberry and his associates. Dogberry mangles traditional sayings, remarking "comparisons are odorous," or "To be a well-favoured man is the gift of fortune; but to read and write comes by nature." But he is the kindliest of constables. When the watchman asks whether he is to lay hands on a thief, Dogberry tells him, "Truly, by your office, you may; but I think that they who touch pitch will be defiled. The most peaceable way for you, if you do not take a thief, is to let him show himself what he is, and steal out of our company." But it is Dogberry and his followers who, in a dogged but stumbling way, help expose the conspiracy against Hero. So all ends happily, and the verbal sharp-shooting of Beatrice and Benedick continues to the end of the play. When they are about to be married, he says, "Come, I will have thee; but by this light, I take thee for pity," and her rejoinder is, "I would not deny you; but by this good day, I yield upon great persuasion; and partly to save your life, for I was told you were in a consumption."

Dogberry and his mates are objects of laughter, yet they are lesser fools in their ignorance than the gentry who are educated and the souls of "honor." In fact, it is precisely because the gentry see themselves in the light of honor that Claudio denounced his inncocent beloved, and that Leonato, Governor of Messina, denounces his darling daughter for having both fallen readily for the trick that Dogberry and his men later expose. Nor do Beatrice and Benedick find any way of expressing their faith in Hero other than for him to fight a duel with his best friend. So Shakespeare has his good-natured fun with the aristocracy.

In *Twelfth Night,* which completes this trio of light-hearted, masterly comedies, the gentry appear to be even greater fools, although any criticism of them in the play is veiled by the pervading atmosphere of poetry, music, love and high spirits. In Shakespeare's comedy cannon it is a minor crime to be foolish; what is a major one is to be malicious, to deliberately seek to hurt people, to be treacherous or dishonest.

The melodramatic thread is provided by the twins, Viola and Sebastian, who are separated by shipwreck and cast ashore on the seacost of the imaginary country of Illyria, neither knowing whether the other is alive. She dresses as a man and finds a post as servitor of the lovesick Duke of Illyria, Orsino, who can think of nothing but how lovesick he is. She promptly falls in love with him but cannot show it because of her male disguise. The woman he desires is a great lady, Olivia, who has renounced all courtship because she mourns the death of her father and brother. But when Orsino sends Viola to Olivia as his messenger of love, Olivia falls in love with the messenger. They engage in an interchange of playfully serious language, embellished with very tender and lovely poetry. The comedy lies in the disparity between the earnestness of their language and the bizarre situations in which they find themselves, fooled by appearances that disguise reality. Orsino is loved by a woman who he thinks is a boy, and Olivia loves that same "boy."

The contrasting line of the plot, with its comic characters, clowns and its witty prose is provided by Olivia's household. There are her sharp-minded maid Maria and her steward Malvolio. The latter is straight-laced, despising the pleasures of mirth, "cakes and ale," yet holding a lofty opinion of himself, and even dreaming of marrying the lady he serves.

In Olivia's household there is also a kinsman, Sir Toby Belch, a propertyless, raucous-mouthed glutton and a drinker, a small chip off John Falstaff's block. He has brought with him Sir Andrew Aguecheek, a thoroughly stupid gentleman whose education, as he himself describes it, consists of "fencing, dancing and bear-baiting." So long as he can buoy up Andrew's hopes of successfully courting Olivia, Toby can drain Andrew of his money. The foolery and "being fooled" here takes a different form, for Maria and Sir Toby Belch are avid practical jokers. They trick Malvolio into believing that his lady secretly loves him, thus causing him to act so strangely that he is confined as a madman. And Toby incites a duel between Viola and Sir Andrew, taking Viola for a very unwarlike youth and knowing Sir Andre to be a notorious coward. That Toby gets a broken head out of this only adds to the fun.

Through the scenes flits Feste, a "wise fool," although not as sharp in his social comments as Touchstone. He sings three of Shakespeare's most beautiful songs: "O, Mistress mine, where are you roaming," "Come away, come away, death," and "When that I was and a little tiny boy." The first two are not rustic-style songs like those in *As You Like It*, but the kind of popular love song, of which the Elizabethan age produced so many lovely examples, to be sung as madrigals or as solo airs with lute. And Feste enables Shakespeare to deliver, through Viola, another little aesthetics lecture on the various kinds of stage fools—contrasting the servant who must keep his wits about him while acting the fool, making sure to keep his eyes on his master, while it is the master himself who loses his wits and becomes genuinely foolish:

> This fellow is wise enough to play the fool;
> And to do that well craves a kind of wit.
> He must observe their mood on whom he jests,
> The quality of persons, and the time . . .
>   . . . This is a practice
> As full of labour as a wise man's art:
> For folly that he wisely shows is fit;
> But wise men, folly-fall'n, quite taint their wit.

Can it be that Shakespeare saw himself, the playwright as, in a way, the "wise fool," who must watch his lords and patrons carefully and "in jest" also be quite ready to show them when they have really lost their own wits?

In the play, the appearance of Sebastian, Viola's twin, brings the tangled skein of appearance and reality to its climax and also manages to unwind it. Taken by Sir Toby Belch and Sir Andrew Aguecheek to be his twin Viola, Sebastian ends by beating up both of them. And taken by Olivia to be the youth she fell in love with, she invites him to marry her and he accepts. This leaves Viola, having found her brother, free to resume her real identity, and she marries the Duke. Sir Toby Belch marries Maria. Only Malvolio leaves the scene unhappily, "I'll be revenged on the whole pack of you," he says. The audience undoubtedly is moved to laughter by his remark. But the question still can be asked: Is Malvolio the greatest fool in the play?

For there are many fools in *Twelfth Night,* and the titled gentry are well represented among them. Of course, Duke Orsino and Olivia are not meant to be regarded as ridiculous people, although they do find themselves in ludicrous situations and really don't possess a full-size brain between the two of them. But their sentiments are endearingly human as they emerge from the lovely poetry their creator has given them to speak.

And in this dreamland, where necessity disappears and with it all social problems, there are no decisions to be made that call for more than a pea brain. But Sir Toby Belch still remains a ridiculous person, a barbarian who stuffs his gut and has no regard for people except to misuse them for his pleasure, and the audience enjoys seeing him get a bloody head. Sir Andrew Aguecheek is a ridiculous person in that he has a title and property, which automatically raise him above ordinary men, combined with insensitivity, ignorance and stupidity that put him below them—a scarecrow. Here Shakespeare uses the gentry for his clowns.

Sir John Falstaff comes back on the stage early in the 17th century in *The Merry Wives of Windsor,* and amiable comedy which, according to a report circulated a century later, was written because Queen Elizabeth wanted a play showing Sir John in love. He is not really the Falstaff of the two parts of *Henry IV,* although Shakespeare links the two characters by having Master Page say of him, "He kept company with the wild Prince and Poins." But in Shakespeare a personality is, as we have pointed out, a social creation. He builds a specific character on the stage through the company he keeps and his relations with him. And the older Falstaff consorted, however clownishly, with princes and leaders of the nation at a time of great national upheaval. He had aspirations beyond seducing a couple of middle-class wives for whatever money he could get to extract from their husbands—which is his aim in *Merry Wives of Windsor*. He still has the gift of gab. But the women make a fool of him, keep their chastity, and and also laugh at their over-suspicious husbands. The butt of the play's ridicule, along with the fat knight, are middle-class figures like Master Ford, who has no confidence in himself as a person but only in the power of money. One of the ludicrous situations comes when Falstaff, having already decided to pay court to Ford's wife, is paid by Ford, who uses an alias, to make love to his wife in order to test her honesty.

And, in fact, Shakespeare jocularly turns Falstaff himself into a kind of bourgeois gentleman by having him talk of the courtship of Mistress Page and Mistress Ford as a kind of mercantile investment: "She is a region in Guiana, all gold and bounty. I will be cheaters to them both, and they shall be exchequers to me. They shall be my East and West Indies, and I will trade to them both. Go bear thou this letter to Mistress Page; and thou this to Mistress Ford. We will thrive, lads, we will thrive."

It is an unusual comedy for Shakespeare in that it focuses on bourgeois characters. They triumph over a silly, old and seedy knight, but not through any manliness of their own, rather by the cleverness of their women. Young love laughs at both the the old order and the new, and it is obvious that Shakespeare does not like the money-motivated mentality.

All's Well That Ends Well is overloaded with plot and weak in characterization. It makes a plea for sexual morality; the women in it are like angels; the men tend to be weak or despicable. Helena, its heroine, is typical of Shakespeare's women in her fight to marry the man she loves, but the man she loves and marries, Bertram, is not very appealing. He is a young, brave lord who at first scorns Helena, but is brought to love her in the end, after a series of tricks, which include getting him to sleep with her while thinking she is someone else. In the process a lascivious braggard, Parolles, who has a bad influence on him, is exposed.

The message of the play with regard to respecting woman does honor to Shakespeare but it is too full of contrivances, and even the society depicted is not credible. It is a misfire in the direction in which two great comedies in which sexual morality as a central motif are aimed: *Troilus and Cressida* and *Measure for Measure.* In both, a living society emerges and a new kind of comedy is shaped, one so bitter and realistic that it has a tragic impact. Social necessity is treated more lightly, but its visage does appear in the fabric to give the comedy a tone of ironic laughter. For, in irony, the butt of the laughter is less directed at a contemptible object than at the teller of the tale, and, by empathy, at his audience. It is the storyteller who is left with unsolved problems—laughter in his only relief.

Troilus and Cressida is a story of the Trojan war, but it follows neither the Homer poems nor Virgil's *Aeneid.* It is closer to Chaucer's long narrative poem, *Troilus and Crisseyde,* but it deviates sharply from this work, too. A crucial difference is in the way Shakespeare treats chivalry, and also in that Chaucer includes the death of Troilus, while Shakespeare's play ends with him alive and strong. Thus the story of the play can be called the education of Troilus from a lovesick youth to a hard determined leader who faces war in all its brutality, with no illusions of chivalry. And integral to this theme is the social picture with its portrayal of chivalry as something outmoded. The Trojans who profess it honestly are made to seem weak in comparison with the Greek princes who make a travesty of it through the brutal possessiveness of their lovemaking, treating woman as whores, as well as through the chicanery with which they fight. The decline of the medieval chivalry of the aristocracy is, indeed, the social theme of the play.

The war is shown as being fought for the most ridiculous of reasons—to drag a faithless woman back to her husband. The Prologue says of the Greeks:

> their vow is made
> To ransack Troy, within whose strong immures
> The ravished Helen, Menelaus' Queen,
> With wanton Paris sleeps; and that's the quarrel.

Some of the protagonists are aware of this foolish wasting of lives. Troilus says in the first scene:

Fools on both sides! Helen must need be fair
When with your blood you daily paint her thus.
I cannot fight upon this argument:
It is too starved a subject for my sword.

This is raised as a purely personal objection. But Hector, the Trojan prince with the most chivalrous sense of dignity and responsibility to others, says in council:

                                                    Let Helen go.
Since the first sword was drawn about this question,
Every tithe soul 'mongst many thousands dismes [tenths-S.F.]
Hath been as dear as Helen.

Among the Greeks, the slave Thersites, amidst the stream of foul-mouthed abuse he pours on his masters, calls them "those that war for a placket." The hard-headed cynic Diomedes tells Paris, Helen's lover:

For every false drop in her bawdy veins
A Grecian's life hath sunk; for every scruple
Of her contaminated carrion weight,
A Trojan has been slain.

To Ulysses, King Menelaus, Helen's abandoned husband, is a pathetic cuckold: "O deadly gall, and theme of all our scorns: / For which we lose our heads to gild his horse."

They fight by the rituals of a medieval tournament of knights. The princes decide for themselves the day they will fight. Aeneas calls out to Troilus, hearing the sounds of battle, "Hark, what good sport is out of town today!"

Troilus courts Cressida through her uncle Pandarus, who, willingly and with no scruples at all, brings a prince and a woman to sleep together. But Troilus genuinely loves her, and she likes him, although at first she plays hard to get. She is not an evil woman but a weak one and somewhat crafty. It is better, she says, to keep men beseeching than to give in to them easily. But the love of Troilus is honest. And, in general, he speaks the best poetry in the play because he is genuinely involved with what he says and is a man of deep feelings who does not try to hide them.

As the story of this love develops, the play contrasts the Trojans' chivalry with the Greeks' lack of it; and it is the Trojans who are more genuinely chivalrous. Troilus, Hector, Aeneas, and Paris (though the lastnamed is shown more as making love to Helen than as fighting) have no guile. The Greek princes are more cunning and brutish and jeer at each other behind their backs. Agamemnon is slow-witted; Achilles is proud and selfcentered and cares nothing for the others. He withdraws from the fighting because he is in love with a Trojan princess and has made a deal with Hecuba, her mother. Ajax is utterly stupid and is secretly laughed at by the others as an obese fool. Diomedes is a woman-chaser without tenderness; Patroclus is, in the words of Thersites, the "masculine whore" of Achilles; Nestor is an old babbling of his youth; Ulysses is practical and cunning. And abusing them all is the slave Thersites. His literary ancestry is Dromio in the early *Comedy of Errors,* a slave who curses his master while he is being beaten. He is built up with Shakespeare's relish of language, here highly vituperative, to a major figure. In one scene, his opening, he says in the hearing of Ajax that he (Ajax) "wears his wit in his belly and his guts in his head"; that Nestor's "wit was mouldy ere your gransires had nails on their toes"; that Patroclus is "Achilles' brach" [a female hound—S.F.]; that Ajax and Achilles are stupid because Ulysses and Nestor have yoked them "like draught-oxen" in order to "plough up the wars." There is none of Shakespeare's humanity in Thersites, but there is truth, and his vitriol is the counterfoil to the inhumanity of his masters.

We meet the Greek leaders in council. The discussion is written in blank verse of a stately rhetoric, adorned with maxims and parables, with impressive figures of speech, but cool—like the speech of men accustomed to public addresses who must keep their image polished, while holding a tight rein on their inner feelings. Agamemnon and Nestor are disturbed that their seige of Troy has ground to a halt. Ulysses puts his finger on the problem, speaking first in generalities. There is no "order"; what is happening to the Greeks is like what happens when the planets "in evil mixture to disorder wander." There is no obedience to a superior. "When degree is shaked . . . the enterprise is sick." When the others agree and ask for details, Ulysses points out how their most powerful warrior, Achilles, lies in his tent with Patroclus, ridiculing the other Greek leaders.

Ulysses' speech for "order" is sometimes taken as an expression of Shakespeare's own political view. But Ulysses' philosophy is not quite Shakespeare's; his concept of "order" resting on "degree" is too much like the medieval upper-class concept of a hierarchy stemming from emperor to kings and barons, with no consideration for the common people, to conform to Shakespeare. The playwright believes in the unity and peace of a nation under a strong king, as opposed to the individualist power and pride of the old-line barons, but an important part of his thinking is that the king, while holding in check the barons, must also feel responsible for the common people. Thus Shakespeare's Henry V says:

> We few, we happy few, we band of brothers;
> For he today that sheds his blood with me
> Shall be my brother.

This, to Henry V, includes the common solidiers; but in Ulysses there is no thought of brotherhood of any kind.

At the council meeting, Aeneas enters from Troy to bring Hector's challenge. It is put in pure medieval chivalric terms. Hector "hath a lady, wiser, fairer, truer, / Than ever Greek did compass in his arms." If no Grecian challenges this, "he'll say in Troy when he retires,/ The Grecian dames are sunburnt and not worth / The splinter of a lance." The crafty Ulysses sees in this proposal for single combat a way of turning it to Greek advantage. The challenge is obviously meant for Achilles. But Ulysses tells Nestor to let them ignore Achilles and choose the "dull, brainless" muscle man Ajax. If Ajax should win, that is all to the good. If he should lose, the Greeks have hardly lost anything. They will still have Achilles. Ulysses talks like a clever business man:

> Let us, like merchants, show our foulest wares,
> And think, perchance, they'll sell; if not,
> The lustre of the better yet to show
> Shall show the better.

There is a council of the Trojan princes to discuss the possibility of returning Helen to the Greeks and to ending the war. Hector is for it, not because of any fear, but because of the wastage of lives. Troilus and, of course, Paris argue against it. Troilus is in love with Cressida and his idealization of love tinges his thinking, influenced by the principles of chivalry. Why employ the timidity of reason?

> Nay, if we talk of reason,
> Let's shut our gates, and sleep. Mankind and honour
> Should have hard hearts, would they but fat their thoughts
> With this crammed reason. Reason and respect
> Make livers pale and lustihood reject.

And Helen is beautiful. Her "youth and freshness / Wrinkles Apollo's and makes stale the morning." They all applauded the taking of Helen, he says. Why renounce her now?

Hector is unconvinced. It is still wrong to keep a wife away from her husband. But since the others think their chivalrous honor is involved ("She is a theme of honour and renown; / A spur to valiant and magnanimous deeds"), he will go along with them. Furthermore, he has already sent a challenge to the Greeks. He expects it will be answered by Achilles.

Then there is the climax of love and a sudden twist of the plot: Pandarus brings Troilus and Cressida together. As against the cynicism of Pandarus, to whom love and lust are synonymous, Troilus speaks of his hope for a constant woman, to keep his integrity. "I am as true as truth's simplicity / And simpler than the infancy of truth." Cressida vows eternal fidelity and they go to bed together. But meanwhile, in the Grecian camp, Cressida's father Calchas, a priest who has treacherously fled to the Greeks, asks in recompense for the information he has given them that Cressida be asked for in exchange for a Trojan prince they have captured. And so, the morning after the night of love, a Trojan delegation headed by Aeneas and the Greek Diomedes comes to the house of Pandarus to deliver Cressida to the Greeks. There is an intensely moving parting between Troilus and Cressida, couched in beautiful poetic language:

> Injurious Time now with a robber's haste
> Crams his rich thiev'ry up, he know not how.
> As many farewells as be stars in heaven,
> With distinct breath and consigned kisses to them,

He fumbles up into a loose adieu,
And scants us with a single famished kiss,
Distasted with the salt of broken tears.

He tells her to be true to him. He will find ways to see her,
through whatever dangers. "For I will throw my glove to Death
himself. / That there's no maculation in my heart." He himself
will be true, and this is no mere self-praise:

> Alas, it is my vice, my fault,
> Whiles others fish with craft for great opinion,
> I with great truth catch mere simplicity;
> Whilst some with cunning gild their cooper crowns,
> With truth and plainness I do wear mine bare.
> Fear not my truth. The moral of my wit
> Is 'plain and true': there's all the reach of it.

But as Diomedes takes her away, the Greek asserts his right as a
warrior to have any woman, and he will accept no admonitions
from Troilus. Diomedes knows no chivalry. "I'll nothing do on
charge. To her own worth / She shall be prized; but that you say
'Be't so,' / I'll speak it in my spirit and honour 'No!" He really
lacks the aristocrat's honor or chivalry.

Hector goes into combat with a chosen Greek. As Aeneas says,
the glory of Troy lies "On his fair worth and single chivalry."
Cressida, among the Greeks, kisses the princes. Ulysses says,
"Her wanton spirits look out / At every joint and motive of her
body." Hector finds his chosen antagonist is Ajax and fights with
him, but then stops the combat because Ajax is his kin. He really
wants to face Achilles, and when he he meets Achilles, who talks
to him contemptuously and says he will kill Hector in the field the
next day, Hector says, "Thy hand upon that match."

The great scene of the education of Troilus follows. He is led
by Ulysses to watch the tent of Calchas from a distance and sees
Cressida flirting with Diomedes. She has no strength to cope with
this man who is brutal and will not even beg her love or wheedle
her to break down her resistance. He asserts his strength over
her, and when she hesitates, he pretends to go off in a huff.
Frightened, she yields. Says Cressida, "You shall not go. One
cannot speak a word / But it straight starts you." Diomedes says

simply, "I do not like this fool ng." She even gives Diomedes the sleeve Troilus had given her as a token of constancy, although she pretends to regret this. Troilus is violently shocked. Shakespeare has endowed him with a straightforward character, uncomplicated and true to itself, and he believes others are like him. Now he is assailed by reality, and his belief in others is shattered:

> This is, and is not, Cressid:
> Within my soul there doth conduce a fight
> Of this strange nature, that a thing inseparate
> Divides more wider than the sky and earth.

He does not hate Cressida. She has been weak in a brutal world, the world of Diomedes with which Troilus must cope. He, however, will be true to his own vision. His love for Cressida is part of this:

> Instance, O instance! strong as Pluto's gates:
> Cressid is mine, tied with the bonds of heaven.
> Instance, O instance! strong as heaven itself:
> The bonds of heaven are slipped, dissolved and loosed: . . .
> The fragments, scraps, the bits and greasy relics
> Of her o'er-eaten faith, are bound to Diomed.

Diomedes' world is a travesty on chivalry; it treats women as objects to be used and thrown away. It is the world of Thersites, who cries, "Nothing but lechery. All incontinent varlets!" Troilus will not give up his integrity and beliefs; he will destroy the brutality that has taken Cressida from him. When Ulysses asks him whether he loved Cressida, he replies:

> Ay, Greek; and that shall be divulged well
> In characters red as Mars his heart
> Inflames with Venus. Never did young man fancy
> With so eternal and so fixed a soul.
> Hark, Greek: as much as I do Cressid love,
> So much by weight hate I her Diomed.
> That sleeve is mine that he'll bear on his helm,
> Were it a casque composed by Vulcan's skill,
> My sword should bit it.

Troilus leaves the Greek camp, for the truce is over. Thersites alone, having also watched the scene from afar, mutters his refrain: "Lechery, lechery! Still wars and lechery! Nothing else holds fashion. A burning devil take them!" His phrase, "Wars and lechery," is an unchivalrous interpretation of Troilus's reference to Mars and Venus.

Through this part of the play Shakespeare has been spinning his counterplot of the Greek leaders attempting to shame Achilles into fighting. They have made their point, with their pretended adulation of Ajax. Fame doesn't live on the past; it must be kept alive. Achilles has promised to meet Hector on the field the next day, but he receives another letter sent him secretly from Queen Hecuba in Troy. All the Greek leaders now know of his love for a Trojan princess. And he has resolved to keep his oath to the Trojan women.

Back in Troy, Hector is arming for combat, despite the warnings of his sister Cassandra and his wife Andromache, for he has promised Achilles to meet him in the field. He tells Troilus, "I am today i' th' vein of chivalry." This turns out to be ironic, for he will be killed in a most unchivalrous manner. Meanwhile Troilus has learned his bitter lesson, and he reproves Hector, his older brother, and the mainstay of the Trojans, in a climactic dialogue:

> *Troilus.* Brother, you have a vice of mercy in you
> Which better fits a lion than a man.
> *Hector.* What vice is that, good Troilus? Chide me for it.
> *Troilus.* When many times the captive Grecian fails,
> Even in the fan and wind of your fair sword,
> You bid them rise and live.
> *Hector.* O, 'tis fair play.
> *Troilus.* Fool's play, by heaven, Hector.
> *Hector.* How now! How now!
> *Troilus.*   For th' love of all the gods,
> Let's leave the hermit Pity with our mother;
> And when we have our armours buckled on,
> The venomed vengeance ride upon our swords,
> Spur them to ruthful work, rein them from ruth!
> *Hector.* Fie, savage, fie!
> *Troilus.*   Hector, then 'tis wars.

In the great battle that follows, the Trojans, especially Hector and Troilus, wreak havoc on the Greeks, doing, in Ulysses' words, "mad and fantastic execution." Patroclus is killed. Then Achilles, enraged at the death of Patroclus, takes to the field accompanied by a band of his serving myrmidons. He seeks no one but Hector and comes upon him near the close of day, when Hector has laid aside his armor. Achilles commands his men to assassinate the unarmed Hector. This is unchivalrous and dishonest—more tha ̀ cowardly. Achilles is apparently obeying the letter of the vow he made to Hecuba and the Trojan princess, while trampling on its spirit.

The desolate word spreads through the Trojan camp that Hector is dead. And as the Trojans are withdrawing from the day's battle, Troilus steps into Hector's place as a leader. The fight from now on will be ferocious. The Trojans must defend their homes without mercy:

> And, thou great-sized coward,
> No space on earth shall sunder our two hates,
> I'll haunt thee like a wicked conscience still, . . .
> Strike a free march to Troy! With comfort go.
> Hopes of revenge shall hide our inward woe.

Troilus's last words, as he passes Pandarus, are to curse him. And Pandarus, left alone on the stage, addresses the audience, reminding it of its own hypocrisy. Why does it employ "traitors and bawds," or traders in flesh, and pretend to despise them? "Why should our endeavors be so loved and the performance so loathed?" It is his comment on the seamy side of pretensions to chivalry.

To Shakespeare, wars were nasty and brutish. If they had to be fought, they had to be recognized as the evil they were. People attacked in their homes had to kill or be killed. Such wars should not be decorated with the myths of chivalry.

This is the theme of *Troilus and Cressida*, which is a comedy in that it ends on a rising note with Troilus's education, but it is not a merry comedy. It is actually a new kind of comedy, which had been projected in *The Merchant of Venice* but not then fully worked out. There is no death of a hero—Hector is not its hero—but it is serious in thought from beginning to end and places the problem not only of war but also of love and sex relations squarely in the lap of society. Cressida is not a heroine but neither is she evil, only victimized by a man's world. And chivalry, with its deification of women is no answer, for even the aristocracy who proclaim it no longer lived by it. Shakespeare raises a new and powerful standard of morality. It is Troilus's "truth," which means truth to oneself and honesty that involves one's whole being. It is realistic in that it faces the actual world. How it fares is an open question, but it is a way of life. And in another comedy, Shakespeare takes up the question—*Measure for Measure.*

Measure for Measure moves with the structural unity of a great tragic drama like *Julius Caesar,* again depicting contrasting sides of life. The play deals with sex and social morality and, showing a technical grasp as firm as its social understanding is profound, unfolds this theme in the parallel worlds of the vulgar streets and the halls of the mighty. Each scene plays a role in both the development of the plot and the development of the thought. There are no characters who function solely as clowns. Those whose language is predominantly comic, like the seedy gentleman Lucio and the whorehouse flunkey Pompey, play a solid role in the dramatic thought and action.

The time of the play is close to Shakespeare's own, and by giving it a setting away from England in a Vienna ruled by a kindly Duke with absolute powers but responsible to his people, Shakespeare is able to disguise central questions of government and morality. The framework of the play is made of the conventions of comedy. Thus in the first scene the Duke, setting off on what he explains is a necessary journey to Poland, hands over his authority to the noble Lord Angelo, and in the third scene the audience learns that the Duke has come back to Vienna disguised as a friar to see what happens in his pretended absence. This is assurance that at the critical time the Duke will throw off his disguise and confound whatever evils he has discovered. The audience is also expected to accept the fact that the Duke's disguise is absolutely impenetrable and that as a strange friar he can gain entry wherever he wishes. But these conventions are transformed in the bitterly ironic meanings that Shakespeare develops through the Duke's secret role. The very conventions provide the irony.

The play is undeniably a comedy, for the element of "necessity" is done away with. The good people are in the end victorious and the evildoers exposed. But it is a bitter play, for its central motif is death, and the struggle for the life of a young gentleman who is condemned by law, but whom everyone of good heart wants to save. Its theme is that human life must be held precious in the face not only of murderers but also of the law, which itself murders and plunders.

In the short first scene the Duke of Vienna says farwell to the aged Lord Escalus, and, referring to the young Lord Angelo, says that he has:

> Lent him our terror, dressed him with our love,
> And given his deputation all the organs,
> Of our own power.

He tells Angelo, "Mortality and mercy in Vienna / Live in thy organs and thy heart." Important is the word "mortality." And the second scene finds Angelo ruling Vienna with fanatic morality. He has brought back to life a law that had long been ignored, and condemned to speedy death a young gentleman, Claudio, who got his beloved Juliet with child without marrying her. They had postponed their marriage until certain questions of her dowry could be settled. But the letter of the law has been violated, and Angelo rules he must die. This scene also introduces three characters who are important to the play because they personify the raucous, lusty, undercover sexual activity of the streets—which could be as true of the streets of London as they are of Vienna. They are Mistress Overdone, a whorehouse madam; Pompey, her tapster; and Lucio, a witty gentleman who is one of her frequent customers.

Lucio, a friend of the arrested Claudio, is told by him to call Claudio's sister Isabella, who is about to take vows in a nunnery and ask her to appeal to Angelo for his life. Lucio does so, after another short scene in which the Duke returns to Vienna disguised as a friar. The reason for this masquerade, he says, is that for 14 years the laws in Vienna have been allowed to slip, so that now dissolution is rampant, "liberty plucks justice by the nose / The baby beats the nurse." For the Duke to reactivate the laws would seem to be tyranny. And so he has left it to the straitlaced Angelo. Now, in disguise, he, the Duke, will see "If power changes purpose."

There is another scene of city corruption. It begins with a discussion between Angelo and Escalus of Claudio's threatened life. Escalus pleads for mercy and understanding. Claudio has been weak, but others, not condemned, and perhaps even the condemners, have been just as weak. But Angelo stays firm. "We must not make a scarecrow of the law, / . . . he must die." Then Pompey, some of the gentry, and the constable Elbow burst in with a weird tale of wrongdoing that Elbow is too slow-witted to get straight. It turns out that part of the breakdown of justice comes about when the local citizens, who are required periodically to act as constables, pay the idiot Elbow to take their place. And as part of the scene, this conversation takes place:

> *Pompey.* Truly, sir, I am a poor fellow that would live.
> *Escalus.* How would you live, Pompey? By being a bawd? What do you think of the trade, Pompey? Is it a lawful trade?
> *Pompey.* If the law would allow it, sir.
> *Escalus.* But the law will not allow it, Pompey; nor it shall not be allowed in Vienna.
> *Pompey.* Does your worship mean to geld and splay all the youth of the city?

Escalus threatens Pompey with whipping if he is brought up again before the law, and Pompey says privately, "The valiant heart's not whipt out of his trade." Thus he mockingly twists the noble sentiments of the gentry. And this abrasion of the life of the gentry against that of the streets, which contrasts the open corruption of the streets with the hidden corruption of the gentry, in language as well as action, creates the atmosphere of the play. The scene ends again with sad talk about Claudio. Escalus is for mercy. "Pardon is still the nurse of second woe: / But yet - poor Claudio! There is no remedy."

A confrontation between Isabella and Angelo takes place. The scene opens with the provost of the prison speaking to Angelo, hoping he will relent on Claudio. His argument is a humanistic one. "He hath but as offended in a dream! All sects, all ages smack of this vice; and he / To die for't!" Angelo is adamant; Claudio must die the next day. Then Isabella enters. She asks mercy for Claudio. Angelo insists, "It is the law . . . / Were he my kinsman, brother, or my son, / It should be thus with him." She grows more eloquent. Shakespeare gives her a distinct ethical feeling; she is about to become a nun, and her argument is that of a convinced Catholic who finds in religion a higher law than mankind's:

>   O, it is excellent
> To have a giant's strength; but it is tyrannous
> To use it like a giant. . . .
>   man, proud man
> Drest in a little brief authority,
> Most ignorant of what he's most assured,
> His glassy essence, like an angry ape,
> Plays such fantastic tricks before high heaven
> As makes the angels weep.

She promises Angelo that she and the nuns will pray for him,

>   with true prayers
> That shall be up at heaven and enter there
> Ere sunrise, prayers from preserved souls,
> From fasting maids whose minds are dedicate
> To nothing temporal.

It is her very saintliness that captures Angelo—not to forgive Claudio but to desire her sexually. He bids her to return the next day and when they are alone discloses how his lust has been aroused:

> O cunning enemy, that, to catch a saint,
> With saints dost bait thy hook! . . .
>   never could the strumpet
> With all her double vigour, art and nature,
> Once stir my temper; but this virtuous maid
> Subdues me quite.

Into the jail comes the Duke disguised as a Friar Lodowick. He
speaks to Juliet, whom Claudio has gotten with child. "Love you
the man that wronged you?" Her answer is "Yes, as I love the
woman who wronged him." Friar Lodowick says that Claudio
"must die tomorrow," and the Provost says again, " 'Tis pity of
him." Then follows the intense scene the next day between
Isabella and Angelo. She does not understand Angelo's hints
until he puts it to her bluntly. "Lay down the treasures of your
body," and Claudio will live. She indignantly refuses. When
Angelo says that her brother must then die, she says,

> And 'twere the cheaper way:
> Better it were a brother died at once,
> Than that a sister, by redeeming him,
> Should die forever.

Isabella is not popular with critics. Charlotte Lennox, an
English writer admired by Samuel Johnson, wrote in the 18th
century that Isabella was a vixen and a prude. Hazlitt is scornful
of her "rigid chastity." But hers is the understandable position of
a Catholic prepared to withdraw from the world and fix her eyes
on the life after death. To lose eternal blessedness for a few more
years of her brother's life would be a bad bargain. This is not
Shakespeare's view. To him, real life is precious. But he respects
her position, and, more important, he is realist enough to know
that she would gain nothing by succumbing to Angelo's black-
mail. Angelo, once he sins, would be led to further sins. As it
turns out, when later Angelo thinks he has slept with Isabella, he
gives orders to have Claudio immediately executed. For he is
afraid that were Claudio to live and some day find out the truth,
he would take revenge. And Angelo already knows the trickery of
his depravity. When Isabella says that she will "tell the world
aloud / What man thou art," his answer is that he would deny it,
and nobody would believe her.

There follows next the great climactic scene of this first part of
the play. Isabella goes to the prison to tell Claudio of the
atrocious offer, feeling that this will reconcile him to die. And at
first he agrees with her; then he says, "O Isabel! . . . Death is a
fearful thing."

Thus a great climax is reached of conflicting views of life. For Claudio's feeling is not morbidity. It is the intense relish for life in a youth who has just begun to live. He speaks as a humanist who finds delight in simply living, moving, speaking. It is expressed in powerful poetry which expresses his visions of death:

> Ay, but to die, and go we know not where;
> To lie in cold obstruction and to rot;
> This sensible warm motion to become
> A kneaded clod; and the delighted spirit
> To bathe in fiery floods, or to reside
> In thrilling region of thick-ribbed ice;
> To be imprisoned in the viewless winds,
> And blown with restless violence round about
> The pendant world; . . .
>   'Tis too horrible!
> The weariest and most loathed worldly life
> That age, ache, penury, and imprisonment
> Can lay on nature is a paradise
> To what we fear of death. . . .
>   Sweet sister, let me live.

This is especially powerful because it sums up in a great outburst all the expressions of concern that have marked the play up to this point over Claudio's awful situation. Isabella is furious at him. "O you beast! / O faithless coward! O dishonest wretch!" She turns away in wrath.

The Duke, as Friar Lodowick, who has been secretly listening to this exchange, takes Isabella aside to propose a solution. He knows a woman, Mariana, to whom Angelo had pledged marriage. Oaths were sworn, but suddenly her brother had died in shipwreck, and with the ship her dowry had been lost. Angelo had renounced her. But in spirit she is his wife. Let Isabella agree to sleep with Angelo, but at a time and place in which Mariana could substitute for her. And so Claudio would be saved and later, when the ruse would be made public, Mariana would have a husband.

The picture of the upper-class, secret corruption of Angelo, is contrasted with a scene of street corruption. Pompey is arrested; bitterly he says, "of two usuries, the merriest was put down, and the worser allowed by order of the law a furred gown to keep him warm." So the poorer scoundrels are punished and the rich scoundrels honored. But still the street corruption, which buys and sells human beings like animals, is no less inhuman. The Duke, as Friar Lodowick, tells Pompey, "Canst thou believe thy living is a life, / So stinkingly depending? Go mend, go mend." Pompey recognizes Lucio as an old customer, and asks him for bail money, but Lucio only wishes him a long stay in jail. Bad as Pompey is, the gentleman Lucio is worse. He is also a lying gossip and prattles dirty stores about the Duke to Friar Lodowick, not knowing, of course, that he is addressing the disguised Duke himself. Mrs. Overdone is arrested. Lucio has informed against her. He has gotten a whore with child and, to escape responsibility, abuses Mrs. Overdone. The Duke as Friar Lodowick ends the scene thinking of Angelo. "He who the sword of heaven will bear / Should be as holy as severe." But Angelo is a hypocrite. "O, what may man within him hide, / Though angel on the outward side!" He must be approached with cunning. "Craft against vice I must apply."

The scheme to have Angelo sleep with Mariana works. There now follow in succession two fantastic scenes in the prison which make wild, bitter humor over the theme of death. The first opens with the Provost asking Pompey, "Can you cut off a man's head?" He gets a lasciviously witty answer, but he is serious about making Pompey a helper to the executioner, who is named Abhorson. The executioner objects, "Fie upon him! He will discredit our mystery." But the Provost says, "Go to sir; you weigh equally." The Duke, still disguised, enters, confident that he has saved Claudio, but he is horrified when a messenger comes from Angelo insisting that Claudio be executed and his head sent to Angelo. The mock Friar convinces the kindly Provost that it would be in accord with the Duke's wishes to give Claudio four days' grace and send Angelo a substitute head. But the question rises, whose head? The bitter comedy reaches extraordinary heights with another prisoner, Bernadine. He is due for execution, and the plan is to send his head to Angelo instead of Claudio's. But Bernadine simply refuses to agree to having his head cut off. He protests he is too sleepy; then, that he has been drinking all night and he is not fit for the execution. Finally he says, "I swear I will not die today for any man's persuasion," and walks off. Providentially, another criminal in the prison has just died of a fever, and his head is sent off to Angelo with the pretense that it is Claudio's. Then Isabella enters, and the Duke (still as a mock friar) tells her Claudio is dead.

The play then moves to its grand finale. The Duke has letters sent to announce his return. He makes his appearnace in his own guise, is met by the city dignitaries, and is approached by Isabella and Mariana with their charges against Angelo. He pretends not to believe them. These women are lying or mentally incompetent. How can a man of such a blameless reputation as Angelo be guilty of such misdeeds? Let the women be arrested and questioned.

Some commentators have found Shakespeare guilty of making the Duke needlessly cruel. Not only has he told Isabella her brother was executed, when he knows he was not, but now he brings further pain to Isabella and Mariana. And the suspense is further prolonged. Friar Lodowick is named as the insidious scoundrel who fostered these charges by the women, and Lucio adds to the slanders about him. The Duke sends for the Friar and disappears. Then he appears disguised as the Friar, and is abused and threatened by the city officials. The malefactors are triumphant. But there is method to this dragged-out pain before the happy ending. Shakespeare is having the Duke act as he probably would have acted had he gone on an actual journey and been met on his return with these strange-sounding charges. How else would he have been able to penetrate the glib lying of the saintly Angelo and the quick-witted Lucio?

Everything is set straight, of course, when Lucio, ingratiating himself with the city officials, pulls off the Friar's hood and, to his astonishment, discovers that he is the Duke. The scoundrels are aghast. Sternly the Duke names their hidden crimes and pronounces sentence. He knows everything, including their most intimate secrets—like one of "God's spies," to quote a phrase from *King Lear.* He condemns Angelo to marry Mariana and then to be executed, because he has planned Claudio's death. Mariana and Isabella both beg mercy for him, but the Duke is adamant. And then it turns out that Claudio has not been killed, and so Angelo is reprieved. The Duke condemns Lucio to be whipped and hanged, and then, rather than having him hanged, he decides that Lucio must merely marry the whorehouse slut he got with child. The principle he has proclaimed is, "Like doth quit like, and Measure still for Measure," giving a sentence that matches the crime. It is a scene like the medieval visions of the Day of Judgment, when all souls appear before the awesome Judge, naked not only in body but in mind. But there is one central difference—these people are all alive and have a life before them. And what is significant is that nobody is killed. Even Barnadino, the condemned criminal, is granted mercy. And the Duke asks Isabella to be his wife.

It is an ending that could only happen in comedy, where social necessity is temporarily suspended. And because of the intense social realism of the body of the play, of its street scenes, its whorehouses patronized by the gentry, its brutal chicanery typified in a gentleman like Lucio, its seamy ways of making a living, its corruption among the highest personages—including one who judges others (as Pompey says, crime is protected when it wears a "furred gown"), this happy ending is of necessity ironic. The irony is intensified by the returning Duke's pretended suspicion of the good people. And the question necessarily arises among the audience: in real life could even the most astute and principled of rulers see the truth behind appearances? Could he penetrate the lies of a Lucio and discern an Angelo's sexual desire behind his icy front?

The question is left up in the air. Shakespeare has no answer. Actually any reasonable answer was to lie far in the future, when justice was to become a social concern and did not rest on the power of an absolute ruler alone. Shakespeare cannot see this answer and the problems attendant on it. But his genius enables him to put the question powerfully and to express his intense hatred for the kind of immoral conduct that harms others as well as his deep sadness for the sorry ways of life forced on people. So by writing the play and addressing it to society, he makes it a presentation of a social problem. And he does have one answer, even if it is not complete—that human life must be considered precious, that people are killed not merely by murderers but by the law, and it is far better not to kill than to kill.

8

LOVE AND THE STATE

Othello

Othello is one of Shakespeare's most perfectly constructed tragic dramas, a great masterpiece in the consistent beauty of its poetry and the abundance of incisive characterizations, each of which plays a decisive role in the drama. The central dramatic conflict involves Othello, Desdemona and Iago, but there are others who play an essential role: Roderigo, a young nobleman enamored of Desdemona; Cassio, Othello's right-hand man; Emilia, Iago's wife and servant to Desdemona; Brabantio, Desdemona's father. Not only do each of them have an internal life that rings true and makes them come alive to the audience, but their relationship to the world around them makes them representative of specific currents of social reality. The world they collectively shape has remarkable vitality, and the tragedy is as much a creation of this world as of the individual personages.

Like the earlier play, *The Merchant of Venice, Othello* is centered in Venice and its period is close to Shakespeare's own time. In both plays there is a scathing critical exposure of evils rising from social phenomena. In the earlier play, as this study has tried to show, the playwright criticized the money-driven mentality and the consequent destruction of its possessor's humanity. In *Othello,* he exposes the rationalized self-centeredness and a new form of psychological duplicity that tries to advance through ruthless war upon all men.

Othello is not a play that relates to the racist practises of today or of the 18th and 19th centuries. This has to be said because productions and discussions have interpreted it in this light. The racism in which the white man is projected as the natural superior of the black man was not a feature of the ancient slaveholding societies, nor of the middle ages, nor of Shakespeare's own time. In ancient slavery, it was conquered people who were enslaved, regardless of color. In the Middle Ages and Renaissance there was enough trade between Europe and Africa to bring widespread knowledge of African kingdoms and civilizations. Europe's slave trade to furnish Europe's slave trade to furnish labor to the Americas ruined these kingdoms, but this trade did not begin until the 16th century. English adventurers in Shakespeare's time, Sir John Hawkins, for example, supplied slaves to Spanish ports. It was only with the establishment of great European empires over Asia and Africa, and with the ruthless use of African labor on American cotton plantations that the theory arose that colored people were innately inferior to whites, and fit only to work in their service. Thus Paul Bohannan writes of the late 18th and 19th centuries, "It was in this era that the idea of the Dark Continent—the phrase was Stanley's—came to the fore . . . . Africa was a prime target for colonial expansion. In order for colonial expansion to take place, it became necessary to consolidate the view of African cultures as savage and barbarian in order to justify one's activities."[1]

In the 19th century there were agitated proposals that Othello should be shown as a light brown man rather than as a black African, although Shakespeare is quite explicit as to his blackness. Coleridge wrote early in the 19th century, "Can we suppose him (Shakespeare) so utterly ingorant as to make a barbarous *negro* plead royal birth? Were negroes then known but as slaves;

on the contrary, were not the Moors the warriors, etc.?"[2] But Coleridge is historically ignorant while Shakespeare is not; there were Africans of royal blood in Shakespeare's time.

The 20th century ascribed to Shakespeare a pseudoethnic theorizing. Mark Van Doren writes of Othello, "there is a great gentleness in him" and also that "the barbarian is very close to the surface. . . . Othello is all of the past trying to forget itself in a moment, he is Africa trying to breathe in Venice."[3] Sir Lawrence Olivier gave a highly studied performance on the stage and in a motion picture, in which he stressed Othello's fancied weird and alien characteristics, to the extent that the actor was unable to give eloquence to Shakespeare's lines. His simulation of Othello as a black man contrasted sharply with the dignity given the role by the great Paul Robeson.

It is true that in Shakespeare's England, black was almost synonymous with ugly, while fairness was associated with beauty. But this was no barrier to marriage between black and white. Portia, in *The Merchant of Venice,* is courted by a black man, the Prince of Morocco. He says, "Mislike me not for my complexion." She assures him that he is a perfectly fit suitor for her hand, although she is glad when he chooses the wrong casket, and says, "Let all of his complexion choose me so." In *The Tempest,* the daughter of the King of Naples marries the black King of Tunis.

Othello is not handsome, he is not young, he is battle-scarred, but at the same time nobody in Venice or Cyprus feels anything amiss in that a black man is their general or that he is a governor of Cyprus, or that he has a white wife. Nobody has any hesitation in taking orders from him. What is surprising to some people in the play is that the young and beautiful Desdemona, daughter of one of the great patrician senators of Venice, should have fallen in love with an unhandsome, black man. But Shakespeare uses the blackness to emphasize Othello's heroic qualities. He makes Desdemona's love explicit a sign of her nobility and independence of mind. She is attracted not to a handsome face nor to a clotheshorse, but to a human being of stature above the ordinary, a noble and heroic personality—an honored guest in her father's house.

The first scene of *Othello* is perhaps the greatest opening scene in Shakespeare's plays for dramatic intensity, breadth of social outlook and the sheer amount of information it conveys in a most natural way. The great event it tells of is the elopement and marriage of Othello and Desdemona, but these two do not appear in it. With consummate artistry and economy, Shakespeare presents the event through its effect on Iago, who hates Othello; Roderigo, who dotes on Desdemona; and Brabantio, her father, while, at the same time, it reveals their personalities and sets the drama in motion with white-hot intensity.

Iago and Roderigo are seen walking on a street in Venice. It is worthy of comment that the qualities that some commentators attribute to Othello when he later succumbs to Iago's wiles, his gullibility and childishness of mind (ascribing them to his blackness), are far more true of Roderigo, a young nobleman who has become a victim of Iago's scheming. It is extraordinary how much the first lines of the play tell us in the most apparently effortless way:

> *Roderigo.* Tush, never tell me; I take it most unkindly
> That you, Iago, who has my purse
> As if the strings were thine, shouldst know of this.
> *Iago.* 'Sblood, but you will not hear me:
> If ever I did dream of such a matter,
> Abhor me.
> *Roderigo.* Thou told'st me thou did hold him in thy hate.
> *Iago.* Despise me, if I do not.
> Three great ones of the city,
> In my personal suit to make me his lieutenant,
> Off-capped to him: and, by the faith of man,
> I know my price, I am worth no worse a place,
> But he, as loving his own pride and purposes,
> Evades them with a bombast circumstance
> Horribly stuffed with epithets of war;
> And, in conclusion,
> Nonsuits my mediators; for 'Certes,' says he,
> 'I have already chose my officer.'
> And what was he?
> Forsooth a great arithmetician,
> One Michael Cassio, a Florentine . . .

We learn from this that Iago has been helping himself liberally to Roderigo's money; that some suspicion has arisen in Roderigo's mind about the friendliness of their relationship; that some military leader in the city has been involved in an important event; that Iago hates him; that Iago is no ordinary soldier but one who has friends in high places and thinks himself worthy of being this great leader's lieutenant or right-hand man, and that the leader can't be bent by influence but has a mind of his own.

As Iago continues his abuse of this eminent leader and the lieutenant he has chosen, it emerges that Iago himself has been named the leader's "ancient" or ensign, third in command. When Iago repeats he hates this leader, this dialogue occurs:

> *Roderigo.* I would not follow him then.
> *Iago.*   O, sir, content you;
> I follow him to serve my turn upon him . .
> In following him, I follow but myself.

A moral difference comes clear, which Iago smooths over with glib speech. Roderigo is a straightforward man, not that he is the soul of honesty but that he lacks craft. He follows the code of his class, the landed gentry. If one doesn't like a leader, one doesn't serve him. Iago's is a different code; he serves the man he hates in order to find ways to destroy him. Life is a cutthroat struggle. "Reason" to him means to recognize this and to fight with all weapons including duplicity. Of course, the simpleton-gentleman Roderigo will not know of Iago's perfidy until the closing scenes of the play. Iago does not have to feel a special hate for a man in order to kill him, for he despises all men and regards them as being either as malevolent as he or as fools.

The scene develops further. The two are before Brabantio's house: Iago tells Roderigo to rouse the father with the news that his daughter has stolen away and to raise an alarm "As when, by night and negligence, the fire / Is spied in populous cities." Roderigo does so, and Iago, while hiding, adds his more brutal comments, "an old black ram / Is tupping your white ewe." Significantly only Iago in the play uses what might be termed racist epithets. They are a product of his own animalistic views of people. So he adds, "You'll have your daughter covered with a Barbary horse. You'll have your nephews neigh to you."

Brabantio thinks that only Roderigo is there and speaking. Iago hopes to stir up an armed conflict between Brabantio's kinsmen and Othello's soldiers. But he keeps hidden in the background. Then he tells Roderigo that he, Iago, must not be seen rousing Brabantio against Othello, since he must pretend to be Othello's loyal follower. And after he tells Roderigo where Othello is staying so he can lead Brabantio's men there, he slinks away. Brabantio is aroused. "Get weapons, ho! / And rouse some special officers of night."

Interestingly, when earlier in the scene Brabantio had first noticed Roderigo, he had said, "I have charged thee not to haunt about my doors . . . . / My daughter is not for thee." At the end of the scene, he tells Roderigo, "O, would you had had her!" It is not that he is an evil old man, but his is a mind of the old aristocratic order. He loves his daughter, but regards her as his property. He had planned a noble marriage for her, someone greater than Roderigo, but even he would do, rather than a scarred, ugly African, however honored.

In the second scene Othello confronts the raging Brabantio and his armed men. It begins with Iago acting before him the role of a sturdy soldier hotheadedly loyal to his superior, but self-critical because he cannot easily murder people who abuse his superior. He warns Othello of Brabantio's search for him, omitting, of course, that he had stirred up Brabantio and has had Roderigo tell him where Othello was. Othello is calm, unafraid, self-confident. He will not boast that he is of royal birth until "I know that boasting is an honour." To him the life of a soldier is freedom, and were is not that he loves the "gentle Desdemona," he says, "I would not my unhoused free condition / Put into circumscription and confine / For the sea's worth." When Iago tells him to flee, he stands his ground. Cassio comes with a notice for him to appear before the Council. Then when Brabantio comes with his men, Iago pretends to want to fight Roderigo. "You, Roderigo! come, sir, I am for you." But Othello calms them all down with good-humored contempt:

Keep up your bright swords, for the dew will rust them.
Good signior, you shall more command with years
Then with your weapons.

They agree that Brabantio will present his charges at the Council, where Othello is being asked to become governor of Cyprus and defend it against the threatening Turks. Othello's character flowers fully in this council scene. Brabantio brings charges against Othello of using drugs and witchcraft, "spells and medicines bought of mountebanks," for how else could Desdemona "fall in love with what she most feared to look on." Othello says, "Rude am I in my speech." He knows little of civilized or city life. For seven years his arms "have used / Their dearest action in the tented field; / And little of this great world can I speak,/ More than pertains to feats of broil and battle." He asks them to send for Desdemona.

Meanwhile, he tells them how he won her. In a wonderful speech, without figures of speech, flowery language or rhetorical effects, he speaks great poetry revealing sensitivity and powers of observation, catching the details that reveal the interior life. Brabantio, he says, had loved him and often invited him to his house to tell of his past life and adventures:

> This to hear
> Would Desdemona seriously incline:
> But still the house affairs would draw her thence;
> Which ever as she could with haste dispatch,
> She'd come again and with a greedy ear
> Devour up my discourse . . .
>   My story being done,
> She gave me for my pains a world of sighs.
> She swore, in faith, 'twas strange, 'twas passing strange;
> 'Twas pitiful, 'twas wondrous pitiful.
> She wished she had not heard it, yet she wished
> That heaven had made her such a man. She thanked me,
> And bade me, if I had a friend that loved her,
> I should but teach him how to tell my story,
> And that would woo her. Upon this hint I spake.
> She loved me for the dangers I had passed,
> And I loved her that she did pity them.

The Duke exclaims, "I think this tale would win my daughter too."

Othello is the kind of commander a rising nation needs to

defend itself, strong, straightforward, incorruptible, loyal. He knows the battlefield, where men must show their courage and cannot dissemble. He knows nothing of civilized city life and its treacheries. And so the ground is laid for the tragedy to come. For, as a trusted public servant, his reputation is linked with that of the state. He must live blamelessly. Any slander aimed at him becomes slander of the state he represents. That is why when the accusation that Desdemona is unfaithful comes to him later, it appears to him incontrovertible, destructive of his career, and his great outcry is, "Othello's occupation's gone."

Desdemona then appears in person for the first time in the play, but she has already been vividly brought to life before the audience by Othello's speech. When Brabantio demands her obedience, she answers that her duty is "divided," for while she respects her father, she has also chosen Othello as her husband. It is plain that she is one of Shakespeare's great heroines. She has a fine mind and deep principles. She has chosen for husband no courtier but a person of deep inner qualities—courage and honesty. This is the third of the opposition of the old and the new moralities through which the drama proceeds. There had been the opposition between Roderigo's code with its relative frankness and Iago's duplicity and cunning; then the opposition between Brabantio's feudal-minded attempt to settle arguments with swordplay and Othello's peaceful restraint and devotion to the state; now the opposition between Brabantio's view of his daughter as his chattel and Desdemona's insistence on the humanist right to choose and marry the man she loves. Shakespeare does not look on Brabantio as an evil man but only as one limited by his narrow and outmoded outlook. He says fiercely that his daughter is "dead" to him, but the audience will later learn that he dies of a broken heart. His final words to Othello are like a curse: "Look to her, Moor, if thou hast eyes to see; / She has deceived her father, and may thee," He speaks from the cynical knowledge of the treacheries with which city life abounds, and the words will haunt Othello's mind. In a way, Brabantio unwittingly assists at the murder of his own daughter.

When Othello is sent to Cyprus, Desdemona pleads to go there with him and she is allowed to do so. This great scene ends with a dialogue between Roderigo and Iago, which further reveals Iago's rationalistic questioning of all moral principles and sentiments. Roderigo, having observed Desdemona's attachment to Othello, announces, "I will incontinently drown myself." Iago laughs at him. A man must learn "to love himself." He must poise "reason" against his "sensuality," and "reason" to Iago means self-service larded with money:

> I say, put money in thy purse. It cannot be long that Desdemona should continue her love to the Moor—put money in thy purse—nor his to her: it was a violent commencement in her, and thou shalt see an answerable sequestration;—put but money in thy purse. These Moors are changeable in their wills: fill thy purse with money. The food that to him now is as luscious as locusts shall be to him shortly as bitter as coloquintida. She must change for youth: when she is sated with his body, she will find the error of her choice. She must have change, she must: therefore put money in thy purse. If thou wilt needs damn thyself, do it a more delicate way than drowning. Make all the money thou canst. If sanctimony and a frail vow betwixt an erring barbarian and a supersubtle Venetian be not too hard for my wits and all the tribe of hell, thou shalt enjoy her; therefore make money.

Roderigo, comforted with the promise that he will possess Desdemona, goes off to raise more money, saying "I'll go sell all my land." Iago, left alone, comments, "Thus do I make my fool my purse." He despises Roderigo, "a snipe"; he hates the "Moor"; knows that Othello has a high regard for him and lays plans to destroy him by using Cassio. He will convince Othello that Cassio is sleeping with his wife:

> The Moor is of a free and open nature
> That thinks men honest that but seem to be so;
> And will as tenderly be led by the nose
> As Asses are.

This ends the first act, and the next four acts take place in Cyprus, where the Venetian governor, Montano, welcomes the fact that he will be replaced by Othello; "'tis a worthy governor . . . . the man commands / Like a full soldier." Iago makes the handsome Cassio his tool by getting him drunk, presumably to honor Othello's arrival, and having Roderigo attack him. In the resulting fight, the blame falls on Cassio, whose wits are too befuddled to know what has happened. Othello, angry, cashiers him. "Cassio, I love thee; / But never more be officer of mine." Cassio's passionate outcry is taken ironically by Iago. "Reputation, reputation, reputation! O, I have lost my reputation! I have lost the immortal part of myself, and what remains is bestial. My reputation, Iago, my reputation!" It is more moving than Iago's later rhetorical homily to Othello, "Good name in man—and woman—dear my lord, / Is the immediate jewel of their souls. / Who steals my purse steals trash . . ." because it is a cry from the heart. And now Iago puts Cassio to further use, advising him to appeal to Desdemona for assistance. This will enable Iago to raise suspicions in Othello's mind.

Commentators are strangely puzzled by Iago, considering him to be a devil or monster, G. Wilson Knight writes, "Iago, if not human or in any usual sense 'realistic,' is quite unique."[4] But Iago's mentality is nothing more than that of the profiteer or capitalist who seeks his own private advantage and must regard all other people as potential enemies or victims. Money, he thinks, is the greatest power, and to have money is the greatest good. Life is a war of all against all. Behind his hatred of Othello lie hopes for his own advancement. He is no common soldier but a man of rank. High personages in Venice thought him fit to be Othello's second in command. Why could he not hope to fill Othello's shoes if the Moor were destroyed? As a matter of fact, later in the play an order comes from Venice calling Othello back and appointing Cassio in his place. Why could this not be Iago?

His psychological manipulation of people is remarkable, so that while posing as a bluff, simple person, he injects thoughts they think have come from their own minds. And this kind of manipulation was an indoctrination technique, used in later historical epochs, reaching its peak with the growth of capitalism and accompanied by party politics, newspapers, publicity, the consumer goods industries, and a concentration on selling the public commodities and political ideas. Shakespeare catches the process in its inception. Today this lack of conscience has become a major force in advertising, politics and diplomacy.

Thus Vance Packard describes it in his book *The Hidden Persuaders:*

> It is about the large-scale efforts being made, often with impressive success, to channel our unthinking habits, our purchasing decisions, and our thought processes by the use of insights gleaned from psychiatry and the social sciences. Typically these efforts take place beneath our level of awareness; so that the appeals which move us are often, in a sense, 'hidden.' The result is that many of us are being influenced and manipulated, far more than we realize, in the patterns of our everyday lives.[5]

Shakespeare, of course, had no special knowledge of modern psychiatry or the social sciences to guide his keen observation of people. But he has described with horror a real process that was to grow in future centuries. And he exposes it with the sensitive perceptions of an artist and the analytic mind of a scientist.

The scene in which Iago manipulates Othello's mind in this way, the third of Act Three, is a masterpiece, so subtle in its gradation of steps that although great changes take place in this one scene, the audience accepts it completely because the process is psychologically so sound. Cassio is speaking with Desdemona in the garden and, following Iago's advice, he leaves when he sees Othello and Iago approaching. The process of manipulation begins with these words:

> *Iago.*   Ha! I like not that.
> *Othello.* What dost thou say?
> *Iago.*   Nothing, my lord: or if—I know not what.
> *Othello.* What not that Cassio parted from my wife?
> *Iago.*   Cassio, my lord! No, sure, I cannot think it,
> That he would sneak away so guilty-like,
> Seeing you coming.
> *Othello.* I do believe it was he.

So Iago plants in Othello's mind the thought that there are secret relations between Cassio and Desdemona, and yet he has said nothing about this; only a muttered exclamation to himself which he immediately withdraws as "nothing," and then a defense of Cassio when Othello names him, into which, with an air of innocence, he injects such words as "sneak" and "guilty-like." And so Othello thinks that the idea of Cassio's interest in Desdemona is his own, while Iago, he believes, is a straightforward man who thinks no harm of anyone.

The drop of poison Iago has injected has a troubling effect on Othello's mind, so that when Desdemona enters talking cheerily and innocently of Cassio, each of her words strikes a chord in Othellos spirit. It is the first disturbance of their relationship. And drop by drop Iago adds what he himself calls "my poison," while simultaneously building his own image before Othello as an open-hearted man who only reluctantly would think ill of another person. At the midpoint of the scene, Desdemona binds Othello's head with a precious handkerchief, which Othello carelessly discards. Emilia picks it up, and Iago purloins it. He now has a new weapon, and can say behind Othello's back:

> Not poppy, nor mandragora,
> Nor all the drowsy syrups of the world,
> Shall ever medicine thee to that sweet sleep
> Which thou owedst yesterday.

And Othello's poignant lament shows how the thought of Desdemona's betrayal has affected not only the personal pride or possessiveness but his public life:

> Farewell the neighing steed and the shrill trump,
> The spirit-stirring drum, th' ear-piercing fife,
> The royal banner and all quality,
> Pride, pomp and circumstance of glorious war!
> And, O you mortal engines, whose rude throats
> Th' immortal Jove's dread clamours counterfeit,
> Farewell! Othello's occupation's gone!

He finds it inconceivable to live by one set of moral principles in private life and another set in public life, for that would be living a lie. A defender of the state represents it and must be one at whom nobody can point an accusing or derisive finger.

It is this that leads to the torment Othello suffers in the second part of the scene. For if the accusations of hidden adultery are true, Cassio and Desdemona cannot be allowed to live. So Othello's derangement of mind begins. To Shakespeare this is a conflict between firmly held illusions and a reality that cannot be reconciled with these illusions. So Othello is torn between the conviction that Desdemona is unfaithful, and the knowledge in his senses and intuition that tells him she is true. "I think my wife be honest, and think she is not." Iago proceeds to the attack, while pretending that his "evidence" is being given reluctantly; it is being dragged out of him; he is permitting this only out of "foolish honesty and love" for Othello. He tells a lie about having heard Cassio in his sleep talking of his love for Desdemona. Of course, to influence Othello to interpret this as indicating a real affair, Iago says, "Nay, this was but his dream." Then Iago tells of the precious handkerchief which he has seen in Cassio's hands, presumably given him by Desdemona. It is, of course, at this very moment in Iago's pocket. The scene ends with Othello commissioning Iago to kill Cassio, thinking of the way he himself will kill Desdemona, and telling Iago, "Now art thou my Lieutenant."

This is the turning point, and the tragedy moves to its conclusion. Othello demands the handkerchief of Desdemona. She, of course, is bewildered, not knowing how it has disappeared. Iago can now venture a direct lie. He tells Othello that Cassio has confessed to him that he had slept with Desdemona, and Othello falls into a babbling fit. "Is't possible? Confess? Handkerchief? O devil!" Then Iago sets up a scene where he will presumably be talking to Cassio about Desdemona, and Othello will look on but not be able to hear. Actually Iago will talk to Cassio about Bianca, his favorite strumpet. Cassio will laugh, and Iago says, "As he shall smile, Othello shall go mad."

The scene takes place and has the planned effect. Furthermore, Bianca then enters, and carrying the handkerchief which Iago has dropped in Cassio's room, she talks to Cassio. He laughs and this inflames Othello still further. He is determined to kill Desdemona. But he is still torn. "O, the world hath not a sweeter creature; she might lie by an emperor's side, and command him tasks . . . . But yet the pity of it, Iago! O, Iago, the pity of it, Iago!" Iago stamps out these reservations. A noble envoy comes from Venice commanding Othello home and appointing Cassio governor in his place. Desdemona says how glad she is, and Othello publicly strikes her.

There is a scene where Othello calls Desdemona "a whore," and, ironically, she appeals for solace and assistance to Emilia and Iago. Emilia speaks with the realism of one who has knocked about the civilized world, has no belief in lofty principles but has tender feelings for those who deserve them. This bit of dialogue reveals how near she comes to the truth, and also shows the difference between her eye-for-an-eye morality and Desdemona's all-forgiving humanism:

> *Emilia.*   I will be hanged if some eternal villain
> Some busy and insinuating rogue,
> Some cogging, cozening slave, to get some office,
> Have not devised this slander. I'll be hanged else.
> *Iago.*   Fie, there is no such man: it is impossible.
> *Desdemona.* If any such there be, heaven pardon him!
> *Emilia.*   A halter pardon him / and hell gnaw his bones!

Roderigo berates Iago and questions his honesty. Iago has drained him of money and jewels which Iago had promised to give to Desdemona. He, Roderigo, will speak to Desdemona. Iago argues him into assaulting Cassio with a sword that night, with Iago nearby for assistance. This, Iago says, will win him Desdemona by removing a rival. It is the last of Iago's planned riots, and he hopes it will end with both Roderigo and Cassio dead.

The last moral opposition takes place; a touching one between Desdemona and Emilia. Contrasted are two opposite sides of the "new"; Desdemona's visionary humanism, which sees the world not as it is but as it should be and will be in some distant future, and Emilia holds to an earthy insistence on existing realities. Desdemona asks her whether there really are women who wrong their husbands, as Othello has accused her of doing. Emilia has no doubt that there are; Desdemona says she does not believe Emilia would behave that way. Emilia says she would if there were enough to be gained by it and Desdemona insists that there are not such woman, while Emilia insists:

> Let husbands know
> Their wives have sense like them: they see and smell
> And have their palates both for sweet and sour

As husbands have. What is it that they do
When they change us for others? Is it sport?
I think it is. And doth affection breed it?
I think it doth. Is't frailty that thus errs?
It is so too. And have not we affections,
Desires for sport, and frailty, as men have?
Then let them use us well: else let them know,
The ills we do, their ills instruct us so.

Desdemona ends with a more realistic version of her humanism:

Good night, good night. God me such uses send,
Not to pick bad from bad, but by bad mend!

Emilia has attacked the prevailing double standard for wives and
husbands, women and men. And Desdemona's conclusion is that
rather than use one evil to justify another, the evil should be
faced so that the world can be improved.

The two big and complex scenes of Act V end the play. The
reluctant Roderigo at night attacks Cassio but misses, and Cassio
wounds him. Iago wounds Cassio in the leg from behind, then
runs off. Roderigo and Cassio cry for help, in the dark. Othello
passes by and thinks he is hearing Cassio dying at Iago's hands.
The puzzled Venetian emissaries enter. Iago enters with torches.
He pretends to run over to help Roderigo and stabs him to death;
Roderigo, in his last moment, realizes Iago's duplicity. "O
damned Iago! O inhuman dog!" Bianca enters, and Iago plans to
slander her and Cassio as the cause of the riot, while the
wounded Cassio is carried off.

In the castle bedroom, Othello kisses the sleeping Desdemona,
and, when she wakes, accuses her of adultery with Cassio. As she
protests her innocence, he smothers her. Emilia rushes in with
the news of Cassio's wound and Roderigo's death and, seeing the
smothered Desdemona, cries, "O, who hath done this deed?"
Desdemona's last words are:

Nobody: I myself. Farewell.
Commend me to my kind lord. O, farewell!

As Othello repeats his accusations to Emilia and repeatedly
mentions Iago's name, she is aghast at the role her husband has

played. When the Venetian noblemen and Iago enter, Othello mentions the handerchief that Desdemona has presumably given to Cassio. Before Iago can stab Emilia, she tells the truth of how she had picked it up, and how Iago had taken it from her. Bit by bit the whole truth comes out, and Othello realizes how he has been fooled. He asks of Cassio:

> Will you, I pray, demand that demi-devil
> Why he hath thus ensnared my soul and body?

Iago's answer is:

> Demand me nothing: what you know, you know.
> From this time forth I never will speak word.

What this could mean is that he himself could not explain it. Whatever motives he could truthfully give would sound ridiculous in the light of this slaughter of good people. It is as if one asked today's armaments manufacturer and his publicists beating the drums for the war why they wanted to kill a couple of million people in Vietnam. As with Iago, they can live with their motives only when they do not see before their face the full horror of what they have been led to do.

Othello wreaks vengeance on himself. His closing speech, as he stabs himself, begins:

> Soft you: a word or two before you go.
> I have done the state some service, and they know't,
> No more of that. I pray you in your letters,
> When you shall these unlucky deeds relate,
> Speak of me as I am; nothing extenuate,
> Nor set down aught in malice. Then must you speak
> Of one that loved not wisely but too well;
> Of one not easily jealous, but, being wrought,
> Perplexed in the extreme; . . .

and it ends:

> And say besides, that in Aleppo once,
> Where a malignant and a turbaned Turk
> Beat a Venetian and traduced the state.
> I took by the throat the circumcised dog
> And smote him thus.
>
> > [*He stabs himself.*]

Thus he reminds them that it was in honest devotion to the state that he shaped his life.

The politics of the play is the picture it paints of the kind of military leader the new national state needs in its defense and the problems this raises for him. The old order does not come off very well. Roderigo is a harshly critical version of a landed gentleman, like Bassanio in *The Merchant of Venice,* who knows how to raise money only by selling his estate and then proceeds to spend it in pursuit of a woman. Brabantio has a tender concern for his daughter but is tyrannical in his insistence on her obedience at the expense of her right to love. On the other side, Othello is the kind of strong, courageous and committed leader a nation needs, but he knows men only by the battlefield and succumbs to the treacheries of the new "civilization." Desdemona is courageous, with profound capacities for love, noble in her choice of a noble mind and personality for a husband, and humanist in the moral standards of faith in others that she sets for herself as well as for others. Iago is the evil in the new civilization, the rationalist without humanity.

The national state took shape through a multitude of forces, but decisive in the process was the pressure of the city middle class and the commercial or trade-minded gentry, who needed a unified state against the divisive interests of the old landed nobility. The national state was to become the capitalist state, and the patriotism which it espoused as a weapon against the feudal-minded nobility would come to be used as a tool for aggrandizement against its colonies and commercial rivals. The Iagos with their gift for mind-manipulation would become its honored publicists and politicians. To say that Shakespeare foresaw this would be ridiculous. But in showing the conflicts in his own age between the old and new moralities, which is the driving thought behind the construction of *Othello,* he also had the insight to discover a conflict within the "new." Alongside of the patriotic devotion to the embattled state, alongside the new humanism of love relations and responsibilities of one person for others, he saw the rise of the rationalism of self-centeredness, ruthlessness in exploiting others, the view of human beings as animals, and the craft of mind-manipulation.

In 1866, the composer Giuseppe Verdi, in his 70's, produced his opera *Otello,* the greatest opera fashioned from a Shakespeare play. The play had to be badly cut, and many of the moral conflicts disappear. But Italy had belatedly fought for and won its national unity and independence. Verdi had procured guns for Garibaldi's troops. And in his opera he caught the theme of a heroic patriot who achieves victory and then is destroyed by a scheming politican, who is a master at deception. At about this time, in 1880, he wrote in a letter: "Shakespeare was a realist, only he did not know it. He was a realist by inspiration; we are realists by design." And in 1870, he wrote: "I can't reconcile the idea of Parliament with the College of Cardinals, a free press with the Inquisition, civil law with the syllabus. . . . If tomorrow we should have a shrewd, adroit Pope, a really crafty fellow, such as Rome has often had, he would ruin us." In 1876 he wrote, "Poor Cavour . . . and poor us!" It is reasonable to believe that these feelings came alive for him in *Otello.* A lover of his own country and a critic of the politicans who proliferated after its heroic emergence, Verdi felt this same theme in Shakespeare's play. Italy had achieved its unity and independence at last in struggle, not only against outside oppressors but against its own Church and medieval-minded aristocracy, and there seemed to be parallels with the emergence of an English nation three centuries earlier.

9

ONE KING
AS FOOL
ANOTHER AS
MURDERER

King Lear
Macbeth

KING LEAR and *Macbeth* are Shakespeare's most searching studies of kingship. In *King Lear,* in a reversal of roles, it is the King who is foolish, while the professional Fool is actually a realist with a goodly measure of hardheaded wisdom. The ruling gentry are depicted as fools, in that they live by grandiose illusions that conflict with reality. Through a cataclysmic struggle the King attains some degree of insight, and although his ordeals have unhinged his reason, he does finally arrive at an awareness that he has been a fool.

Macbeth studied the King as murderer. But if he is a relatively ruthless murderer, like Richard III, he is also a human being with a complex internal life, and he realizes too late that his murders of others are also murders of himself.

Because of Shakespeare's detailed analysis of King Lear's internal life, his personality looms larger than that of anyone else in the play. His two evil daughters, Goneril and Regan, and Regan's husband, the Duke of Cornwall, are hardly distinguishable from one another. Edmund, the treacherous bastard son of the Earl of Gloucester, is a primitive Iago, who has a rationalist and inhuman view of reality that leads him to cut the throat of the man next to him lest his own might be threatened. He regards all good-hearted people as victims and fools. Of these, Cordelia is lovable for her sweetness, tenderness and honesty, but is not explored in depth; the Earl of Gloucester is a naive old man; his son Edgar lacks depth of treatment; the rugged, brave and loyal Duke of Kent is two dimensional. So is the Duke of Albany, Goneril's husband. The Fool plays an important role in the first part of the play, but less as a personage than as the first strong voice of the reality that Lear ignores, and he disappears when reality begins to play its own active role in the drama. Virtually the entire interior conflict of the drama is that undergone by Lear. Shakespeare's most sweeping portrayal of such a conflict, it reaches shattering proportions in madness, and in the end causes changes in Lear's character. It is a supreme achievement in portraying graphically and effectively the conflict and consequent growth that takes place in the mind. Perhaps it was only by going back to the legendary antiquity of pre-Christian England that Shakespeare could safely create an English king like this, but his mental life belongs to Shakespeare's time.

In the first scene of *Othello* Shakespeare had carefully built up an immense psychological and social picture, flaring into high drama. In the first three scenes of *King Lear* he moves rapidly to get past the essential preliminaries of his story so that he can get to what really interests him—the beginning of Lear's and Gloucester's tragic conflict. These are the two interlocking lines of plot: Lear's deprivation by his older daughters, and Gloucester's deprivation by his illegitimate son Edmund, who also is conspiring against his half-brother Edgar.

Shakespeare quickly covers Lear's decision in his old age to cut his kingdom in three and give each of them to one of his daughters to run, preserving for himself only "the name and all th'addition of a king"; his demand of his daughters that they tell him how much they love him; the flattery of the two older daughters; his rage against Cordelia, who speaks honestly; his disowning Cordelia, and his banishment of the Duke of Kent,

who dares to protest. And we also see Edmund, whom Gloucester has jocularly introduced as his "whoreson," inveigling his
father through a forged letter to believe that his legitimate son
Edgar is plotting against him. Gloucester, disturbed by Lear's
actions, is all to ready to believe this as a sign that "machinations,
hollowness, treachery and all ruinous disorders follow us dis-
quietly to our graves." In Scene 3, Goneril, at whose house Lear
is staying with the hundred knights he has asked to retain, begins
to rob her father of his sense of royalty by telling her steward,
Oswald, to treat the King and his knights with disrespect; she
writes to Regan to do likewise.

The drama goes into high gear. Scene 4, a profound one in
which the Fool is given his greatest role in a Shakespeare tragedy,
depicts the Fool facing Lear with the bitter truth that in giving
away his material power he has given away the royalty that he
thought was innate in him, and tells Lear he has left himself a
"nothing" in the eyes of those to whom he has given the power.
The scene also presents a motif for the entire play through the
dual meaning of the term "fool." On the one hand, there is the
wise fool who knows exactly what he is doing. Clear in his mind
but helpless except for the protection of his wits, he entertains his
masters with pretended nonsense but has a common man's
awareness of the hard realities of life and the cruelties of which
the upper class is capable. And, on the other hand, there are the
members of the ruling class who are intensely serious but are
actually fools in that they live in delusions, think they are the
masters of their own and others' lives but are in for rude and
harsh shocks when their plans miscarry.

The scene begins when Kent enters in disguise and enlists
himself as a common servitor of Lear. It is a loving action, this
effort to protect the old King against the consequences of his own
foolish actions. The Fool offers Kent his coxcomb. And when
Kent asks, "Why, fool?" the Fool answers, "For taking one's part
that's out of favour." In a way this is a compliment, for if the
disguised Kent knows exactly what he is doing, he is also a "wise
fool," embracing the weaker side.

Then the Fool twits Lear and offers him his coxcomb, and
when Lear threatens the whip, the Fool says, "Truth's a dog must
to kennel; he must be whipped out." It is a prophetic statement,

for later Lear will discover some fundamental truths of life only when "whipped," that is, completely impoverished and wandering on the heath in a violent storm. But Lear doesn't know this. And when the Fool sings a pointed ditty about the two kinds of fool, the "sweet and bitter fool, the sweet fool being in motley and the other being "out there," Lear asks, "Dost thou call me fool, boy?" The Fool answers, "All thy other titles thou hast given away; that thou wast born with."

Then the Fool sings another ditty, and when Lear asks, "When were you wont to be so full of songs, sirrah?" the Fool answers, with one of Shakespeare's most vivid images of ordinary life: "I have used it, nuncle, e'er since thou mad'st thy daughters thy mothers; for when thou gav'st them the rod and put'st down thine own breeches,

> Then they for sudden joy did weep,
>   And I for sorrow sung,
> That such a king should play bo-peep,
>   And go the fools among."

So again he calls Lear a fool. More bitter quips follow. When Goneril enters, he says, "Thou hast pared thy wit o' both sides and left nothing i' th' middle. Here comes one of the parings." And when Lear complains of her frowning look, the Fool delivers a broadside. "Thou wast a pretty fellow when thou hadst no need to care for her frowning. Now thou art an O without a figure. I am better than thou art now: I am a fool, thou art nothing."

It is of course to Goneril that Lear is a "nothing," but he doesn't realize this yet. Much later in the play, however, when the cruelty of Goneril and Regan has sunk in and he has gone mad, he meets with his old fellow-sufferer, the Earl of Gloucester, blinded and homelessly wandering. And he develops one of the Fool's thoughts, saying:

> I will preach to thee: mark . . .
> When we are born, we cry that we are come
> To this great stage of fools.

And when Lear still later is comforted by Cordelia, he will say, "I am a very foolish fond old man." This will be the beginning of his wisdom.

Meanwhile, in the latter part of this scene, Goneril berates her father, while the Fool continues his sardonic comments, like "May not an ass know when the cart draws the horse?" She tells Lear that a hundred knights are too many for him; furthermore, they carouse too much. She reduces Lear's regiment to fifty. He renounces her as his daughter. But he has another "kind and comfortable" daughter, Regan. He'll resort to her and he will be master again. "I'll resume the shape which thou dost think / I have cast off forever." Goneril's husband, the Duke of Albany, is puzzled and disturbed at her conduct, although he himself begins to take his share in it. She accuses him of "silky gentleness" and "want of wisdom." And in Scene 5, the Fool tells Lear that Regan will be like Goneril. He continues to pick on Lear's illusions. "If thou wert my fool, nuncle, I'd have thee beaten for being old before the time . . . . Thou shouldst not have been old till thou hadst been wise." Lear's exclamation is prophetic; "O, let me not be mad, not mad, sweet heaven! / Keep me in temper; I would not be mad!"

In Act II, Lear's rising rage as he is increasingly frustrated by the harsh treatment inflicted on him increases to the point of madness. At first there is the victory of treachery in the Gloucester family. Edgar, pursued for reasons he cannot understand, disguises himself as the poorest of beggars, Tom of Bedlam, naked, filthy, covered only with a blanket. Edmund ingratiates himself with Regan and the Duke of Cornwall, who presumably recognize him as one of their own crooked, inhuman cast of mind. Kent, who is Lear's servant, beats Oswald, Goneril's lackey, and is thrown into the stocks by the Duke of Cornwall, who recognizes an honest man and is also all too willing to insult King Lear. And Lear is offended by seeing his servant thus treated. And the Fool sings, "Fortune, thou arrant whore, / Ne'er burns her key to th' poor," Lear cries, "down, thou climbing sorrow," He asserts that he is still King. He complains to Regan of her sister and she defends her. "O, sir, you are old . . . you should be ruled and led." He curses Goneril, and Regan says, "so will you wish on me." When Goneril enters, and the two women take turns at sniping at him. Their aim is to reduce him to a nothing. He says to Goneril, "I prithee, daughter, do not make me mad. / I will not trouble thee, my child: farewell." But Regan is equally vicious. He tells her, "I gave you all." She answers, "And in good time." She cuts his number of knights down to twenty-five. He turns to Goneril, who at least allowed him fifty, but she says he doesn't need any at all, and Regan agrees with her. Then Lear makes the wild speech of stifled rage which also shows him at the point of madness.

> No, you unnatural hags,
> I will have such revenges on you both
> That all the world shall—I will do such things—
> What they are, yet I know not, but they shall be
> The terrors of the earth. You think I'll weep;
> No, I'll not weep.
> I have full cause of weeping; but this heart
> Shall break into a hundred thousand flaws
> Or ere I'll weep. O fool, I shall go mad!

He goes out into the heath, and the closing words of the act are Cornwall's: "Shut up your doors, my lord: 'tis a wild night. / My Regan counsels well. Come out o' th' storm."

To Shakespeare, mental derangement is almost always a conflict between firmly held illusions and a reality that denies them and beats in upon the mind. So it is with Lear. His illusions were not merely that his older daughters love him. Shakespeare cuts wider and deeper. His greater illusion is in his own innate majesty, so that he thinks he can give away his land and power and still be honored as a king. The truth which now beats in on his mind is his own nothingness other than that of an ordinary human being, and the social truths that he should have recognized and taken into account, had he been a proper king. So, in his deprivations, these truths are "whipped out."

Early in his madness, when it is coming on and he cries, "O, Regan, Goneril! / Your old kind father, whose frank heart gave all— / O, that way madness lies: let me shun that," he is taken by Kent and the Fool to a poor hovel for shelter from the storm. He discovers in himself concern for others and tells the Fool. "In, boy, go first." Then, with the storm beating down, he reveals that this solicitude now includes a recognition of all the poor and

homeless and how he as a king should have taken measures about
this. Only his own desolate condition has awakened him to their
poverty; it has been a "physic" to him. He says:

> Poor naked wretches, wheresoe'er you are,
> That bide the pelting of this pitiless storm,
> How shall your houseless heads and unfed sides,
> Your looped and windowed raggedness, defend you
> From seasons such as this! Take physic, pomp;
> Expose thyself to feel what wretches feel,
> That thou mayst shake the superflux to them
> And show the heavens more just.

Later in his madness, the reality that breaks in upon him is
ordinary humanity. "They flattered me like a dog . . . To say 'ay'
and 'no' to everything I said! 'Ay' and 'no' too was no good
divinity. When the rain came to wet me once and the wind to
make me chatter; when the thunder would not peace at my
bidding; there I found 'em, there I smelt 'em out. Go to, they are
not men o' their words: they told me I was everything. 'Tis a lie' I
am not ague-proof." And he comes upon Gloucester, blinded,
watched over by his son Edgar. Lear cries to him, "Your eyes are
in a heavy case, your purse in a light. Yet you see how the world
goes." When Gloucester says, "I see it feelingly," Lear answers,
"What, art mad?" Thus being mad is akin to being a blind man
who feels deeper truths than those who have sight. And Lear
then puts his finger on the fundamental inequity of class society.
Justice doesn't operate for the poor; the law doesn't protect them.
Justice is what suits the rich and powerful. He says, "Thou hast
seen a farmer's dog bark at a beggar? . . . And the creature run
from the cur? There thou mightst behold the great image of
authority: a dog's obeyed in office." He then expands the thought:

> The usurer hangs the cozener
> Through tattered clothes small vices do appear;
> Robes and furred gowns hide all. Plate sin with gold,
> And the strong lance of justice hurtless breaks;
> Arm it in rage, a pygmy's straw does pierce it.
>   . . . . Get thee glass eyes,
> And like a scurvy politician, seem
> To see the things thou dost not.

Edgar mutters, "Reason in madness."

Lear's madness is fully expressed in only four spaced-out scenes. Yet it creates the tone of all of Act III and Act IV, except for its last scene, because of the extensive reverberations Shakespeare has given it. There is the pelting storm throughout Act III; there is the setting, like a world upside down; the King is in a poor farmhouse and, along with the King, Edgar unclothed and, acting the part of Tom of Bedlam, deliberately talking gibberish. And there are the dreadful deeds of "sane" people—Edmund's treachery in having his father condemned, and Cornwall's violence in putting out Gloucester's eyes. When Lear recovers his sanity, he becomes not the old Lear but a much different man, far more humble and far more of a human being who is capable of loving others. This is the reason why A. C. Bradley can write, "There is nothing more noble and beautiful in literature than Shakespeare's exposition of the effect of suffering in reviving the greatness and eliciting the sweetness of Lear's nature."[1]

Lear's madness is powerfully dramatized. Seeing Edgar naked, as Tom of Bedlam, he tears off his own clothes. He will owe nothing to anyone; not even to a silkworm his silk, to a sheep, his wool, to some other animal his leather. He will be honestly a man, a "poor, bare, forked animal" like Edgar. Then, in a farmhouse to which the kindly Gloucester has taken him, with Kent, the Fool and the disguised Edgar, he imagines he sees his evil daughters before him and puts them on trial. Edgar, the Fool and Kent are appointed the judges. Meanwhile the rain pours down, Gloucester enters, warning the others to carry off Lear in a litter to Dover, where Cordelia has landed with a French army. There is a plot, he says, against Lear's life.

While this is going on, Gloucester has trustingly told Edmund that he does not like the way the Duke and Duchess of Cornwall have taken over his own house; that he does not approve of the vile treatment of Lear, that there is trouble between the Dukes of Albany and Cornwall, and that help is on the way for Lear. He is in touch by letter with Lear's friends. And this gives Edmund a weapon to use against his father. He betrays Gloucester to Cornwall and Regan. Then when Gloucester returns to his castle, he is seized and Cornwall has his eyes put out. Cornwall's servants are the decent people here. One of them fights to save Gloucester, and Regan stabs the servant from behind, killing him, but not before he gives Cornwall a mortal wound. The other two servants help Gloucester when Cornwall leaves.

Shakespeare develops the characters of Edgar and Gloucester. Edgar is young and can stand adversity; he does not give up. At first alone and bewildered, he finds strength in joining with others who suffer. Discovering Lear's miserable treatment, he says, "How light and portable my pain seems now, / When that which makes me bend makes the King bow, / He childed as I fathered." He will stay to support the King. Later he finds his father blinded and wandering. He attaches himself to Gloucester, not disclosing his identity. Gloucester is seeking to kill himself. To him the world is absurd. "As flies to wanton boys are we to th' gods; / They kill us for their sport." This suggests the "absurd world" of modern existentialism. He asks the disguised Edgar to lead him to the cliff of Dover and plans to throw himself over the cliff. "This world I do renounce." To cure him of the desire to kill himself, Edgar tells him he is standing on the verge, and when he falls to the ground that he has really fallen down the cliff and has been saved by a miracle. Gloucester will no longer try to kill himself. "Henceforth I'll bear / Affliction till it do cry out itself / 'Enough, enough' and then die."

Oswald enters and tries to kill Gloucester, which is his mission, but Edgar interposes himself and in the fight kills Oswald. Edgar then discloses himself to his father and reads the letter in Oswald's pouch. It is from Goneril to Edmund, asking him to find a way to kill her husband in the forthcoming battle so that they can marry. Still later, when the forces of Cordelia are defeated, Gloucester will not move from his spot and flee until Edgar speaks his philosophy. "What, in ill thoughts again? Men must endure / Their going hence, even as their coming hither: / Ripeness is all."

The evil sisters come to a bad end because, hating people as they do, they also hate each other. They squabble over Edmund whom Regan is ready to marry because her husband, Cornwall, is dead. Goneril wants her husband Albany killed, so that she can marry Edmund. Goneril poisons Regan, and when it appears that her misdeeds are known, she kills herself.

The play is extraordinary in that despite the fact that Lear dies,
Shakespeare gives the play an enormous lift in the end. For Lear,
in becoming sane again, discovers his humanity. He is a new
man. For a while he will not face Cordelia but, after a night's
sleep, waking to find loving people about him, he recovers his
wits and speaks with humility. With all its seeming plainness, his
speech contains the greatest poetry:

> Pray, do not mock me.
> I am a very foolish fond old man.
> Fourscore and upward, not an hour more nor less;
> And to deal plainly,
> I fear that I am not in my perfect mind.
> Methinks I should know you and know this man;
> Yet I am doubtful; for I am mainly ignorant
> What place this is, and all the skill I have
> Remembers not these garments, nor I know not
> Where I did lodge last night. Do not laugh at me;
> For, as I am a man, I think this lady
> To be my daughter Cordelia.

Even when Cordelia's French army loses the battle, and she
and Lear are prisoners, Lear's happiness is untouchable. Having
found himself, he is impervious to any more misfortunes. For he
has Cordelia with him. He loves and is loved. This evokes a most
gaily beautiful passage:

> Come, let's away to prison,
> We two alone will sing like birds i' the cage,
> When thou dost ask me blessing, I'll kneel down
> And ask of thee forgiveness; so we'll live,
> And pray, and sing, and tell old tales, and laugh,
> At gilded butterflies, and hear poor rogues
> Talk of court news; and we'll talk with them too,
> Who loses and who wins, who's in, who's out;
> And take upon's the mystery things
> As if we were God's spies: . . .

The Duke of Albany, the victor, plans to treat Lear and
Cordelia kindly. But Edmund secretly induces a captain to hang
Cordelia. Then he is challenged as a traitor by Edgar, who has
been hiding in a knight's armor and helmet, and Edmund is
mortally wounded. When his evil deeds are made known, when

Kent and Edgar are revealed in their true persons and the bodies of Goneril and Regan are brought in, the dying Edmund tells of his secret order, but it is too late. Lear enters carry Cordelia's body. He dies, hoping she is still alive. Kent says to those who would help Lear, "He hates him / That would upon the rack of this tough world / Stretch him out longer." Here, too, ripeness is all. He has lived his full life. Gloucester dies happy. His heart, "twixt two extremes of passion, joy and grief, / Burst smilingly." Edgar is left to rule. He says, "The weight of this sad time we must obey, / Speak what we feel, not what we ought to say." The play has spoken what Shakespeare feels about kingship.

A few words about the Fool's "prophecy" in the second scene of Act II. It links the situation to an England beyond Shakespeare's time. The Fool explains the references to priests and churches—for this is presumably pagan England—to the fact that it is a prophecy "Merlin shall make." It appears on first reading to be impossibly confused, but if the 11th and 12th lines are moved up to become the fifth and sixth and to end the first stanza, it makes good sense. The first stanza then becomes a derisive attack upon the corruptions of a land very much like England. The second stanza paints a Utopian society where honesty reigns, law is just, people are not hounded for debt, usurers count their money openly instead of secretly, and whores build churches. With the position of the two lines altered, it reads as follows:

> When priests are more in word than matter;
> When brewers mar their malt with water;
> When nobles are their tailors' tutors;
> No heretics burned but wenches' suitors'
> Then shall the realm of Albion
> Come to great confusion.

> When every case in law is right;
> No squire in debt, nor no poor knight:
> When slanders do not live in tongues,
> Nor cutpurses come not to throngs;
> When usurers tell their gold i' th' field,
> And bawds and whores do churches build:
> Then comes the time, who lives to see't,
> That going shall be used with feet.

It is a sad picture; *King Lear* altogether is not a happy play. But it makes a challenging case about the neglect of the poor and the corruption of justice in high places. It promises no cure of this, for it cannot honestly do so. It shows wickedness in full operation and reveals the harm this does. But it makes a dramatic case for human values, of living with honesty, knowledge, devotion and love for others. And it says that life must be faced and its problems fought through. Those who live by human values may not always triumph, but they have a strength that misfortune cannot overcome.

To Shakespeare, the entertainer, playwright and, in a sense, court "fool," makes himself the educator of kings. And if some kings will not learn, there may be others who will concern themselves with poverty and injustice. People may ask impatiently today why, with so great an awareness of the limitations of absolute rule, he did not advocate doing away with the institution. In effect, he does so, for the demands he makes of kingship—that it concern itself with poverty and with the perversion of justice by the rich—are really impossible for royalty to meet. But the question remains: What would have replaced monarchies at that time? A quarter century after Shakespeare's death there was a revolution in England against absolute rule by a king, and step by step England became a democratic capitalist society. Yet to this day the questions of poverty and the perversion of justice are on the agenda. The rule of an absolute monarch was not the only inequity; it was the division of society between exploiters and exploited. And that, under capitalism, is still with us—more rampant than ever before. Lear's demands could only have been met by a classless society.

Macbeth could be said to have a happy ending, at least in the sense that a murderous king is himself killed; and Scotland, where the action takes place, is subsequently ruled by a good-hearted king of legitimate descent. But the focus is on Macbeth, the murderer, and Shakespeare here evolves a new level of tragedy, in which a murderer can be a tragic protagonist. For he exhibits human qualities and, in the course of the tragedy, he becomes more and more aware of the breakdown of his moral fibre.

In this play there are witches, whether Shakespeare believes in them or not. Basically he is a realist and he makes them personifications of impulses already existent in the minds of his characters. At the outset of the play it is important to note that their presence evokes differing attitudes from Macbeth and Banquo. Both have fought bravely in defense of King Duncan, Macbeth so much so that when Duncan hears of it he makes Macbeth the new Thane of Cawdor, having executed the previous Thane, who proved to be a traitor. Both Macbeth and Banquo encounter the witches on the heath. They hail Macbeth as the Thane of Glamis, which he is, and the Thane of Cawdor, which he doesn't yet know he is, and then they hail him as the king "hereafter," which makes him start. Banquo notices this, "Good sir, why do you start, and seem to fear / Things that do sound so fair?" Then Banquo addresses the witches with strong skepticism:

> Are ye fantastical, or that indeed
> Which outwardly ye show? . . . .
> If you can look into the seeds of time
> And say which grain will grow and which will not,
> Speak then to me, who neither beg nor fear
> Your favours nor your hate.

The third witch tells Banquo, "Thou shall get kings, though thou be none." Macbeth is convinced that the witches are true prophets and demands to know more. "Stay, you imperfect speakers, tell me more. / . . . Speak, I charge you." When the witches vanish, he says, "Would they had stayed!" Banquo is still skeptical:

> Were such things here as we do speak about?
> Or have we eaten on the insane root
> That takes the reason prisoner?

Macbeth's mind is still captured by the prophecies. When two noblemen enter to tell him that King Duncan has made him Thane of Cawdor, he speaks as if the witches rather than the King have given this honor to him. He asks Banquo:

> Do you not hope your children shall be kings,
> When those that gave the Thane of Cawdor to me
> Promised no less to them?

Banquo answers drily, "That, trusted home, / Might yet enkindle you to the crown." He warns Macbeth,

> And often times, to win us to our harm,
> The instruments of darkness tell us truths,
> Win us with honest trifles, to betray's
> In deepest consequence.

But Macbeth is absorbed by the witches' prophecies, for they correspond to his own ambition to be King and even to thoughts of murder that have lurked in his mind. He says to himself:

> The truths are told,
> As happy prologue to the swelling act
> Of the imperial theme. . . .
> . . . why do I yield to that suggestion
> Whose horrid image doth unfix my hair
> And make my seated heart knock at my ribs,
> Against the uses of nature? Present fears
> Are less than horrible imaginings.
> My thought, whose murther yet is but fantastical
> Is smothered in surmise, and nothing is
> But what is not.

The thought comes to Macbeth that he might simply wait. "If chance will have me King, why, chance may crown me / Without my stir." But he is still in brooding conflict, which takes fire in the next short scene when he meets King Duncan, and the King announces that he has established his "estate" upon his oldest son, Malcolm, who will be the Prince of Cumberland. Macbeth is horrified, for this seems to be a barrier against his ever getting his Kingship.

> The Prince of Cumberland! That is a step
> On which I must fall down, or else o'er leap,
> For in my way it lies. Stars, hide your fires:
> Let not light see my black and deep desires . . .

The next episode is the murder of Duncan when he visits Macbeth's castle. Significantly, Shakespeare intensifies Macbeth's psychological course by interweaving it with, and yet opposing it to, Lady Macbeth's, for they are very different. She is at first the more unreflecting murderer, willing to use the knife herself; he hesitates and knows the murder is wrong. Later in the play, she will crack up in madness, while he becomes a hardened killer. And so, when Macbeth writes to his Lady of the prophecies of the witches, she determines that Duncan must die and deplores only that Macbeth's nature is "too full o' th' milk of human kindness," and that she must harden his will to the murder. She tells Macbeth when he comes that Duncan must never leave their house alive. But when, in a soliloquy, he decides not to go through with the deed, it is not simply his "milk of human kindness." Duncan, he says, is also his kinsman and his chief and his guest, and there are the repercussions that would come from the deed to consider. "If it were done when 'tis done, then 'twere well / It were done quickly." And there is also the "consequence" of the deed. It will give people "bloody instruction," which will return to plague him. And Duncan is so gracious a King that after his killing, "his virtues / Will plead like angels trumpet-tongues against / The deep damnation of his taking-off."

So Macbeth tells his Lady, "We will proceed no further in this business," but she shames him for his vacillation. For she knows the desire is in his mind. Will he "live a coward" in his own esteem? He answers, "I dare do all that may become a man," but he still asks, "If we should fail?" To her everything is simple. She will get Duncan's two chamberlains drunk and put the guilt on them. He agrees, knowing he has embarked on a new life of falsehood; "False face must hide what the false heart doth know."

Shakespeare handles the murder through the minds of Macbeth and Lady Macbeth. It is a temporary triumph of the forces of darkness, both darkness of nature and darkness in the mind, the deepest night, when "Nature seems dead" and there are evil dreams, witchcraft and prowling murder. Macbeth's mind is tormented; he sees a dagger before his eyes, and then it covers itself with blood. He knows "There's no such thing. / It is the bloody business which informs / Thus to mine eyes." Even Lady Macbeth feels a slight crack in her steely determination. She had been in the room of the sleeping Duncan, preparing the daggers of his grooms, but could not bring herself to kill Duncan. "Had he not resembled / my father as he slept, I had done't." Macbeth does the deed but he is troubled because when he was in Duncan's room, the grooms momentarily awoke and muttered "God bless us!" and he could not bring himself to say, "Amen," however much he wanted to. He cannot smear the grooms' daggers with blood. Lady Macbeth goes back to do this for him. Then comes the knocking at the door, the first break of day into the murky night atmosphere, nature is again alive; there is teeming humanity and sanity.

Macbeth cries in horror:

> Will all great Neptune's ocean wash this blood
> Clean from my hand? No! this my hand will rather
> The multitudinous seas incarnadine,
> Making the green one red.

Lady Macbeth's hands are also bloody, but she says, "A little water clears us of this deed, / How easy is it then!" This is ironic, for he will wash the blood from his hands and eventually out of his mind, while she, later in her madness, will be agonized that she cannot apparently wash the blood off her hands. But meanwhile he laments, "Take Duncan with thy knocking! I wish thou couldst!" They go to put on nightgowns and pretend to have slept.

The shock of the entrance of day and life is intensified by a touch of ribald humor. A porter ambles to the door, playfully imagining that he is porter of "Hell Gate," calling on Beelzebub, and pretending that he is a "devil-porter" opening the gates of hell for the entrance of sinners. When Macduff and Lennox enter and ask him why he was so slow to open, he explains they were drinking and says, "drink sir is a provider of three things . . . nose-painting, sleep and urine. Lechery, sir, it provokes and unprovokes: it provokes the desire, but it takes away the performance." The murder is discovered; Macbeth kills the two grooms in pretended horror at their deed; Lady Macbeth faints or pretends to faint, and the King's sons, Malcolm and Donalbain, flee quickly for safety.

The next great episode is the murder of Banquo, which also brings on its turning-point. Banquo is suspicious of Macbeth, meditating that Macbeth now has all that the "Weird Women" promised, for he is now King, "and I fear / Thou playd'st must foully for't?" Banquo, who is to attend a festive supper given to the lords of Scotland by King Macbeth and the Queen, will ride with his son Fleance for some hours before the time arrives. Macbeth calls two murderers to waylay Banquo and his son and kill them, thus removing the threat posed by the witches' prophecy that Banquo's progeny would replace Macbeth's as kings. The unnamed murderers appear but briefly in the play, but Shakespeare examines their minds—since this is the theme of the play itself: what makes men kill? And so in only seven lines he creates two quite different human beings who have turned to murder, giving each, if not exculpation, at least a social reason for his crime:

> *Second Murderer.*   I am one, my liege,
> Whom the vile blows and buffets of the world
> Hath so incensed that I am reckless what
> I do to spite the world.
>   *First Murderer.*   And I another
> So weary with disasters, tugged with fortune,
> That I would set my life on any chance,
> To mend it or be rid on 't.

Macbeth appears to have made his peace with Duncan's murder. "After life's fitful fever he sleeps well." He tells Lady Macbeth, "O, full of scorpions is my mind, dear wife!" But he means that he plans to sting others, like Banquo and his son. The plan, however, partly misfires; Banquo is killed but his son escapes. Macbeth gets the report as the banquet is about to begin. But then the Ghost of Banquo enters to sit in Macbeth's seat, seen by Macbeth alone. Macbeth is shaken, shouts at the Ghost and when it leaves, speaks the lines that sum up the entire play up to this point:

> Blood hath been shed ere now, i' th' olden time,
> Ere humane statute purged the gentle weal;
> Ay, and since too, murthers have been performed
> Too terrible for the ear. The time has been
> That when the brains were out, the man would die,
> And there's an end; but now they rise again,
> With twenty mortal murthers on their crowns,

And push us from our stools. This is more strange
Than such a murther is.

Thus Shakespeare states through Macbeth the new humanist morality. A human being cannot kill another like an animal; the dead will come back to haunt the mind; the killer must kill his own humanity.

The theme of the remainder of the play is Macbeth's increasing dehumanization, along with Lady Macbeth's madness. When the guests leave, he tells her:

I am in blood
Stepped in so far that, should I wade no more
Returning were as tedious as go o'er.

He goes off to consult the witches. From this point on, he makes no pretense at innocence. He will rule with an iron hand and with blood-letting and war. The witches, the forces of darkness, will tell him the future. The apparitions they stir up delude him with half-truths. They tell him to beware of Macduff, but that "none of women born" will have Macbeth, and he will never be vanquished until Great Birnam Wood comes against him on Dunsinane Hill. They also tell him, however, that Banquo's progeny will be kings.

There is a terrifying scene in which Macduff's wife and son are killed by Macbeth's agents, Macduff having fled to England; then a scene in England between Macduff and Malcolm, King Duncan's son, in which Macduff urges Malcolm to take up arms against Macbeth. It firmly states Shakespeare's belief in the unity of a nation. Malcolm says first that he is avaricious and then that he is lecherous, and Macduff is willing to put up with both these evils. But then Malcolm says that if he became the ruler, he would create disunity, "Pour the sweet milk of concord into hell," and Macduff is heartsick. Malcolm, he says, is not only unfit to rule but unfit "to live." Then Malcolm explains that he was only testing Macduff in fear of agents in Macbeth's pay. They set off with forces against Macbeth, and Macduff learns of the butchery of his wife and children.

But the main point of the latter part of the play is what happens in the minds of the characters. First, back in Dunsinane, Lady

Macbeth has gone mad. She walks in her sleep, trying vainly to wash imaginary blood off her hands—"All the perfumes of Arabia will not sweeten this little hand. Oh, oh, oh!" Her mind is fixed in desperation on the murder of Duncan. Their plot has not worked out as she expected. It had not proved to be so simple; one man dead and then a happy kingship for Macbeth with herself as Queen. Instead of a broadening field of activity, she and Macbeth have become more isolated, more alone. He has become aware of this and continues to play the only part left for him. As for her, it is precisely because she had been so much more uneasy in the beginning, because she had to stifle such qualms as that Duncan looked like her father, that her mind has now cracked and that she is finally led to killing herself.

Macbeth is more firm, but not more happy. He accepts the fact that happiness is not for him and reveals his desolation:

> I have lived long enough. My way of life
> Is fall'n into the sere, the yellow leaf;
> And that which should accompany old age,
> As honour, love, obedience, troops of friends,
> I must not look to have; but, in their stead,
> Curses, not loud but deep, mouth-honour, breath,
> Which the poor heart would fain deny, and dare not.

He will hang those that talk of fear. He would like to cure Lady Macbeth, but knows this impossible, for she is not sick in the ordinary sense:

> Canst thou not minister to a mind diseased,
> Pluck from the memory a rooted sorrow,
> Raze out the written troubles of the brain,
> And with some sweet oblivious antidote
> Cleanse the stuffed bosom of that perilous stuff
> Which weighs upon the heart?

He knows it cannot be done even as he asks it, and he cries, "Throw physic to the dogs, I'll none of it." He clings to the fact that the witches have told him he cannot be defeated until Birnam Forest comes to Dunsinane, and this, he knows, is impossible. But Malcolm's soldiers have reached Birnam wood and each man has been told to cut down a bough and hold it as a kind of camouflage. Thus the forest does, in a sense, seem to move. Meanwhile Macbeth is told that the Queen is dead, and there follows his great speech, "Tomorrow, and tomorrow, and tomorrow . . . ," and ends that life "is a tale told by an idiot, full of sound and fury, / Signifying nothing." What is important about this is that it is not Shakespeare's philosophy but Macbeth's as Shakespeare sees it. The world seems irrational, because Macbeth, who had once possessed human and rational possibilities, had chosen an irrational course for his life. The world seems to be "a tale told by an idiot," because he has renounced contact with people whom he can love and trust. The news comes then that Birnam wood appears to be moving toward Dunsinane. But there is one hope still remaining—the witches' prophecy that no man born of woman could harm him. He says, "I 'gin to be a-weary of the sun," but he will fight to the end. "At least we'll die with harness on our back."

In the fighting that follows, Macduff says, "I cannot strike at wretched kerns, whose arms / Are hired to bear their staves." It is again the contrast between old and new, between the system whereby poor foot-soldiers had to fight for whoever owned them, and the system whereby they had rights and minds of their own. He runs into Macbeth, whom he had been seeking. Macbeth does not want to fight him. "My soul is too much charged / with blood of thine already." He believes he cannot be killed by anyone born of woman. But Macduff says he was from his mother's womb "untimely ripped."

Thus Macbeth finally knows that although the witches told him truth, they told only that part of it which pleased him. He will not fight, but when Macduff says, "Then yield thee, coward," and threatens to exhibit him to the public as a monster, Macbeth fights on and is killed. The new order takes over. Malcolm is King of Scotland, and those who were Thanes are now Earls, and there is a legitimate descent.

Macbeth is the "butcher" and his wife the "fiend-like Queen" that Malcolm calls them in his final speech, but this is only one side of the story. Shakespeare has also told the other side: that they are human beings who have been corrupted, who could have been different and who came to have no joy in life long before the final punishments caught up with them. In this sense, the drama is an expression of the new humanism.

There is an implied distinction in the play between killing and murder, for Shakespeare felt that not all killing was murder. Macbeth and Banquo kill in defense of their country and King, and are brave men. Killing someone who means no harm for personal advantage, however, is murder. Even today to kill in defense of one's country is not murder; indeed, it is considered a brave deed. Yet the concept of the preciousness of human life makes this distinctio. that has been imposed by society—it is not eternal. And its removal is on the order of our own day.

In Shakespeare's time, a world of peace was inconceivable and unrealistic. The old order did have a vision of a world theoretically without war, all ruled by a central pope and emperor, but even this was limited to Europe and in actuality there were constant wars in Europe. The common people were considered nobodies, expendable. There was no peace for them; at best a short oppressive life, while the ruling class lived in ease and comfort. But even the satisfactions of the privileged strata was only relative; they were constantly fighting among themselves for riches and power, and their wars made the oppression of the people even worse, with the result that they were constantly challenged by insurrections.

The rise of the national state made the change in this system that peace and law could presumably prevail within the nation. The matter of murder could be raised on a national scale, as Shakespeare raised it. But as a great artist, he cannot limit himself to legal forms; he deals with politics in human terms, and these, involving the value of life and the psychological effect on one person of killing another, go beyond legal limitations.

He could not foresee the competitiveness inherent in the national state when it is run by a greedy, oppressive class. He could not foresee, for example, that the Dutch Republic, which, as the Netherlands, England was guardedly helping against Spain, would after his death be warring with England. The fight of England against Spain and France was to him the fight of the new order against an older, oppressive one—the national state fighting for its existence against backward and feudal forms. But he raises the cry against murder both because it is an outrageous crime and because it destroys the murderer. Macbeth is shattered internally as a human being before he is physically destroyed. (This truth is manifested today on a wider scale than Shakespeare ever dreamed of.)

And the playwright has Macduff say, "I cannot strike at wretched kerns, whose arms / Are hired to bear their staves." The common people are part of the nation and have rights of their own. Macduff also speaks for the new nation—one with internal "concord." In what form the rights of the common people were to be realized Shakespeare did not know, nor that they would be realized only when the people themselves were running affairs. But he knew the demand for their rights to be justified, that it was on the agenda of history.

With Lear and Macbeth, Shakespeare moved far beyond his own times and was able to put kingship itself under the microscope, with a modernity of thinking that was remarkable even in the Elizabethan Age. The King, he showed, was like every other human being, but with great responsibilities that he had to answer to or suffer both externally and internally. And less than a half-century after Shakespeare's death, the ruling King of England was brought before the bar, judged, and executed.

10

A CRITICAL LOOK AT THE OLD AND NEW ORDERS

Anthony and Cleopatra
Coriolanus
Timon of Athens

IN SHAKESPEARE'S last three tragedies, *Antony and Cleopatra*, *Coriolanus* and *Timon of Athens*, he takes a penetrating look at the old order of nobility and an even more critical look at the new money-minded order. In *Antony and Cleopatra*, he reveals some indulgence in his attitude toward the old-style nobleman. Yes, Antony is heroic, gallant and fearless, but he is also tremendously self-centered. He sees the world as his own possession, as if he were a king. But his foothold is slippery; he is being discarded by the real world, which has no use for him. The play is supremely skillful in its organization of an abundance of characters put together in a coherent whole; profound in its analysis of personality, always aware of human values, which find expression in continuously exalted poetry. *Coriolanus* is bleaker in its humanity and poetry. *Timon of Athens* has powerful sections, but its people and poetry are also somewhat bleak, so much so that the question of whether it is entirely Shakespeare's has seriously been raised.

The Antony of *Antony and Celopatra* is historically the same

198

figure as the Antony of *Julius Caesar*, and in its events it could be considered a sequel to the earlier play. But it is an entirely different kind of play, different in theme and in its picture of society. Shakespeare creates a quite different personality for Antony—not the cunning demagogue, playing second fiddle to Julius Caesar and even Octavius Caesar, as in the earlier play, but a magnificent soldier and lover who plays second fiddle to nobody and is virtually worshipped by his followers. Even his enemies see him as almost superhuman, and when he falls, an epoch seems to come to an end. Octavius Caesar, when told of his death, says, although Antony was his enemy:

> The breaking of so great a thing should make
> A greater crack. . . . The death of Antony
> Is not a single doom; in the name lay
> A society of the world.

The main personages of the drama are Antony, Cleopatra, Octavius Caesar. Pompey is a lesser character. An extraordinarily important part is played by a group of military officers: Philo, Enobarbus, Menas, Ventidius, Maecenas, Dolabella, Scarus, Agrippa, Canidius, Thidias. They resemble one another and are almost like a social brotherhood, feeling a kind of fellowship even when they fight on opposite sides. Brave men, their business is war; they obey their masters, who rule the events. Strong men of a military society on which the entire order of the play is erected, they nevertheless have minds of their own. They are limited in imagination but shrewd, hard and practical. While they speak a rough soldier's language, it frequently breaks into inspired poetry. The most completely developed among them is Enobarbus, who gains added strength because he typifies them all, and who rises to become a tragic figure in his own right. A unique and central feature of the play is the continuous counterpoint of the comments made by these captains on the foolishness and high-flown dreams of their masters.

The very opening of the play is a speech by one of the military captains, Philo, who is deploring Antony's "dotage" on Cleopatra. Antony's eyes once "glowed like plated Mars;" he had a "captain's heart, / Which in the scuffles of great fights hath burst /

The buckles on his breast," and now he only cools a "gipsy's lust;" he is "The triple pillar of the world, transformed / Into a strumpet's fool." The imagery that paints Antony seemingly larger than life may appear grandiose, but not in Shakespeare's hands. It permeates the play and evokes the qualities Antony possesses that make him a demi-god to his followers.

Cleopatra enters and speaks with the cunning of a Queen in love, desperately trying to keep Antony in Egypt. A messenger has come from Rome, and Cleopatra tells Antony to listen to him, but her words are designed to stir up his resentment of Roman authority. Perhaps, she says, Fulvia, Antony's wife, "is angry," or the "scarce-bearded Caesar"—who is Octavius, heir to the former slain leader—is sending "His powerful mandate to you: 'Do this, or this.'" Antony is "Caesar's homager." He is being scolded by his wife, "shrill-tongued Fulvia." Antony answers in sweeping terms, "Let Rome in Tiber melt and the wide arch / Of the range empire fall." His place is with Cleopatra. This is "the nobleness of life." And so when she says again, "Hear the ambassadors," he answers as she wishes, "Fie, wrangling queen!" He will stroll through the streets with her. They leave, and Philo laments, "He comes too short of that great property / Which still should go with Antony."

So the image of Antony is struck: a mighty soldier, almost worshipped by his men, who walks on the earth as its master and scorns anything that pretends to have authority over him. Like one of the old-style great English noblemen, he is a law unto himself. He will consort with Cleopatra because that is his wish.

The demand that Antony attend to affairs in Rome is overwhelming, and Cleopatra schemes to keep her hold on him not merely as a woman in love but as a Queen. The erotic atmosphere about her is beautifully created through her two attendants, Iras and Charmian, with their light, gay, bawdy humor.

Antony listens to the messengers; he is losing ground in Asia. He says, "These strong Egyptian fetters I must break / Or lose myself in dotage." Another messenger tells him that his wife has died. Pompey, son of Pompey the Great, whom the previous Caesar had slain, is now raising a rebellion against the present

Caesar in Rome. He counts on exploiting the popularity of his father and the unpopularity of young Caesar. Pompey has built up considerable strength at sea. So Antony says, "I must from this enchanting Queen break off; / Ten thousand harms, more than the ills I know, / My idleness hatch." Another captain, Enobarbus, is with him and maintains the counterpoint of the play. When Antony says they must leave, Enobarbus is bluffly satiric. Cleopatra will instantly die. "I have seen her die twenty times upon far poorer moment."

This has its effect. Antony is determined to leave for Rome, and Cleopatra must consider how to continue holding him even at a distance. When Charmian advises her, "In each thing give him way, cross him in nothing," Cleopatra says, "Thou teachest like a fool: the way to lose him." And so she is bitter to him: "O, never was there a queen / So mightly betrayed!" She has him begging her to believe he still loves her and, on leaving, he says, "I hence fleeting here remain with thee."

In the Roman part of the world, Pompey is contempuous of Caesar, who, he says, "gets money where / He loses hearts." He also has little regard for Lepidus, the other member of the triumvirate that is ruling Rome. But he is shocked to hear that Antony is returning, for this is a soldier whom he respects.

There is a great scene in which the triumvirate meets. Antony and Caesar are cool to one another, with Lepidus trying to act as peacemaker. Antony will not accept Caesar's criticisms and when he is accused of breaking his oath of support, he answers:

> Neglected rather,
> And then when poisoned hours had bound me up
> From mine own knowledge. As nearly as I may,
> I'll play the penitent to you: But mine honesty
> Shall not make poor my greatness, nor my power
> Work without it.

When Enobarbus suggests that they bury their differences at least until they dispose of Pompey, Antony shuts him up. But another officer, Agrippa, suggests that Caesar's sister Octavia might marry the widowed Antony, and Antony accepts the idea. And the counterpoint of the play continues, for this scene ends with a meeting of another triumvirate: Enobarbus, Agrippa and Maecenas. They speak with the hard-boiled realism of soldiers. That they are of different factions does not disturb their good-fellowship. Factions are their masters' business, and the officers will fight faithfully when they have to, for that is their profession. But when there is no battle, they can be friends. And so Enobarbus tells the others of Egypt and when he gets to Cleopatra, he speaks glowing poetry:

> The barge she sat in, like a burnished throne,
> Burned on the water. The poop was beaten gold;
> Purple the sails, and so perfumed that
> The winds were lovesick with them; the oars were silver,
> Which to the tune of flutes kept stroke and made
> The water which they beat to follow faster,
> As amorous of their strokes. For her own person,
> It beggared all description. She did lie
> In her pavilion, cloth-of-gold of tissue,
> O'erpicturing that Venus where we see
> The fancy outwork nature. On each side her
> Stand pretty dimpled boys, like smiling Cupids,
> With divers-coloured fans, whose wind did seem
> To glow the delicate cheeks which they did cool,
> And what they undid did.

This is not simply Cleopatra, but Cleopatra the Queen, the jewel in its setting and more descriptive of the setting than of the jewel. The rich description continues, emphasizing the sensuous pleasure that Cleopatra represents. And so when Maecenas says, "Now Antony must leave her utterly," the practical Enobarbus knows better:

> Never! He will not
> Age cannot wither her nor custom stale
> Her infinite variety.

Then the three soldiers go off to dine.

The duality between master and man takes on a sardonically critical tone in a scene about Pompey. He has been given an offer by Caesar, Lepidus and Antony to take command of Sicily and Sardinia if he will end his revolt. He accepts, although it means he is giving up hope of ever ruling the Roman Empire. Pompey's captain, Menas, says in an aside, "Thy father, Pompey, would ne'er have made this treaty." But it is Antony's presence that has convinced him to take the easier way, and this will be his doom. For, as we will later learn, Caesar will use him and then put him to death.

Meanwhile Pompey has still another chance. There is a scene of wild feasting on Pompey's galley, where he has invited the triumvirate to celebrate their agreement. Amid the singing, dancing and drunkenness, Menas suggests to Pompey that he cut the ropes that moor the galley and then slaughter the three. The Empire will then be his. Pompey answers:

> Ah, this thou shouldst have done,
> And not have spoken on't. In me, 'tis villainy;
> In thee 't had been good service. Thou must know,
> 'Tis not my profit that does lead mine honour;
> Mine honour, it.

His, however, is a shaky honor, which gladly would have profited had the act been done without his knowledge. Caesar will not treat him with any honor. The atmosphere is that of an old order of great warriors passing away. The only one who really retains this greatness is Antony, and he is now bound to Cleopatra. Enobarbus says, "He will to his Egyptian dish again." And throughout these scenes, Enobarbus and Menas comment on their leaders like hardened, down-to-earth soldiers. About each other they have no illusions. Enobarbus says to Menas, "Give me your hand, Menas. If our eyes had authority, here they might take two thieves kissing." And Menas offers him a bed for the night.

During this time Cleopatra is desperate with fear. She writes daily to Antony. When a messenger comes who humbly tells her that Antony has married Caesar's sister Octavia, Cleopatra beats and threatens to kill him. It is a remarkable scene, comic in its extravagance and yet with a vein of poignant tenderness; it has Shakespeare's remarkable ability to find outer actions that portray inner feelings. It ends as Cleopatra says, "Pity me, Charmian, / But do not speak to me. Lead me to my chamber."

Shakespeare's use of officers to fill out the social picture is worthy of note. Antony sends an officer, Ventidius, to Syria to combat a Parthian revolt. He wins a smashing victory and could extend it by pursuing the refugees into Mesopotamia. But he halts, saying, "I could do more to do Antonius good, / But 'twould offend him, and in his offence / Should my performance perish." A follower should not appear to be bigger than his leader. This becomes another facet of Antony's decline in idleness. His captains are losing confidence in him. Meanwhile the triumvirate is disintegrating. While Antony is in Athens with Octavia, Caesar makes war upon the weakened Pompey, defeats him, and imprisons Lepidus. He is ready now to break with Antony, who has been a friend to Pompey. He sends Octavia back to Rome and returns to Cleopatra. The political maze has cleared up; two antagonists are left, and the shrewd politician Caesar now unchecked in Rome holds the stronger hand.

The outbreak of war between Caesar and Antony is the turning point of the drama, and from now on what is important is the mentality of Antony as he suffers setback after setback. Actions that appear to be mistakes have their own logic. Antony is a disabled leader, whose ailment follows from his concept that his stature is that of a demi-god; he refuses to obey orders from persons or circumstances, insisting on his love for Cleopatra as the center of his life. Meanwhile Caesar is the careful, practical calculator.

Antony's first mistake is to fight by sea. His officers Enobarbus and Canidius tell him his ships are heavy, and his seamen are newly impressed while Caesar's had gained experience against Pompey. A common soldier warns him of this, too. But the pressure emanates from Cleopatra, "By sea: what else?" And she offers 60 ships which prove to be worthless.

In leading her fleet beside Antony's, Cleopatra tries to play a man's role, but Shakespeare paints her as weakly feminine, lacking the brave spirit. Her 60 ships turn tail and flee and, what is worse, Antony then flees, too. So the battle is lost, and Canidius, Antony's land officer, abandons him to surrender to Caesar. He tells this frankly to Enobarbus, who says, "I'll yet follow / The wounded chance of Antony, though my reason / Sits in the wind against me."

Antony loses touch with reason and behaves with wild irration-
ality. At one point, completely dejected, he says, "The land bids
me tread no more upon't." He tells his followers to abandon him
and to take his treasure. He expostulates to Cleopatra: "thou
knew'st too well / My heart was to thy rudder tied by th'strings, /
and thou shouldst tow me after." Then he goes off with her and
sends an ambassador to Caesar asking to be treated as a private
citizen. Caesar is practical and hard. His officer Dolabella points
out that Antony is "plucked," by sending his schoolmaster as
ambassador, "Which had superfluous kings for messengers / Not
many moons gone by." Caesar's aim is to cut Antony apart from
Cleopatra and Egypt. When Antony's offer is refused by Caesar,
Antony madly offers to fight him hand to hand. Caesar's unhero-
ic answer to this is, "Let the old ruffian know / I have many other
ways to die, meantime / laugh at his challenge." Antony, in a fit
of rage, has Thidias, Caesar's ambassador to win over Cleopatra,
whipped—a breach of military courtesy—but it makes him feel
like a commander again. He suddenly conceives the hope that he
can beat Caesar militarily. He will fight another battle. "I will be
treble-sinewed, hearted, breathed / And fight maliciously." He
goes off with Cleopatra to drink meanwhile, swearing "I'll make
death love me, for I will contend / Even with his pestilent
scythe." Enobarbus correctly appraises this:

> Now he'll outstare the lightning. To be furious
> Is to be frighted out of fear; and in that mood
> The dove will peck the estridge; and I see still
> A diminution in our captain's brain
> Restores his heart.

Enobarbus abandons Antony, but not before a dinner at which
the mercurial Antony talks sadly of past greatness and tells his
followers that they are free to leave him. Enobarbus goes through
a struggle. "Look, they weep, / And I, an ass, am onion-eyed." In
the conflict between reason and sentiment, reason tells him to
leave Antony for Caesar, and he does so. Antony, finds that
Enobarbus has left behind his treasure and sends it after him,
saying, "O, my fortunes have / Corrupted honest men." But
reason in this situation is barren. Nobody loves a turncoat.

Caesar plans to use the deserters in the front ranks of the fight against Antony. It is not for this reason, however, but for a more profound one—the loss of the human fellowship he had with Antony—that Enobarbus dies of a broken heart. "I am alone the villain of the earth, / . . . I will seek / Some ditch wherein to die. The foul'st best fits / My latter part of life." Part of Antony's greatness as a soldier is that he could command such loyalties—a frequent phenomenon in the old order.

There is a land battle where Antony wins a temporary victory. An officer, Scarus, says, "I had a wound here that was like a T, / But now 'tis made an H." Antony loses the main battle, which is at sea. Again the Egyptians have surrendered; he curses Cleopatra and drives her away, believing that she has betrayed him. Frightened, she has word sent to him that she is dead and, at this news, his love returns in full blast. "I will o'ertake thee, Cleopatra, and / Weep for my pardon."

He determines to kill himself and asks an officer, Eros, to use a sword to slay him. But Eros instead kills himself. And so Antony falls on his own sword, but although he is mortally wounded, he does not die. Then he is told that Cleopatra is not dead, that she had lied to him out of fear, and that she has not yielded herself to Caesar. He asks his woebegone attendants to carry him to her, telling them not to sorrow, and that when punishment comes, "We punish it / Seeming to bear lightly." He is drawn up to the monument where she has taken shelter and as he dies he kisses her, saying that when alive he was "the greatest prince o' th' world," and that he had yielded to no one but was taking his own life.

Caesar is moved by the news of Antony's death. "The breaking of so great a thing should make / A greater crack." He is ready to make longer laments, but realizes there is no time for them. He must guard Cleopatra and keep her from killing herself so that he can bring her in triumph back to Rome. She thinks she has time to maneuver, but he sends men who trick and seize her. Antony becomes a glowing fantasy in her mind.

> His face was as the heavens, and therein stuck
> A sun and moon, which kept their course and lighted
> The little O, the earth. . . .

His legs bestrid the ocean. His reared arm
Created the world. . . .
                    In his livery
Walked crowns and coronets. Realms and islands were
As plates dropped from his pocket.

Caesar speaks gently to her; he needs her alive. But one of his captains, Dolabella, moved by her beauty and torment, tells her the truth: she will be led as trophy in Caesar's triumph. That she will not do; she is a Queen, which is why Antony loved her. Sometimes, to preserve her empire she had to go against his interests, but she will die a Queen.

Cleopatra is a remarkable creation—not a staunch, firm and noble woman, not a Juliet or Desdemona. She has frailties and fears; she is the only heroine like this in Shakespeare's tragedies. Even near the end, she tries to deceive Caesar by giving him a list of all the money, plate and jewels she owns and keeping hidden more than half. But she dies a noble death. A countryman comes in, as arranged, with a basket of figs in which are hidden poisonous asps. There is a short comic-poignant scene; "I wish you joy of the worm," he says. Then dressed in robe and crown, she says:

Husband, I come!
Now to that name my courage prove my title!
I am fire and air; my other elements
I give to baser life. So: have you done?
Come then and take the last warmth of my lips.
Farewell, kind Charmian, Iras, long farewell.

She applies the asp to her breast. Caesar enters, to find her dead, as are Iras and Charmian.

And so an old order—the great noblemen-warriors, each of whom was a law unto himself—passes. Shakespeare has a lingering fondness for this order, even though he recognizes its limitations and why it must be moved off the stage of history. It lacked the sense of social responsibility, it lacked humanistic concern for ordinary people. It was wasteful of life, capricious, winning great fortunes and tossing them away; it made the world subservient to the whims of a leader. But it did have certain human qualities—the leaders were warlike and took their chances like anyone else, sharing the comradeship of the battlefield. The new order was hard, practical, utterly lacking in sentiment. It promised peace but could it fill human needs? Could Caesar arouse the love that Antony aroused among his officers and soldiers? Those were the questions left by the play.

And they are raised again in *Coriolanus.* Here he presents a less attractive figure of the old order than Antony, but also speaks with franker detestation of some aspects of the new order. What is unattractive about Coriolanus is that he has no love for anyone, even for his wife Vergilia, whom he respects without affection, and whom he abandons without a qualm. True, he has some feeling for his comrate-in-arms, Comenius, and for the old patrician Menenius, whom he accepts practically as a foster father, but he easily crushes even these feelings. And this affects the entire play—it has no lyricism, no warmth, no outpouring of love for people or for nature.

Coriolanus remains a hero, nevertheless. He has two qualities which to Shakespeare are great and necessary—absolute courage and absolute honesty. But there is nobody in the play to stand alongside him, sharing his good qualities yet speaking with more love—if only of one other person. There is Coriolanus on one side, who will not curry favor with the people he despises. And there are the two tribunes on the other side, Sicinius Velutus and Junius Brutus, who pretend to speak for the common people but who actually despise them, showing it by continually lying to them and manipulating them.

The central theme of the play is the life of the nation, in this case Rome, but it could be any nation. Coriolanus, after his banishment, turns against his native land. "My birthplace hate I," he says, and this, combined with his honesty, his lack of any craftiness, proves to be his downfall. Against him are two politicians who likewise see nothing in the nation but a chance for their own advantage. Nowhere in the play is there the rhapsodic national feeling that was expressed, for example, in *Henry V.* Could it be that now, after the death of Queen Elizabeth and the accession of King James, Shakespeare feels that the nation is torn between self-seeking elements on opposite sides, a nobility with no regard for the people and a middle class with regard only for its own rights.

The drama opens with a mutiny. There is a "dearth," and the people want bread. As always, Shakespeare shows the people divided, some eager to burn and destroy, and some opposing them. The popular and breezy old patrician Menenius tries to calm them with a parable found in Plutarch about the patrician-senate being the "stomach" of the national body, sending food to all its limbs and organs. And the news comes that another contingent of plebeians has won the concession of having tribunes speak for them. Caius Marcius (afterwards known as Coriolanus) enters with his customary vituperation against the commoners. But news comes that the Volsces are carrying war to Rome, and he eagerly enlists in the fight against them, although not without a last remark that the "rats"—namely, the commoners—will find plenty of corn to "gnaw" in the bins of the Volsces. Left on the stage are the two tribunes, Sicinius Velutus and Junius Brutus, who speak of their hatred of Caius.

These two are the villains of the play, and the way in which he builds them up indicates that Shakespeare is obviously thinking of his own England rather than of ancient Rome. They talk for the people, but are not of them; they are moneyed, middle-class persons and magistrates, who raise the cry of rights for the people because that is the way they can get standing in the state against the patricians. Shakespeare depicts them as hypocrites.

There is a scene of the Volsces in their city, Corioli, who have a spy in Rome writing them of the dissension there. And there is a scene of three women: Volumnia, Caius Marcius's mother, a Roman matron who wants her sons to be brave fighters with a fierceness that is almost repellent, glad even when they die in battle. Vergilia, his wife, is a much softer person, with a tender respect for him. And there is their friend Valeria, who wants Vergilia to visit with her, but Vergilia refuses to leave the house until Caius Marcius returns.

There follows the battle, in and around Corioli. Caius Marcius distinguishes himself as a great hero, bitter, reviling his own soldiers who are not as fearless as he, and threatening to treat them like the enemy. At one point he is alone in the city of Corioli, because the others are afraid to follow him through the gates. But he beats off the Volsces and later finds himself face to face with their leader, Tullus Aufridius, an old antagonist. Only the intervention of other Volsces saves Aufridius. When the battle is over and Corioli is taken, Caius Marcius refuses all spoils and even praise. The leaders of the Roman army, Cominius and Lartius, are thoroughly unselfish, giving him full credit for his exploits and officially titling him Coriolanus.

Act II begins with Coriolanus welcomed home as the hero he is, while the two tribunes Sicinius and Brutus plot more viciously against him because the people are cheering him. His fierce mother is happy that he comes home wounded. She applauds his killing of others. "Death, that dark spirit, in 's nervy arm doth lie; / Which, being advanced, declines, and then men die." The great election episode follows, covering the latter part of Act II and all of Act III. Coriolanus is chosen consul by the Senate, but he must also get the approval of the people. He does this, speaking honestly and curtly to them, and they find him worthy of the office. But the tribunes, Brutus and Sicinius, are enraged, Shakespeare has them cleverly confuse the people. Since Coriolanus out of pride had not shown them his wounds, Sicinius taunts the people with "childish friendliness," then Brutus says:

> Did you perceive
> He did solicit you in free contempt
> When he did need your loves; and do you think
> That his contempt shall not be bruising to you
> When he hath power to crush? Why, had your bodies
> No heart among you?

Thus the very honesty of Coriolanus is twisted cunningly into a seeming dishonesty. And when the people are convinced to demand another election, both tribunes hide their tracks by asking the people to say that they were led to vote for Coriolanus by the tribunes. Brutus says, "Lay / A fault on us, your tribunes." Sicinius says, "Say, you chose him / More after our commandment than as guided / By your own true affections." Meeting Coriolanus, the tribunes deliberately enrage him by claiming the people are now making charges against him. They then accuse him of "manifest treason." When his anger has risen, they call for help, pretending that they are being attached. The plebeians enter and the tribunes inflame them. There is a scuffle, in which Coriolanus beats back the people and the tribunes. Coriolanus is advised by his mother and by Comenius to speak peacefully to the people, but at the coming meeting in the Forum, the tribunes plan not to let him speak temperately. They contrive to keep the people excited:

> And when such time they have begun to cry,
> Let them not cease, but with a din confused
> Enforce the present execution
> Of what we chance to sentence.

Then, when alone, Brutus says, "Put him to choler straight." And when the meeting comes, they challenge him with what will most kindle his fury, "You are a traitor to the people." He forgets all his reluctant promises to speak equably and instead breaks out in anger. The tribunes sentence him to banishment from Rome. And when friends, like Comenius, try to speak, Sicinius says, "He's sentenced; no more hearing," and Brutus, "There's no more to be said but he is banished / As enemy to the people and his country." And this is exactly what they succeed in making of him.

Coriolanus could have been of use to the Roman state, but he is rebuffed. From hatred of the Roman common people to hatred of all Rome is, Shakespeare shows, an easy step. He goes to the Volsces and Aufidius and tells them they can kill him if they want or accept him as an ally. He hates Rome. He is happily accepted and made a leader in the war against Rome. Aufidius still hates and fears him but plans to make fullest use of him before he finds means to do away with him. "When, Caius, Rome is thine, / Thou art poor'st of all; then shortly are thou mine."

There is consternation in Rome when the news comes that Coriolanus is leading a Volscian army against them; Brutus and Sicinius are especially affected.

A strong defense of these two tribunes is made by John Palmer, writing of Coriolanus in *Political and Comic Characters of Shakespeare*:

> For better or worse, these tribunes are Shakespeare's counterfeit presentment of two labour leaders. They are the natural products of a class war in the commonwealth. They use their wits to defend the interests of the popular party and to remove from power a declared enemy of the people. . . . In working for their party they

do not claim to be working disinterestedly for the nation. . . .
They regard themselves as watchdogs of the people. . . .[1]

Of the chicanery they showed in the elections, Palmer writes:

> Admittedly it is dishonest. But do political leaders in the heat of
> an election always tell the truth? There is assuredly no question of
> double-dealing. . . . They also want the senators to feel that the
> rejection of Marcius is a spontaneous and representative act of the
> people. Is this manoeuvre so uncommonly disgraceful? . . . These
> then are the tact. s of the popular front.[2]

Not only does Palmer write of the play as if its characters are
personages in a 20th century social novel, although Shakespeare
could, of course, know nothing of labor leaders, political parties
and popular fronts, but also, even in writing of the tribunes as if
they were living today, Palmer makes no distinction between
dishonest and honest labor leaders. Nor does he discuss the
difference in Great Britain between Labor Party politicians who
talk of socialism but in practice support the capitalist system at
the expense of the workers, and those who are honest with them
and genuinely represent their interests.

To Shakespeare, the dishonesty of Sicinius and Brutus, and
their scorn for the poor and unlettered citizens (none of which is
in Plutarch) are the decisive elements in their characterization.
And when Brutus, on hearing that Coriolanus is marching
against Rome tells Sicinius, "Would half my wealth / Would buy
this for a lie!" it is clear that he is a wealthy tradesman, quite
different from the poor commoners. This is also Shakespeare,
not Plutarch. The tribunes are a counterpart of the wealthy
merchants in Shakespeare's England who were still "nobodies" in
respect to state rights.

Shakespeare builds his play on material from Plutarch, but not
only does he leave out Plutarch's voluminous detail but he also
ignores Plutarch's picture of Roman politics and society. He is
not interested in providing a historical picture of ancient Rome; it
is England that occupies his mind; and the picture he presents is
peculiarly of his own time—men of wealth who are scorned by
the aristocracy, allowed no rights in the state, and who therefore

assume domination over the poor commoners. The human elements he creates resound ringingly today, but not his politics. Too much has changed. In fact, to appreciate properly today the splendor of his human insights, we have first to see how much they sprang from his sensitivity to the issues of his own day.

In Shakespeare's Rome the play builds up to a time of shock, and the only salvation appears to be to send the friends of Coriolanus as emissaries to beg him not to destroy the city. First is Comenius, whom Coriolanus rejects. Then Menenius, who was looked upon by Coriolanus as a foster father, but who is also rejected, although Coriolanus tells Aufidius later that it was with a "cracked heart." Then his mother, wife, child, and Valeria come, and his mother's pleading persuades him to make peace. Her compelling argument is that if he tramples on Rome, he will trample on her, too, and this he cannot face. To Shakespeare, the old order of nobility knew no nation, but did have strong ties of family. And so in Rome there is joy: Coriolanus returns to the Volsces, pointing out that he has won them much booty and is no lover of Rome. But he has given Aufidius an opening to have his conspirators slay him, which they do.

The core of the drama is that whatever wrongs Coriolanus suffers (and Shakespeare shows these as being greater than those related by Plutarch), are real and grievous, it is unforgiveable for him to desert his country and join its enemies. This judgment is delivered, as always in Shakespeare, not as morality handed down from heaven but as an act of life. A man's country is not something he can drop or change like a garment. When Coriolanus takes the step of joining Rome's enemies, he dooms himself. For even had he not listened to his mother, he would have been surrounded by those who hated him.

The drama is powerfully written and organized, and yet is less in greatness than the tragedies from *Hamlet* through *Antony and Cleopatra,* because it gives less scope for Shakespeare's humanistic love of life. He has not changed his politics; he is not a democrat in this play, but then he never was a political democrat. He felt affection for the common people, but he never felt that political leadership was for them. How could he have felt otherwise? Uneducated as they were, could they run a country? Here his bitterness is aimed at both old and new: at the old order, to the extent that however brave its protectors may be, they have no feeling for the nation, which to Shakespeare must include feeling for the common people; and at the new order, to the extent that it is represented by the moneyed commoners who seize leadership of the people in order to promote their own self-interest in running the state along with the aristocracy. The bitterness is more marked because there is practically no relief. Shakespeare creates Coriolanus as honest, hard and grim; the state can use him but he cannot speak for it. Menenius, who "converses more with the buttock of the night than with the forehead of the morning," is too much the old clown. Others, like Comenius and Vergelia, are insufficiently developed. The mother Volumnia speaks for the nation, but she wins Coriolanus over not because of the nation but because, standing with it, she is also his mother. It is a despairing play because Shakespeare despairs of the oldline aristocracy and has no confidence in the middle-class tradesmen or money minds.

To the modern reader, the play appears to attack democracy. But it does not attack the common people, whom it shows as divided and basically fair-minded, if easily deluded by those who claim leadership over them. What it attacks is middle-class democracy, the rule of the money-controlled mind. Shakespeare had the acumen to see that the middle class (like Junius Brutus, who says, "Would half my wealth would buy this for a lie") was raising the cry of people's rights but using the movement only to gain its own rights and enter the state along with the patricians.

Shakespeare had no foreknowledge that in 1640-48 an Oliver Cromwell would show his ability to lead men in fighting as well as, or better than, any aristocrat. But Cromwell could be hard and cruel, too, as in his massacre of the Irish. And Shakespeare equally had no foreknowledge of the coming rise of industrialism and the great transformations that middle-class capitalist democracy would bring about. He had no way of knowing that the working class would also become educated because the middle class needed universal education. But, of course, before they could set up a state of their own the working people would also have to become class-conscious, aware that exploitation was a class phenomenon evoked by the economy and not a matter of personal villainy. But at least he did point out the difference between the ordinary commons and the wealthy commoners. Shortly after his death this issue was to become relevant in English politics, with the rise of a communist-minded faction, the Diggers and Levellers, under Gerald Winstanley, who opposed the men of property.

Nevertheless it is possible to appreciate the fact that Shakespeare criticized the middle class even if he did not expect it to find solutions the age could not provide. At least he raised the problem of a rising class who would become capitalists and despise the people. And this concern is continued in *Timon of Athens,* where the hatred of the money-controlled mentality becomes a bitter scream.

Timon of Athens is a weak play by Shakespearean standards, since it has no people in it with any depth, and no Shakespearean conflict of personalities. Almost the entire society of the mock Athens in the play is made up of money-controlled characters, with the exception of a few servants, who play no important role, and of Timon, who has an incredibly naive faith in people in the first part of the play and an equally incredible hatred for them in the second part. The thought of E. K. Chambers that it is a sketched-out but incomplete play has a good deal of plausibility. It is magnificently written in parts but it has only flickers of dramatic life, out of which ideas emerge about money which are in line with Shakespeare's thoughts but are nowhere else put so sharply.

Lord Timon gives money and other gifts to everyone about him. He thinks people should never worry about money. When they need it, somebody should give it to them and the giver should be confident that if he ever is in need, he will get it from somebody else. In other words, money should be a medium of friendship. He says:

> Why, I have often wished myself poorer, that I might come nearer to you. We are born to do benefits: and what better or properer can we call our own than the riches of our friends? O,

what a precious comfort 'tis to have so many like brothers
commanding one another's fortunes!

Timon sells or mortgages his land and borrows from usurers, so
that he may always have money on hand. He is confident that
those who take his gifts share his views. And, in general, he is a
kindly person who looks forgivingly at a professional cynic like
Apemantus (who talks with hatred of everybody but feeds at
Timon's table); he is friendly with a hardened warrior like
Alcibiades; sympathetic with those caught by the law because
they are short of money and considerate of the poor who cannot
marry for want of money. And he is taken advantage of: he is
given gifts by people who know he will immediately return
something tenfold in worth. As one senator, who is also a usurer,
says, "If I want gold, steal but a beggar's dog / And give it to
Timon, why the dog coins gold."

Timon's faithful steward Flavius, who says "I bleed inwardly
for my lord," tries unavailingly to warn him that his coffers are
emptying. But the bitter awakening comes when the usurious
senator and two other moneylenders demand payment of the
sums they have given Timon on his bond. They have milked
Timon of gifts, but that is of no account. And Flavius tells Timon
that his estates, once large, are gone, either sold or hopelessly
mortgaged. Flavius weeps but Timon is cheerful, for this gives
him an opportunity to test his friends.

He tells Flavius, "You shall perceive how you / Mistake my
fortunes. I am wealthy in my friends." He sends his servants to
the senators and various lords to ask for money. Timon has done
"great deeds," and saved the state with his "sword and fortune,"
but Flavius has already tried the senate and found its members
consider the season a bad one for giving money. As for others
who Timon thought were his friends, they all refuse him,
differing only in their excuses. One thinks it is bad policy to lend
money only on friendship with no security. Another says he is
caught short. A third flies into a huff because he is asked third
instead of first and this suffices as reason to give nothing. All of
them have, of course, liberally accepted Timon's money.

A secondary plot is set in motion around Alcibiades, who

pleads for the life of a brave soldier who has fallen afoul of the law. Alcibiades is denied by the self-righteous and legalistic senate and is himself banished. When Timon invites his former friends to a dinner, they come, apologizing for refusing his money, and when the dishes are uncovered, they are seen to contain only water and stones. Timon pelts them and drives them out with abuse: "Most smiling, smooth, detested parasites, / Courteous destroyers, affable wolves, meek bears, / You fools of fortune, trencher friends, time's flies, / Cap-and-knee slaves, vapours, and minute-jacks! . . . . Athens! henceforth hated be / Of Timon, man and all humanity!"

The most eloquent part of the play follows. Timon calls down curses on all the inhabitants of Athens, goes outside the city to live on roots as one who has renounced all civilization, and hopes that "his hate may grow / To the whole race of mankind, high and low." Flavius divides what money he has with the other servants and makes a touching speech:

> O' the fierce wretchedness that glory brings us!
> Who would not wish to be from wealth exempt,
> Since riches point to misery and contempt? . . . .
> Poor honest lord, brought low by his own heart,
> Undone by goodness!

Timon withdraws from all society, crying, "Destruction fang mankind!" Then, while digging for roots, he comes across a great store of gold. This inspires another powerful speech. (Marx comments on it in his early economic and philosophical manuscripts because of its insight into the perverting role of money in human society):

> Thus much of this will make black white, foul fair,
> Wrong right, base noble, old young, coward valiant.
> Ha, you gods! why this? What this, you gods? Why this
> Will lug your priests and servants from your sides,
> Pluck stout men's pillows from below their heads.
> This yellow slave
> Will knit and break religions, bless th'accursed;
> Walk the hoar leprosy adored; place thieves,
> And give them title, knee and approbation
> With senators on the bench.

Marx comments: "He who can buy bravery is brave, though a coward. As money is not exchanged for any one specific quality, for any one specific thing, or for any particular human essential power, but for the entire objective world of man and nature, from the standpoint of its possessor it therefore serves to exchange every property for every other. . . ."[3]

In two long and powerful scenes, Timon is confronted by various personages, some of whom have heard that he has found money. His scorn is like a catalogue of social hypocrisy. He beats off Apemantus, the cynic, for reviling civilization yet accepting it by living with it; a poet and a painter, for serving villains; senators, for upholding a corrupt city. He gives gold to all who openly and unhypocritically are enemies of society; Alcibiades, for carrying war to Athens; his two whores, so that they may spread diseases; some bandits whom, unwittingly, he almost convinced to follow honest paths by his description of the life of crime he is encouraging them to pursue. The one exception to his hate is Flavius, who comes to offer his services. Timon says:

> I do proclaim
> One honest man—mistake me not—but one!
> No more, I pray,—and he's a steward.
> How fain would I have hated all mankind!
> And thou redeem'st thyself. But all, save thee,
> I fell with curses.

Instead of accepting the money Flavius proffers, he gives him a great sum, but only on the condition that "thou shalt build from men, / Hate all, curse all, show charity to none . . ." Then Timon dies, as Athens surrenders to Alcibiades, who "brings the olive with the sword," and announces a regime of "justice," promising to punish all who wrong him and Timon.

The ending is weak because Alcibiades is not filled out as a character; he remains fragmentary, while Timon's violent hatred of civilized life dominates the play. *Timon of Athens* has been called a study of ingratitude, but although this is an element it is not the main one. What Timon wants is not gratitude but friendship. He has always thought of money as a way of easing relations among people, of making it possible for them to live truly as human beings. He looks upon his money as a kind of servant; and his discovery was that money is the master, not the servant. People did not want simply to be friends; they were money-corrupted; it powered their minds; it dictated values, replacing human values.

There remains Flavius, the one person in the play with genuine humanity. He is not a leading character. A steward at that time could not be the hero of a play. He has no ambition other than serving Timon respectfully and with affection. And the treatment of a character with simplicity of heart occurs in other plays. In his last three, all comedies, *Cymbeline, The Winter's Tale,* and *The Tempest,* Shakespeare would turn away from court life and city life to a kind of pastoral atmosphere in which simple human values existed and where there could be a regeneration of humanity.

11

A VISION OF REGENERATED MAN

Cymbeline
The Winter's Tale
The Tempest

After expressing his violent hatred of the money-centered spirit in *Coriolanus* and *Timon of Athens,* Shakespeare rounds out his work with three comedies that project thoughts of regeneration. They are *Cymbeline, The Winter's Tale,* and *The Tempest.* All three show a furious contempt for the life and atmosphere of the court. What is new about them is not the recognition of a change in society, but the wish or dream that somehow those fated to rule people could be transported in childhood to pastoral surroundings, living simply and close to the earth and ignorant of court intrigues or money rivalries—as a result of which they might emerge as regenerated human beings. In *Cymbeline* and *The Winter's Tale* he tells an involved story which he must make especially preposterous in order to encompass this theme. Finally, in the great masterpiece *The Tempest,* he finds the right form for his thought. The writing in all three is beautiful.

Cymbeline presents a thoughtless King dominated by his Queen, his second wife, whom he married when she became a widow. She is malignantly evil, and her son Cloten is stupid, arrogant and murderous. In the beginning we are told by court gossip that Imogen, the King's daughter by his first wife, has been imprisoned by the King because she refused to marry the stupid Cloten, instead marrying an orphaned gentleman, Posthumus Leonatus.

The setting is England at the time of the Roman Emperor Augustus, but characters talk like courtiers of Shakespeare's own time. Posthumus pledges devotion to Imogen when he is banished, and goes to Rome to live with a man who had been his father's friend. When the mindless King reviles Imogen for marrying Posthumus, she says, "Would I were / A neatherd's daughter, and my Leonatus / Our neighbor-shepherd's son." She has no attachment to courtly pomp, and while the hypocritical Queen pretends affection for her, she plans to poison her by supplying her servitor with a deadly poison and telling him that it is a wonderful elixir of life. But because the chemist who made the potion hates her, he has actually mixed a liquor which will cause the person who drinks it to only appear to be dead for some hours. Meanwhile, in Rome, Posthumus is baited by an Italian, Iachimo, about his beautiful beloved, and a wager is made that she will prove to be unfaithful. (This part of the story is taken from Boccacio.)

Iachimo travels to Britain, tells Imogen that Posthumus lives loosely—which she doesn't believe—tries to make love to her and is coldly repulsed, then tells her he was only testing her. Then he persuades her to keep his trunk in her room that night for safety. That night he emerges from the trunk, examines her room and her sleeping form, takes from her arm a bracelet Posthumus had given her, and hides in the trunk again. Back in Rome he presents Posthumus with this evidence that he made love to her successfully, and Posthumus swears vengeance on her. He writes to his servant Pisanio in England to kill her. And Imogen gets a letter telling her to meet him at Milford-Haven, in Wales.

So far we have a Renaissance tale oddly set in ancient Britain, but the play now takes on a different tone and introduces two young princes, Arviragus and Guiderius, in a cave in Wales, watched over by one Belarius. The two boys have grown up strong in body and with very sweet minds. They have had no dealings with money; they feel no selfishness, rivalry or hatred for others. It is not that they are entirely happy with their secluded life. Belarius, a nobleman who had been loved by Cymbeline as a brave soldier and had been wrongfully denounced by evil people as being in league with the Romans, had stolen the princes away when they were two and three. And in these years when he lived "at honest freedom," he had told them much about "the city's usuries," and the life of the court "whose top to climb / Is certain falling, or so slippery that / The fear's as bad as falling."

He has told them of "the toil o' th' war" and the drive for "fame and honour, which dies i' th' search, / And hath as oft a sland'rous epitaph / As record of fair act." But recognizing the evils he has described, they yet have a vitality that chafes at what the older brother, Guiderius, calls a "quiet life," and a "prison." The world of action and intercourse with other men calls to them. There can be brave actions. And the younger, Arviragus, says:

> What shall we speak of
> When we are as old as you? When we shall hear
> The rain and wind beat dark December, how
> In this our pinching cave shall we discourse
> The freezing hours away? We have seen nothing. . . .

Shakespeare is no advocate of a life of seclusion. It is really education he is talking about: a life away from the corruptions of civilizations in which human beings can grow up decent and unspoiled, and with this strength go out to play their part in the world. Eventually one must leave the countryside. But, as with a good education, its sweetness stays and strengthens the spirit. Shakespeare may be thinking here of his own poetry; it enters into all the nooks and crannies of intellectual life; it takes up all the corruptions of people in a civil society, yet it never loses the foundation of an affectionate closeness to nature. And in these "pastoral" sections, a special quality of the poetry is its lovely nature imagery.

Imogen's torment reaches its peak. In the wilds of Wales, with the servant of Posthumus, Pisanio, he shows her the letter in which Posthumus told him to destroy her for being a strumpet.

But he will not do this. "My master is abused," he says; "Some villain, / Ay, and singular in his art, has done you both / This cursed injury." But she will not go back to the British court to be plagued by Cloten. And so he tells her to dress as a boy and go to the Romans, who are landing at Milford-Haven. For war has broken out between Britain and mighty Rome, since Cymbeline, urged by the Queen and Cloten, has been foolhardy enough to stop paying tribute to Rome. And with the Romans, Pisanio says, Imogen might get to the residence of Posthumus and be near him even though in disguise. So she goes off, dressed as a boy and calling herself Fidele.

The court discovers that Imogen has fled to Milford-Haven. The brutish Cloten decides to pursue her; he engages the helpless Pisanio to get him the clothes of Posthumus. With a peculiar logic, he wants an "honest" servant who faithfully will do whatever evil he commands. "If thou wouldst not be a villain, but do me true service, undergo these employments wherein I should have cause to use thee with a serious industry, that is, what villainy soe'er I bid thee do, to perform it directly and truly."

So Cloten intends to pursue Imogen and rape her while in Posthumus's clothing, then "knock her back" to the court. Pisanio must get him the clothes, but hopes he will not find her. He has a better morality: "true to thee / Were to prove false, which I will never be, / To him that is most true."

Imogen, wandering and hungry, comes upon the empty cave of Belarius and the two boys. She eats some food she finds there. When they come upon her, she offers to pay for the food, and Guiderius scorns it, while Arviragus says, "All the gold and silver rather turn to dirt! / As 'tis no better reckoned but of those / Who worship dirty gods." She is afraid they are angry, but they tell her affectionately she is "amongst friends." She is really their sister, although none of them know it. But a warm love suffuses them.

The next morning, Fidele feels ill and drinks the Queen's drug (which actually will only make her sleep like death for a while). She goes into the cave. Then Cloten appears, rude and, as always, surprised that no one does him homage. He speaks contemptuously to the boys, scorns them as slaves and thieves, proudly tells them his name is Cloten, and when they do not shudder, tells them he is the Queen's son. Guiderius has no fear at hearing this. "Those I reverence, those I fear, the wise: / At fools I laugh, not fear them." So Cloten resorts to the last argument he knows, force. He will kill Guiderius. They go off fighting, and Guiderius returns with Cloten's head. Then Arviragus goes into the cave and is horrified to find Imogen apparently dead. They mourn for "Fidele" in touching, simple nature images:

> With fairest flowers,
> Whilst summer lasts, and I live here, Fidele,
> I'll sweeten thy sad grave. Thou shalt not lack
> The flower that's like thy face, pale primrose, nor
> The azured harebell, like thy veins; no, nor
> The leaf of eglantine, whom not to slander,
> Outsweetened not thy breath. . . .
> Yea, and furred moss besides, when flow'rs are none,
> To winter-ground thy corse.

They then utter one of Shakespeare's most beautiful lyrics. It is not added casually, as if it were a lyric that could be replaced by any other, like the beautiful "Hark, hark! the lark at heaven's gate sings," which occurs earlier, but is an organic part of the play. It celebrates the pastoral life, accepts the finality of death before which all are equal, dwells on the hardships which the working people especially face, and yet is saturated with a life of life:

> Fear no more the heat o' th' sun,
>   Nor the furious winter's rages;
> Thou thy worldly task hast done,
>   Home art gone and ta'en thy wages.
> Golden lads and girls all must,
> As chimney-sweepers, come to dust.
>
> Fear no more the frown o' the great;
>   Thou are past the tyrant's stroke;
> Care no more to clothe and eat;
>   To thee the reed is as the oak.
> The sceptre, learning, physic, must
> All follow this and come to dust.
>
> Fear no more the lightning flash,
>   Nor the all-dreaded thunder-storm;
> Fear not slander, censure rash;

Thou has finished joy and moan.
All lovers young, all lovers must
Consign to thee and come to dust.

No exorciser harm thee!
Nor no witchcraft charm thee!
Ghost unlaid forbear thee!
Nothing ill come near thee!
Quiet consummation have,
And renowned be thy grave.

Then Cloten's headless body, dressed in the clothes of Posthumus, is laid beside that of Fidele, and they leave. Imogen (Fidele) awakens, and falls moaning on the body, which she thinks is that of Posthumus. The Roman officers enter, and taking Imogen for a boy page, enlist her with them.

The play ends melodramatically. Back on British soil with the Romans are Iachimo and Posthumus, who regrets his wretched treatment of Imogen, even though he does not know how he was deceived. He deserts from the Romans and fights with the British, dressed as a peasant. Guiderius and Arviragus cannot keep away from the fray. According to Shakespeare, their princely blood asserts itself. At first the British fly, and Cymbeline is captured, but Guiderius, Arviragus and Belarius do miracles of valor, rally the British, rescue Cymbeline, and lead to a British victory. Then, in a final scene, all hidden identities are revealed and all machinations exposed. The Queen dies, confessing first that she always hated her husband, Cymbeline, and that she had plotted to kill him and to make Cloten king. Iachimo confesses to his evil stratagems against Posthumus and Imogen; Imogen who has been captured with the Romans reveals her true identity; Posthumus who, after the battle had resumed his Roman dress and expected to be killed as a prisoner, reveals his true identity; Belarius tells Cymbeline that the noble boys Guiderius and Arviragus are his stolen sons. And so all but the dead are happy. Finally, in agreement with what he knows of British history, Shakespeare has Cymbeline agree to resume his tribute to Rome.

Structurally it is a strange play, for the sections dealing with Belarius, Guiderius and Arviragus can be excised completely and edges easily sewn up, leaving a complete comedy melodrama with a tangled plot and a happy ending, with Posthumus the hero, Imogen the heroine, The Queen, Cloten and Iachimo the villains. Yet those deletable sections are the most poetic and the most deeply Shakespearean, giving the play a special dimension and character. Against a court picture exhibiting a King who is too credulous, an insanely evil Queen, her imperious and thickheaded son and a malicious courtier—all making things overwhelmingly difficult for two honest people—there is this fanciful picture of an education close to the soil and free of civilized corruptions. It made Shakespeare's pen sing and it foreshadows Rousseau, who wrote his book on education, *Emile,* 150 years later in the "Age of Enlightenment." Shakespeare's critique of society gained even greater cogency when it appeared in a later, more advanced age. For this age, too, had its absolute monarchs and ridiculous courts, and Rousseau's thinking became relevant to the French Revolution.

Equally savage and idiotic are the kings and court affairs in *The Winter's Tale.* It opens in the Kingdom of Sicilia with a picture of blissful peace. Camillo, a Sicilian lord, and Archidamus, a Bohemian lord, talk of the mutual affection of their respective kings, who "were trained together in their childhoods," and Archidamus says, "I think there is not in the world either malice or matter to alter it." But it does alter very quickly. King Leontes of Sicilia has been entertaining his friend King Polixenes of Bohemia for nine months, and Polixenes says he must leave. Leontes entreats him to stay, but he refuses. Leontes then asks his wife Hermione to add her arguments, and when she does so and Polixenes agrees to stay, Leontes suddenly conceives a siege of violent jealousy. He is convinced there is an affair between his wife and Polixenes.

The thought breeds fierce action. He tells Lord Camillo to poison Polixenes, or himself die. The unhappy Camillo knows his suspicions are groundless, but his arguments make no effect on a King whose whim is law. And so he tells Polixenes of the plan to murder him, and Polixenes steals away, taking Camillo with him to serve him in Bohemia. Leontes is furious and imprisons Hermione, who is big with child, and separates her from her young son who adores her. Others expostulate to Leontes, but he is adamant. To quiet them, however, he sends messengers to the oracle of Apollo at Delphos to get confirmation of his wife's guilt.

In prison, Hermione gives birth to a daughter, and a noblewoman Paulina takes the baby to Leontes, hoping the sight will make him relent. But he savagely orders a protesting nobleman to take the baby and abandon it in some desert place far from his kingdom. All this is while his messengers to Apollo's oracle are in transit. Then there is a trial, in which he charges Hermione with adultery. She bears herself nobly. In the midst of the trial, the messengers appear, and the oracle's message says that Hermione and Polixenes are completely innocent. But news comes that the young prince, son of Hermione and Leontes, has died because of the separation from his mother. Hermione faints and appears to be dead, Meanwhile, on a deserted "seacoast of Bohemia," the baby is abandoned by Antigonus, who is then pursued and killed by a bear. The ship that carried him flounders, and all on it are drowned, Act III ends as a shepherd and his son come upon the baby and take it home.

The fantastic unreality of the situation is intensified by the number of unlamented deaths: the young prince, the nobleman Antigonus, the mariners. The audience is not expected to take these events seriously. The play is like a parable, intended to make a point; or, like the story of Job, when his sons and daughters die as a test for him. Here, the point, if playfully made, is the unchecked arrogance of Leontes, who as a King can do whatever he wants. There is nothing to stop him.

Sixteen years pass; the scene changes to Bohemia; and King Polixenes there is as arrogant in his own way as Leontes. Camillo has served him faithfully and now wants to return to Sicilia. But this is refused. The tone of the play changes in the pastoral scene of the shepherds merrymaking at a sheep-shearing festival. There is hilarity, rough humor and dancing. In the midst of this, Perdita, the abandoned child who has grown into a lovely young lady, is being courted by Prince Florizel, the son of Polixenes, under an assumed name. Their language is characterized by a lovely, simple nature imagery, like Florizel's "When you do dance, I wish you / A wave o' the sea, that you might ever do / Nothing but that." The shepherds good humor is not even spoiled by the depredations of a rogue among them, a former court servant, Autolycus, who is a ballad-monger, peddler and crafty pickpocket. Although he robs them, the gold he takes is not a vital part of their way of life. They make their living by struggling with nature and are not obsessed with money. And Autolycus is a jolly rogue. The evil comes from the court, for Polixenes has disguised himself to follow his son, and unmasking himself, condemns the old shepherd, presumably Perdita's father, to be hanged as he threatens to disinherit his son.

Prince Florizel is unabashed and indignant. When his father leaves, he tells of his pl. is to take Perdita with him on the ship and sail away, never to return to Bohemia. Where he will sail, he does not know. Camillo convinces him to sail for Sicilia and say he is sent there by Polixenes. He and Perdita will be royally received. Then Camillo tells Polixenes of this so that Polixenes will follow and take Camillo with him. Thus Camillo will return to his homeland. And it is Autolycus who, out of sheer knavery, unwittingly helps clear up the tangled situation.

Autolycus is dedicated to dishonesty. "Ha, ha! What a fool Honest is! and Trust, his sworn brother, a very simple gentleman!" And so when the old shepherd and his son pass by carrying to the king the cradle in which they found the baby, in order to convince him that the shepherd is not Perdita's father, Autolycus misleads him and puts him instead on Florizel's ship. Florizel and Perdita, hotly pursued by the angry Polixenes, arrive in Sicilia. But the shepherd is with them, carrying the relics he found with the abandoned baby, 16 years before. Leontes and Camillo recognize Hermione's jewel and mantle and Antigonus's handwriting on a letter.

So Perdita is disclosed to be the long-lost princess. Leontes embraces his rediscovered daughter and also embraces Polixenes. The honest shepherd and his son are made gentlemen. Autolycus, who says on seeing them, "Here comes those I have done good to against my will," decides to reform himself. Florizel has Perdita. Even Hermione, who had not died but had been living quietly and secretly with Paulina, is restored to Leontes. And Paulina, whose husband had been eaten by a bear, is given another husband, Camillo.

What emerges from this fantastic comedy is, on the one hand, the foolishness of kings who have absolute power to do good or evil and, on the other hand, the decencies of life among the simple folk. It is not that Shakespeare says life is really better among the shepherds. After all, the honest shepherd is rewarded by being made a prosperous gentleman. It is, however, that Shakespeare finds human virtues of honesty, tenderness, trust and openhearted love at the furthest remove from court or "civilized" life. He projects an area where the relations of friendliness and brotherhood can flower uncorrupted by the pressure of money or power and by the fear that enemies may appear everywhere. This peace of mind he implies, can be carried to civilization.

Finally, in *The Tempest,* Shakespeare carries this line of thought to its full fruition, creating a form in which he can dwell at leisure on this pastoral escape from the rivalries and murders of court life, create more reasonably human characters into whose minds he can delve, and not expend all of his effort on the melodramatic tangles of the court. For the action of the play takes place on the island ruled by Prospero's magic. The evil acts have taken place long before the play begins, and much of it deals with the grotesque reflections of these acts in the friendly atmosphere of the island.

Like *The Merchant of Venice* and *Othello, The Tempest* has suffered from critics who have fastened on the play meanings not intended by Shakespeare. Prospero's half-human slave, Caliban, has been turned into the equivalent of an American Indian or an African victimized by colonialists. The portrayal of Caliban is attacked by those who support the struggles for independence of oppressed peoples, or it is pointed to triumphantly by racists as evidence that black people are not quite human and ought to be ruled by white Europeans.

It is true that by about 1611, when the play was written, colonization of the Americas had long been accomplished by Spain and was being begun by England. But this play is not about colonization. Prospero, its hero, is no Raleigh. He has no interest in developing the products of the island on which he finds himself. There is virtually no population on the island on which he finds himself. A blue-eyed witch named Sycorax, from a city called "Argier," perhaps the city in the play *King John,* had been banished to the island when she was pregnant with Caliban and had died some time after he was born. The sprite Ariel had been her servant, and this lovable character is as much a native of the island as Caliban. Caliban is often shown as dark-skinned; Ariel almost never is. Caliban is not an admirable character. He has sexual cravings for Prospero's daughter, knows no moral principles, and is easily victimized by liquor.

But Shakespeare's interest in the play is in the really despicable characters who are familiar with moral principles only to flout them; Antonio, the usurping Duke of Milan; Alonso, the King of Naples, who plots with Antonio to take over Milan; Sebastian, Alonso's brother, who plots to kill Alonso; Trinculo and Stephano, servants who aim to kill Prospero. *The Tempest* is no play for white supremacists; in fact, Alonso, the King of Naples, has just celebrated the marriage of his daughter to an African, the King of Tunis. But Shakespeare's partial humanization of the witch's son Caliban, making him a half-man, has played into the hands of those who would like to believe that his characteristics are shared by the dark-skinned people who were oppressed, enslaved or killed by the Europeans and their descendants in America.

Four remarkable scenes make up the first two acts, each scene with its own particular human tone, characterization and language color. The first, a short one, concerns the mariners and noble passengers on a ship at sea, apparently foundering in a wild storm. Shakespeare, using boisterous language, gives the scene a comic tone without in any way burlesquing the seeming disaster. The racy language is that of the seamen who, lowly as they were in those times, as people who worked with their hands, suddenly take on the high stature of men who have mastered their difficult and dangerous job, and fight with nature's evils, while all the nobles and gentlemen on board are helpless and can only vent their fears in futile cursing. The gentry are driven below deck:

> *Boatswain.*   I pray now, keep below.
> *Antonio.*   Where is the Master, Boatswain?
> *Boatswain.*   Do you not hear him? You mar our labour.
> Keep your cabins: you do but assist the storm.
> *Gonzalo.*   Nay, good, be patient.

> *Boatswain.* When the sea is. Hence! What care these
> roarers for the name of King? To cabin!
> Silence! Trouble us not!
> > *Gonzalo.* Good, yet remember who thou hast
> > aboard.
> *Boatswain.* None that I love more than myself . . . .
> If you can command these elements to silence
> and work the peace of the present, we will not hand
> a rope more . . . . Out of our way, I say! . . . .
> > *Sebastian.* A pox o' your throat, you bawling, blas-
> phemous, incharitable dog!
> *Boastswain.* Work you, then!

This is one of Shakespeare's notable comments on working people.

The next scene, a long one, presents the inhabitants of the mysterious island. It is distinguished by its beautiful, lucid, unaffected poetry. There are the two great figures about whom the play revolves, who have a finely worked-out relationship to each other—tender, affectionate—even though they are opposites Prospero and Miranda, father and daughter—the old man who has shouldered heavy burdens and the young girl who has been brought up in this magical pastoral environment—the old generation and the new. Miranda's speech shows her lovely tenderness of heart:

> If by your art, my dearest father, you have.
> Put the wild waters in this roar, allay them . . .
> > > > O, I have suffered
> With those I saw suffer! A brave vessel,
> Who had, no doubt, some noble creature in her,
> Dashed all to pieces. O, the cry did knock
> Against my very heart! Poor souls, they perished!

When Prospero tells her, "Tell your piteous heart / There's no harm done," she still answers, "O, woe the day!"

Prospero assures Miranda that "The direful spectacle of the wreck, which touched/ The very virtue of compassion in thee" was so controlled by him that no one in the vessel came to any harm. He then recounts, to her sweetly agitated comments, the cruel machinations that forced them, 12 years before, when she was three, upon this deserted island. He had been the Duke of

Milan, beloved by the people. But in devoting himself to the study of the liberal arts, he had let his brother Antonio manage the state, and he, filling the government with his own followers, conspired with Alonso, King of Naples, to deprive Prospero of his Dukedom. Antonio opened the gates of the city to the troops of the King of Naples. Prospero and Miranda were put on a leaky ship to founder and die. One person, a Neapolitan counsellor named Gonzalo, had a good heart. He furnished the ship with food, water, clothing, linens and, best of all, Prospero's books. They landed on the island, where Prospero was able to perfect his study of magic. And now that fortune had brought all his enemies near the island on the ship, Prospero has magically aroused a mock sea storm to bring them into his power.

The two servants on the island speak in beautiful, poetic language. The ethereal Ariel, whom Prospero rescued from a spell cast by the witch, can take on a multitude of forms, make himself invisible, cast spells, and make music. He serves Prospero cheerfully on the promise that he will soon be free. Caliban, who does the heavy work, remains brutish. Thus Ariel reports on his mission to make the ship appear to sink in a storm:

> Safely in harbour
> Is the King's ship: in the deep nook, where once
> Thou calledst me up at midnight to fetch dew
> From the still-vexed Bermoothes, there she's hid:
> The Mariners all under hatches stowed,
> Who with a charm joined to their suffered labour,
> I have left asleep.

Even Caliban speaks of love in poetry, although Shakespeare gives it the stamp of a rough mind and makes it close to the things of nature:

> When thou cam'st first,
> Thou strok'st me, and made much of me, wouldst give me
> Water with berries in't, and teach me how
> To name the bigger light, and how the less,
> That burn by day and night: and then I loved thee,
> And showed thee all the qualities of the' Isle,
> The fresh springs, brine-pits, barren place and fertile.

> Cursed be I that did so! All the charms
> Of Sycorax, toads, beetles, bats, light on you!
> For I am all the subjects that you have,
> Which first was mine own king, and here you sty me
> In this hard rock . . . .

For Caliban had been treated as a companion until he tried to violate Miranda, after which Prospero had to keep him in submission. Caliban still gloats over the thought. "Thou didst prevent me: I had peopled else / This Isle with Calibans."

Ariel also sings lovely lyrics, like the famous:

> Full fathom five thy father lies,
>   Of his homes are coral made;
> Those are pearls that were his eyes:
>   Nothing of him that doth fade,
> But doth suffer a sea-change.
>   Sea-nymphs hourly ring his knell:
> Hark! Now I hear them—Ding-dong bell.

He now comes back on the scene, leading Ferdinand, the young son of the King of Naples. Ferdinand and Miranda are enraptured with one another. But Prospero, who is pleased that the two have fallen in love, acts harshly, for he wants to put Ferdinand through further ordeals to test him. And so he puts a spell on Ferdinand and tells Miranda that Ferdinand is like a Caliban compared to other men. But Shakespeare's heroines are firm in love and even defy their fathers. Her answer is, "My affections / Are then, most humble: I have no ambition / To see a goodlier man."

Now, under the spell of this island ruled by gentleness, love and kindly people, come the reigning figures of the courts from the outside world. They are the old Neapolitan counsellor Gonzalo; the King of Naples, Alonso; his brother Sebastian; and Antonio, the usurping Duke of Milan. The effect of the enchanted island is to turn them inside out, revealing their inner life in all its ugliness. The writing is in part prose, in part poetic and dramatic rhetoric. But for Gonzalo, they are a scurvy lot. Goodhearted Gonzalo imagines a Utopian community he can create on this island, without rich and poor, arms or magistrates.

The others jeer at him. And when Alonso and Gonzalo fall asleep, Antonio and Sebastian set out to murder them in order to make Sebastian King of Naples. Ariel awakens the sleepers in time, and the killers with drawn swords pretend that they heard animals howling.

In the following scene the magic island throws into sharp relief the dissoluteness of the court servants. They are Stephano, a butler who has floated ashore on a hogshead of wine, and Trinculo, a feeble jester. The tone is one of raucous tavern humor. Caliban comes upon Trinculo, is frightened of him, and acts as if he were dead. Trinculo takes cover from the storm under Caliban's cloak. Stephano thinks he has come across a two-headed monster and feeds him wine. Caliban thinks that Stephano is a god, for he has "celestial liquor." He enlists himself in the service of the drunken Stephano, thinking him to be a far more potent master than Prospero.

And so, in the radiant amosphere of this magic island, young Ferdinand, who is truly modest and humble, as yet undistorted by the court world, finds his true love, while the selfishness, cruelty and murderous corruption of the outside world appear in sharp delineation. The next three short scenes intensify the picture. Ferdinand is set by Prospero the task of carrying logs, but the love he feels for Miranda makes the labor light. She, as always, brims over with pity:

> Alas, now, pray you,
> Work not so hard. I would the lightning had
> Burnt up those logs that you are enjoined to pile!
> Pray, set it down, and rest you. When this burns,
> 'Twill weep for having wearied you.

She even offers to carry the logs for him. It is a radiant love scene, which Prospero watches, unseen by the lovers, and pleased.

The drunken Stephano and Trinculo flounder about with Caliban, who offers to lead them to Prospero when he is sleeping, so that they may kill him. Stephano gloats over the thought of ruling the island. "Monster, I will kill this man: his daughter and I will be King and Queen,—save our Graces!—And Trinculo and

thyself shall be Viceroys. Dost like this plot, Trinculo?" Ariel
teases them, unseen. It is a travesty on the plot of the highborn—the usurping Duke of Milan and the brother of the King of
Naples. But Caliban speaks an earthy but extraordinarily beautiful poetry because he is a creature of this island:

> Be not afeard: the isle is full of noises,
> Sounds and sweet airs, that give delight, and hurt not.
> Sometimes a thousand twanging instruments
> Will hum about mine ears; and sometimes voices,
> That, if I had waked after long sleep,
> Will make me sleep again: and then, in dreaming,
> The clouds, methought, would open, and show riches,
> Ready to drop upon me, that, when I waked,
> I cried to dream again.

The nobility, Antonio and Sebastian, are about to resume their
plot to kill Alonso and Gonzalo, but they are plagued by the
invisible Ariel and by Prospero, who says, "some of you there
present / are worse than devils." To their amazement, Antonio,
Alonso and Sebastian are reminded by fantastic figures of their
own past evil deeds. Then when the three run off, Gonzalo says:

> All three of them are desperate: their great guilt,
> Like poison given to work a great time after,
> No 'gins to bite the spirits.

The turning point of the play is a subtle one. Prospero conjures
up a classical poetic masque to celebrate the love of Ferdinand
and Miranda and their forthcoming marriage. The mythological
figures in the masque, such as June, Ceres and Iris, speak a cool,
well-bred decorative poetry. Then suddenly Prospero dismisses
the revels and speaks a passage of truly great poetry, which also
brings a new note into the play:

> Our revels now are ended. These our actors,
> As I foretold you, were all spirits, and
> Are melted into air, into thin air:
> And like the baseless fabric of this vision,
> The cloud-capped towers, the gorgeous palaces,
> The solemn temples, the great globe itself,
> Yea, all which it inherit, shall dissolve,

> And like this insubstantial pageant faded,
> Leave not a rack behind. We are such stuff
> As dreams are made on; and our little life
> Is rounded with a sleep. Sir, I am vexed:
> Bear with my weakness. My old brain is troubled.
> Be not disturbed with my infirmity.

It is not only the pageant that is dismissed but, by implication, all the magic of the island. For a real human being has appeared, old and tired, willing to relinquish the world to the young.

The dismissal of the magic of the island is suspended, for the plot has to be cleared up. There is another comic scene where Stephano, Trinculo and Caliban are prowling about trying to find Prospero and kill him, but Stephano and Trinculo are drawn away from the plan by seeing some fine clothes hanging on a line. They immediately steal them, while Caliban mutters, "The dropsy drown this fool! What do you mean / To dote thus on such luggage." Then Prospero resumes his soliloquy:

>   I have bedimmed
> The noontide sun, called forth the mutinous winds,
> And 'twixt the green sea and the azured vault
> Set roaring war . . . . But this rough magic
> I here abjure; . . . I'll break my staff,
> Bury it certain fathoms in the earth,
> And deeper than did ever plummet sound
> I'll drown my book.

The audience is left with the realities of youth and age in the real world. The noble refugees from the ship are assembled before Prospero, and the Boatswain and Master are also brought in. Prospero discloses his real identity and shows them Ferdinand and Miranda playing chess. Alonso is overjoyed at seeing his lost son, and Ferdinand is overjoyed at seeing his lost father. Miranda cries the wonderful welcome of the youth to the world:

>   O wonder!
> How many goodly creatures are there here!
> How beauteous mankind is! O brave new world,
> That has such people in't.

Prospero says drily, "'Tis new to thee." It is, of course, new to all young people. And the thought the play leaves in the mind is not simply whether it will all pass away, as of course it will, but how wonderful life can be before it does pass away. The play adds the thought that it can be more wonderful if people will act with love for one another, instead of trying to destroy others and in the process destroying themselves as human beings.

Thus the enchanted island reforms people. Prospero is restored as the Duke of Milan, although he later says, "Every third thought shall be my grave." The others are contrite. As the good Gonzalo says:

> In one voyage
> Did Claribel her husband find at Tunis,
> And Ferdinand, her brother, found a wife
> Where he himself was lost. Prospero his dukedom
> In a poor Isle, and all of us ourselves
> When no man was his own.

Ariel is set free to go where he wishes, and Caliban says, "and I'll be wise hereafter, / And seek for grace." The company sails back to civilization, presumably having been made into honest people.

The theme of the play is that in the pastoral island, people have "found themselves." It does not say, of course, that the people will remain honest. What it does impart, however, is its conviction about the potential for good in human beings, so that when they do evil, it is a distortion of themselves. In a wonderful way, Shakespeare has written a play which is all fantasy, and yet is conceived with both feet in the real world. This world appears altered in the fantasy-glass but, magically, the alteration is not a distortion. Rather it is as themselves, in their true guise, that people appear, while their life in the real world is the distortion of their possibilities.

And this carries over far beyond the time *The Tempest* was written. For if Shakespeare had no illusions about the real world, he still had a grasp of the potential sweetness of human life and brotherhood when it was not soured by a corrupt society. And the challenge was (and still is) to create a society that will not corrupt men.

12

HUMANIZATION AND ALIENATION

WHAT PROGRESS has been made since Shakespeare's time?

The fundamental thread of progress is the development of human freedom, resting on the continuous development of man's power to transform nature for his own use, with the accompanying knowledge this process gives of the laws of reality itself. Engels writes in *Anti-Dühring:*

> Freedom does not consist in the dream of independence from natural laws, but in the knowledge of these laws, and in the possibility this gives of systematically making them work towards definite ends . . . . Freedom therefore consists in the control over ourselves and over external nature, control founded on knowledge of natural necessity. It is therefore necessarily a product of historical development. The first men who separated themselves from the animal kingdom were in all essentials as unfree as the animals themselves, but each step forward in the field of culture was a step towards freedom.[1]

But in a society based on antagonistic classes, the freedom won by some has always rested on the deprivation of others. Engels puts it thus in *The Origin of the Family, Private Property and the State:*

> Since the exploitation of one class by another is the basis of civilization, its whole development moves in a continuous contradiction. Every advance in production is at the same time a retrogression in the condition of the repressed class, that is, of the great majority. What is a boon for the one is necessarily a bane for the other; each new emancipation of one class always means a new oppression of another class. The most striking proof of this is furnished by the introduction of machinery, the effects of which are well known today.[2]

One ruling class replaces another. And it is only in its earlier stages, when it is destroying the obstructive institutions of a previous ruling class and actively carrying on progress in mastering nature, that a new ruling class most feels its freedom. It then exercises genuine leadership, combining "head" and "hand." It consists of doers and thinkers. But after it consolidates its power, it is faced by the increasing challenge of the class it now exploits. It must repress this class, and it becomes the slave of its own repressive machinery. As its wealth increases, it becomes more and more parasitical. It relegates management to its hirelings, and its servants become more skilled and better informed. Its very pressure upon production gives birth to new techniques and skills that demand different social institutions to enable them to work properly. A new, compelling need appears, not that of mastering the laws of the real world but of saving the domination of the new class. Each step this class takes in repression increases the angry resistance of those whom it exploits. Each move the masters now make results quite differently from what was planned, and its leadership of society becomes a disaster.

As the class which replaces it rises to power, the thread of progress is taken up again on a higher level. The new ruling class has a broader base then the preceding one. Marx and Engels put it this way in *The German Ideology:*

> The class making a revolution appears from the very start, if only because it is opposed to a *class,* not as a class but as the whole mass of society confronting the one ruling class. It can do this

because, to start with, its interest really is more connected with the common interest of all other non-ruling classes, because under the pressure of hitherto existing conditions its interest has not yet been able to develop as the particular interest of a particular class. Its victory, therefore, benefits also many individuals of the other classes which are not winning a dominant position, but only insofar as it now puts these individuals in a position to raise themselves into the ruling class. When the French bourgeoisie overthrew the power of the aristocracy, it thereby made it possible for many proletarians to raise themselves above the proletariat, but only insofar as they became bourgeois. Every new class, therefore, achieves its hegemony only on a broader basis than that of the class ruling previously, whereas the opposition of the non-ruling class against the new ruling class later develops all the more sharply and profoundly. Both these things determine the fact that the struggle to be waged against this new ruling class, in its turn, aims at a more decided and radical negation of the previous conditions of society than could all previous classes which sought to rule.[3]

Since Shakespeare's time, there has been enormous progress for a great many people. The development of capitalism, on the threshold of which Shakespeare wrote his plays, has brought into being new and mighty productive forces and created hitherto unknown enhancements of life for many. There was a growth in the knowledge of natural processes and of the sciences far exceeding all the past discoveries of the laws of reality put together. But capitalism had also to create a new kind of educated working class and to exploit it.

In accomplishing this progress, the economy of the individual farmer producing his needs from the soil had to be wrecked and supplanted by large-scale capitalistic farming. This was done, as Marx writes, "with merciless vandalism and under the stimulus of passions the most infamous, the most sordid, the most meanly odious."[4] Masses of people were driven to the cities to live in frightful slums. There was unrelieved misery for the working class, unlimited use of child labor, and fierce rivalry among the capitalists themselves. Marx writes in *Capital:*

> The villainies of the Venetian thieving system formed one of the secret bases of the capital-wealth of Holland to whom Venice in

her decadence lent large sums of money. So also was it with Holland and England. By the beginning of the 18th century the Dutch manufacturers were far outstripped. Holland had ceased to be the nation preponderant in commerce and industry. One of its main lines of business, therefore, from 1701-1776, is the lending out of enormous amounts of capital, especially to its great rival England. The same thing is going on today between England and the United States. A great deal of capital, which appears in the United States today without any certificate of birth, was yesterday, in England, the capitalized blood of children.[5]

Even today when the working class, under bitter conditions of repression and martyrdom, has organized strong unions, won recognition for them and mitigated some of the more inhuman kinds of labor exploitation, the richest and most advanced capitalist countries have widespread poverty, unemployment and misery.

Capitalism has created the most monstrous weapons of human destruction. Driven by the need for profit and more profit, it has despoiled the earth's resources, destroyed the forests, poisoned the water, the air, and the food people eat. The capitalist nations of Europe and then the United States have carried on the rape of Africa, the robbery and murder of the American Indians and the wreckage of Asian civilizations. Even today a war by the United States has been going on for more than ten years in Indochina, the ostensible reason for which is the furtherance of democracy, while its actual imperialist objectives have been hidden from the American people. This war has cost from one to two million Asian lives. Close to 50,000 American soldiers are dead. The monetary costs of the war are placed largely on the backs of the American working people through high taxes and inflation, while profits are derived from the production of arms, the exploitation of resources (oil, rubber and metals), and the creation of great ports for American vessels. All of these are designed to promote the interests of monopoly capital.

Despite the growth of a practical capitalist "science of economics," capitalism cannot control its own system. In its predictable rejection of Marxism, which sees economics itself as a social and historical development with changing laws, capitalist economics must regard the fierce competition it engenders as a "law of nature." The capitalist becomes a slave to the laws of the competitive marketplace in which he makes his profits. Marx writes, "Free competition brings out the inherent laws of capitalist production in the shape of external coercive laws having power over every individual capitalist"[6]

Out of the race for profit come periodic overproduction and crises, with the weaker business going bankrupt and being absorbed by the stronger. "One capitalist always kills many."[7] Among monopolies there are international rivalries that bring on devastating wars. The capitalist is forced to create the conditions that will cause him to be supplanted. "Fanatically bent on making value expand itself, he ruthlessly forces the human race to produce for production's sake; he thus forces the development of the productive powers of society, and creates those material conditions, which alone can form the real base of a higher form of society, a society in which the full and free development of every individual forms the ruling principle."[8]

In defense against the burdens of untrammeled exploitation and periodic unemployment and hunger, the working class organizes itself and eventually embraces an economic and social theory that puts capitalism itself in perspective. Socialism appears, as in Tsarist Russia in 1917, and in spite of all the attacks of the capitalist world, it proves to be indestructible. World War II forced major devastation upon the socialist Soviet Union, but the socialist country defeated the fascist onslaught and brought about a great spread of socialism.

Capitalist science has been unable to fathom what its rule has done to the human mind. Despite its real contributions to psychology and the treatment of mental illness, it sees the patterns engendered by capitalist society as "eternal laws of the mind." And the most striking intellectual changes appear in the arts. The conflicts and frustrations within the human mentality are aroused by the society in which the individual works and lives; they are reflected with greater intensity when their social origins are not recognized. Even when capitalist society is seen as hateful, there seems to be no hope or intention of overthrowing it. Capitalism has produced a plethora of the most debased art in history, has created formulas for turning the arts into a lucrative manufactured commodity. In spite of the prevalence of money-corrupted art, works of relative integrity and taste are often produced under capitalism—notably in literature. These reflect the realities of the decay of society and a destestation of its depredations, even when they portray them as unchangeable. And at propitious times, a critical spirit of this kind, asserting independence of money control, has broken through in the "popular" or mass-manufactured arts. A vast amount of the art produced in capitalist society today nevertheless reflects the alienation that is so pervasive in real life.

Shakespeare's art represents the highest literary peak of what can be called "humanized reality," because it embraces an entire world of nature and people observed objectively and at the same time enriched by the emotional coloring of a responsive interior life. Marx writes in his early *Economic and Philosophical Manuscripts:*

> It is only when the objective world becomes everywhere for man in society the world of man's essential powers . . . that all *objects* become for him the *objectification of himself,* become objects which confirm and realize his own individuality, become *his* objects: that is, *man himself* becomes the object . . . . Thus, the objectification of the human essence, both in its theoretical and practical aspects, is required to make man's *sense human,* as well as to create the *human sense* corresponding to the entire wealth of human and natural substance.[9]

Following this thought, we can find in Shakespeare the highest development of the human senses or the real world that becomes beautiful—not that it is prettified but because it shows that reality is a factor in man's growth and in the realization of his individuality. Thus Shakespeare's varied characters are humanized and, as such, more true to themselves. They represent good and evil and every stage in between, but even the evil characters remain humans corrupted by forces we are enabled to understand. A profound analyst of the relationship between the outer world of human strivings and the inner world of feelings, he is a great realist; and central to his realism in his view of man, in all his individuality, as an essentially social being.

It is this view that the "revolutionary art" of the 20th century has revolted against in its surrender to alienation, or in its conviction that the surrounding world in not a determining factor in human growth but only a cause for despair. And many of the critics who evaluate this art gravitate to the belief that such an attitude is a discovery of some fundamental "truth," while the artists who express it are found the most interesting of our day. M. L. Rosenthal writes in *The New Poets:*

> To begin, then, I want to propose that since the end of the war of 1939-45 the most striking poetry in the English language has taken on a new coloration, in effect a new sense of unease and disorder. Behind it is the feeling, perhaps, that the humanist way, which traditionally educated and romatic modern men still propose to protect, and indeed to project into a Utopian future, has already been defeated and is now no more than a ghost. It is that feeling on which Robert Lowell in one of his poems calls, self-ironically, 'our universal *Angst'*—a heart-heavy realization that remorseless brutality is a condition not only of the physical universe but also of man himself.[10]

This is a symptom of alienation. Alienation is not an awareness of being exploited or of laboring for someone else's profit, for these might lead to collective rebellion. Alienation is the individual's estrangement from himself and his seeing the rest of nature and humanity in the despairing picture he finds when he regards himself. He externalizes his internal frustration by accepting it as an eternal law of reality—the way things are and must be. If the stages of humanized reality are stages of freedom, alienation rises out of the fact that in class society each stage of freedom turns into the unfreedom of both the exploited and the exploiters. And the exploited begin to lose their stage of alienation only when they collectively begin to struggle against all exploitation.

There must have existed something that could be called alienation in past stages of class society. But at a lower level than that of today. For just as each stage in humanized reality is a loftier peak in its real knowledge and command of nature and the mind, so each stage of alienation that follows is more sweeping and bitter in its intensity. Thus Marx writes in his early *Economic and Philosophical Manuscripts* of European medieval society:

Feudal landed property is already by its very nature huckstered land—the earth which is estranged from man and hence, confronts him in the shape of a few great lords.

The domination of the land as an alien power over men is already inherent in feudal landed property. The serf is the adjunct of the land. Likewise, the lord of an entailed estate, the first-born son, belongs to the land. It inherits him.

But if alienation exists, it does not master the mind to the extent of making it anti-human. Marx adds:

But in feudal landed property the lord at least *appears* as the king of the estate. Similarly, there still exists the semblance of a more intimate connection between the proprietor and the land than that of mere *material* wealth. The estate is individualised with its lord: it has its rank, is baronial or ducal with him, has his privileges, his juridiction, his political position, etc. It appears as the body of its lord . . . . Similarly, the rule of landed property does not appear directly as the rule of mere capital. For those belonging to it, the estate is more like their fatherland. It is a constricted sort of nationality . . . . Those working on the estate have not the position of day *labourers;* but they are in part themselves his property, as are serfs; and in part they are bound to him by ties of respect, allegiance, and duty. His relation to them is therefore directly political, and has likewise a human, *intimate side.*[11]

In *Capital,* Marx writes of the worker of pre-capitalist society that "the laborer is the private owner of his own means of labor set in action by himself; the peasant of the land which he cultivates, the artisan of the tool which he handles as a virtuoso."[12]

It is noteworthy that Shakespeare, while acutely aware of the cultural meagreness of life on the land and the narrow limitations of the feudal mentality, nevertheless illustrates the human qualities of the older social life, even while they are in process of being driven out by the new. It may be seen, for example, in the relative happiness and untroubled mind of the shepherds in *The Winter's Tale* when they are not afflicted by an outburst of their lords' harshness. It may also be seen in the warm attachments of Antony with his captains and soldiers in *Antony and Cleopatra.* Shakespeare lived, of course, long before Marx, but what is important in his feeling for reality and its pyschological patterns. He shows these older patterns even while he is also acutely aware of the appearance in society of new, sophisticated forms of thinking, of the money-motivated mind, dominated by what Marx calls in the same essay as above, "filthy self-interest"; Iago in *Othello,* for example, and the commercial mentality of both Shylock and the rulers of the Venetian state in *The Merchant of Venice.*

The alienation that rises under capitalism is far more intense than any which could have arisen in previous societies because it reverses the high peak of humanism reached in the 16th century and early 17th. One of the virulent forms it takes is the complete perversion of labor. Most labor under capitalism is inescapable and hateful, and to the bourgeois mind this compulsion becomes an eternal truth of life.

To Marx and Marxism labor was and will again be one of the joys of life insofar as it manages nature for human use. It is the basis for the growth of the mind and senses, for the development of skills, for the creation of something new that enhances life, for the humanization of reality. And indeed the growth of the senses of the medieval artisan can be seen in the individuality and beauty that are found in his finished work.

Under capitalism the worker must regard his labor, his existence as a worker, as something not his own but belonging to someone else. In fact, in working he may become his own enemy: He has to work to live, but the more he works, the more the surplus he creates may throw him out of work. Marx writes in the early *Economic and Philosophical Manuscripts:*

> What, then constitutes the alienation of labor?
> First, the fact that the labor is *external* to the worker, i.e., it does not belong to his essential being; that in his work therefore, he does not affirm himself but denies himself, does not feel content but unhappy, does not develop freely his physical and mental energy but mortifies his body and ruins his mind. The worker therefore only feels himself outside his work, and in his work feels outside himself. He is at home when he is not working, and when he is working he is not at home. His labor is therefore not voluntary but coerced; it is *forced labor.* It is therefore not the

satisfaction of a need; it is merely a *means* to satisfy needs external
to it . . . . External labor, labor in which man alienates himself, is
a labor of self-sacrifice, of mortification. Lastly, the external
character of labor for the worker appears in the fact that it is not
his own, but someone else's, that it does not belong to him, that in
it he belongs, not to himself, but to another.[13]

Capitalist manufacture not only breaks the work process down
into separate details but frequently gives the worker no idea of
what part his own work plays in the total process of production.
Marx puts it this way in *Capital:*

> It converts the labourer into a crippled monstrosity, by forcing
> his detail dexterity at the expense of a world of productive
> capabilities and instincts; just as in the State of La Plata they
> butcher a whole beast for the sake of his hide or his tallow. Not
> only is the detail work distributed to the different individuals, but
> the individual himself is made the automatic motor of a fractional
> operation.[14]

Marx sums it up in *Capital:*

> In handicrafts and manufacture, the workman makes use of a
> tool; in the factory, the machine makes use of him . . . . By means
> of its conversion into an automaton, the instrument of labour
> confronts the labourer, during the labour-process, in the shape of
> capital, of dead labour, that dominates, and pumps dry, living
> labour-power.[15]

But it is not the factory worker alone who suffers from
alienation. Capitalism has marshalled a vast number of intellectual and artistic workers into its service, and if their pay and
standards of living are generally much higher than those of the
factory worker, their creativity, which demands freedom, is
constricted to the task of selling merchandise and making profit
for someone else; it is carried on under the dictatorship as well as
the judgment of the man who signs the checks. Living under the
threat of unemployment, their working hours tend to become
"death in life."

And the man who makes the money, the capitalist as well as his
skilled agents, is also alienated. Marx writes:

> Private property has made us so stupid and one-sided that an object is only *ours* when we have it—when it exists for us as capital, or when it is directly possessed, eaten, drunk, worn, inhabited, etc.,—in short, when it is *used* by us . . . . All these physical and mental senses have therefore—the sheer estrangement of all these senses—the sense of *having*.[16]

There is, on the one hand, the austerity which the drive for money engenders.

> The less you eat, drink and buy books; the less you think, love, theorize, sing, paint, fence, etc., the more you *save*—the greater becomes your treasure which neither moths nor dust will devour—your capital. The less you *are*, the less you express your own life, the greater is your *alienated* life, the more you *have*, the greater is the store of your estanged being . . . . All passions and all activity must therefore be submerged in greed.[17]

And, on the other hand, there is wild spending:

> There is a form of inactive, extravagant wealth given over wholly to pleasure, the enjoyer of which on the one hand *behaves* as a mere *ephermeral* individual frantically spending himself to no purpose, knows the slave-labour of others (human *sweat and blood*) as the prey of his cupidity, and therefore knows man himself, and hence also his own self, as a sacrificed and empty being. With such wealth, contempt of man makes its appearance, partly as arrogance and squandering of what can give sustenance to a hundred human lives, and partly as the infamous illusion that his own unbridled extravagance and ceaseless, unproductive consumption is the condition of the other's *labour* and therefore of his *subsistence*.[18]

The alienated bourgeois accepts the erosion of human relations as a law of life. He is an active element in a society composed of fragmented individuals whose very activity intensifies this fragmentation. Engels writes in an early essay included with Marx's manuscripts:

> One estate stands confronted by another, one piece of capital by another, one unit of labor power by another. In other words, because private property isolates everyone in his own crude solitariness, and because, nevertheless, everyone has the same

interest as his neighbor, one landowner stands antagonistically confronted by another, one capitalist by another, one worker by another. In this discord of identical interests resulting precisely from this identity is consummated the immorality of mankind's condition until now; and this consummation is competition.[19]

This alienation of the individual from himself, and so from other human beings, involves also an erosion of love relations. The intercourse between man and woman has a biological foundation, but it grows into a more complex relationship with the development of human sensitivity. Shakespeare explores the humanity of this relationship, as with Romeo and Juliet, Othello and Desdemona, Beatrice and Benedict, and all his true lovers. Of this relationship Marx writes, on the one hand:

> It . . . reveals the extent to which a man's *natural* behavior has become *human*, or the extent to which the *human* essence in him has become a *natural* essence—the extent to which his *human nature* has come to be *nature* to him. In this relationship is revealed, too, the extent to which man's *need* has become a *human* need; the extent to which, therefore, the *other* person as a person has become for him a need—the extent to which he in his individual existence is at the same time a social being.[20]

But he says, on the other hand:

> . . . the alienated person who dwindles in social being 'only feels himself freely active in his animal functions'—eating, drinking, procreating . . . and in his human functions he no longer feels himself to be anything but an animal.
>
> Certainly eating, drinking, procreating, etc. are also genuinely human functions. But abstractly taken, separated from the sphere of all other human activity and turned into sole and ultimate ends, they are animal functions.[21]

Not everyone born in capitalist society is alienated, and there are forms of resistance to alienation, of building a humanized life. There is a variety of reasons for this salutary effect. In the 20 years between Marx's Economic and Philosophical Manuscripts of 1844 and the writing of *Capital*, the first volume of which appeared in 1867, there were changes in the conditions of life brought about by the rise of powerful organizations among the working class. In the *Manuscripts of 1844,* when such organizations were relatively few and weak (and even to speak of organizing a trade union was to be considered a communist), Marx wrote:

> When communist *artisans* associate with one another, theory, propaganda, etc., is their first end. But, at the same time, as a result of this association, they acquire a new need—the need for society—and what appears as a means becomes an end. In this practical process the most splendid results are to be observed whenever French socialist workers are seen together. Such things as smoking, drinking, eating, etc. are no longer means of contact or means that bring together. Company, associations, and conversation, which again have society as their end, are enough for them; the brotherhood of man is no mere phrase with them, but a fact of life, and the nobility of man shines upon us from their work-hardened bodies.[22]

There was another quality in this kind of organization—one that might be called realistic or scientific. In this respect, another remark Marx makes in these early manuscripts may be apropos:

> When I am active *scientifically,* etc.—when I am engaged in activity which I can seldom perform in direct community with others—then I am *social,* because I am active as a *man.* Not only is the material of my activity given to me as a social product (as is even the language in which the thinker is active); my *own* existence is social activity, and therefore that which I make of myself, I make of myself for society and with the consciousness of myself as a social being.[23]

Perhaps the enormous developments in these areas impelled Marx in *Capital* not to stress the alienation of the worker as he had done in earlier writings. Although he is relentless in adducing examples of the brutality visited on the worker, he concentrates on the dehumanization of the capitalist class and its middle-class agents, as in such concepts as "the fetishism of commodities." All the rich qualities that things produced have as things, and the producers' interest in them vanish when they are seen abstractly and judged for their convertibility into cash only. He writes: "There is a definite social relation between men that assumes, in their eyes, the fantastic form of a relation between things."[24] A gun and a book are measured only by their cash value.

In the hundred years and more since *Capital,* there have been more monstrous developments in the capitalist world: the intensified plunder of much of Africa, Asia and Latin America; the outbreak of two of the most disastrous wars in history; the birth in the womb of capitalism of German fascism, with its coldblooded murder of all Jews, Communists and Slavs it could lay its hands on—in the interests of a greater Germany. And in resistance to this, the breakaway of a great section of the world to socialism, the rebellion of colonial Africa and the strengthening in the capitalist world of great labor organizations.

In this capitalist world there is no purity for labor organizations like trade unions and labor parties. They can be corrupted, turned into dictatorships, and pressed into the service of capitalism. Nonetheless, labor has taken a long step away from the lowest pit of alienation, through cooperation and increasingly scientific attitudes, while alienation has intensified throughout the bourgeois community. Of a mass of political servants, Senator Fulbright, himself wealthy and capitalist-oriented, wrote in *The New York Times* of April 23, 1967:

> A whole new intellectual community has arisen in our country, dedicated to the development of an ever more sophisticated global strategy. These scholars have introduced new concepts such as "graduated deterrence," the "blance of terror," "acceptable level of megadeaths," all measurable with a fine precision by the playing out of "wargame scenarios." It all sounds so fascinating, so modern, so antiseptic that it is easy to forget that what is being talked about coldly and scientifically, is the prospect of the most hideous carnage in the history of the human race.

The war carried on by the United States in Vietnam and all Indochina, supported by other capitalist governments, has brought to the foreground another aspect of alienation for the great middle-class community: the realization that they have no control whatsoever over what their government does, and that simply accepting the standard political party machines and elections they are only giving legitimacy to much that appals them.

Most striking in the 20th century has been the spread of alienation in the arts. The traditional greatness and beauty of the arts have been their contribution to the humanization of reality, the constant exploration of the richness of human response to the unfolding qualities of nature and people. Alienation has supplanted this tradition, not only within the pseudo-revolution against "copying nature"—as if any truly realistic artist simply copies nature—but in the art works that, while professing realism, describe humanity with shocking coldness, bitterness and cruelty.

Here are son. illustrations of alienated writing. In poetry, T. S. Eliot is a virtuoso in alienation that is expressed in such finely controlled language and deep conviction that many estimable critics called him the greatest living poet in English. He begins his major poem, *The Waste Land:*

> April is the cruelest month, breeding
> Lilacs out of the dead land, mixing
> Memory and desire, stirring
> Dull roots with spring rain.

In another major poem of perhaps 15 years later, *Four Quartets,* he thus describes man and woman cavorting in "matrimonie":

> Round and round the fire
> Leaping through the flames, or joined in circles,
> Rustically solemn or in rustic laughter
> Lifting heavy feet in clumsy shoes,
> Earth feet, loam feet, lifted in country mirth,
> Mirth of those long since under earth
> Nourishing the corn . . . .
> Eating and drinking. Dung and death.

In his verse play *The Cocktail Party,* this speech by a leading character, an all-wise psychiatrist, describes alienation as a pervading truth of all life:

> What we know of other people
> Is only our memory of the moments
> During which we knew them. And they have changed
>   since then.

To pretend that they and we are the same
Is a useful and convenient social convention
Which must sometimes be broken. We must also remember
That at every meeting we are meeting a stranger

Here is a typical passage from the novel *Couples,* by the intensely serious and highly regarded novelist John Updike:

> The evenings before Christmas are gloomy and exciting in downtown Tarbox: the tinfoil stars and wreaths hung from slack wires shivering audibly in the wind, the silent crèche figures kneeling in the iron pavilion, the schoolchildren shrieking home from school in darkness, the after-supper shoppers hurrying head-down as if out on illicit errands and fearful of being seen, the Woolworth's and Western Auto and hardware stores wide-awake with strained hopeful windows and doors that can't help yawning.

These are not isolated examples of alienated writing—they typify a trend, generally carried out on a much lower level of literary polish. Among the better writers this style expresses a genuine, despairing feeling and worldview. The outer world is repulsive. Whatever humanization exists finds expression in poignant personal laments or in the sheer subtle control of the tools of writing themselves.

It is against this kind of negative realism that Shakespeare stands. He is not the genius who miraculously foreshadowed the modern age, but a giant of humanistic realism, who necessarily shared some of the ignorance of his age, but whose creative genius encompassed the entire scope of society, from the way kings ruled to the way peasants lived. He applied to all beliefs his critical sense of what was real and true. He accurately charted the decline of the old-style great feudal-minded nobility as it was being pushed off the stage of history or removed from control over events. From the new-style rulers of the unified state he raised not only his own but history's demand that they pay attention to the way all the people lived, including especially the poorest. He raised before them a new standard of social responsibility and hailed the rise of humanistic love between man and woman as more powerful and important than the restrictions of caste or class. He contemplated the rocky road that love traversed and demanded that it be cleared of obstacles. Within the rising of new social forces he touched with horror on the appearance of antihumanism—the mind controlled by greed and self-interest to the extent of the loss of all feelings or concern for others.

Today, when these forces rule in capitalist society, we can give them names of "capitalism" and "alienation." He developed the concept of morality by exhibiting how the human mind was not to be mechanically pigeonholed in categories of "good" and "evil," but was to be judged with a full understanding of the forces at conflict within that mind. And, a great realist, he traced the relation between these internal forces and the conflicts and pressures of the society surrounding the individual. The human mind was not that of an automaton; it was often a victim of social pressures. Nevertheless, it could make choices. And his plays triumphantly but without illusions present a humanist basis for these choices. It is love and concern for others and full respect for the preciousness of human life. And he showed this not as a moralistic mandate laid down from above. Man, he showed, was above all a social being and was richest as an individual when he joined with others to fulfill their mutual needs.

Shakespeare's achievement was due not only to his genius, but also to the opportunities his age provided for him to realize it. It was undeniably an age of muck and dirt, of poverty, meanness, wars and brutality. He closed his eyes to none of this. But it was also an age in which the new forces, largely middle class, that would later give birth to industrial capitalism, had not yet coalesced into their own narrow exploitive interests. Living under institutions that were still medieval, he was raising a profound critique of these institutions from a standpoint of human needs. The impelling factor was the rise of the English nation, with the demands it was making for unity and internal peace against the divisiveness of the old-line nobility, as well as for the consideration of those without political rights. In this sense, the new forces represented all of those who were resentful of the outmoded order. There was a movement to freedom in the air, of which Shakespeare himself, middle class and without rights but with a voice and a platform, could take full advantage. He explored this freedom to its limits. He could discern the human qualities in the old order, raise new human standards of social responsibility that were outside the vision of those who stood for the old order, and discern the inhumanity already arising amidst the new forces. Because of the scope of his human endowments, he became the great political dramatist of his age, with no solutions to offer, but a host of questions that remain on the unfinished agenda of society.

Shakespeare could not envision a communist society—"From each according to his capacity, to each according to his need!" Yet only such a society could have answered the questions he raised; a society in which all the world is all mankind's domain to enter, manage and enjoy. None of it should be cut into pieces as "private property," while the mass of people labored for their own subsistence and are permitted to do even this if their labor can create fortunes for the owners. The basis for such a communist society is now at hand. The capitalist class, which accomplished miracles in production and the mastery of nature to serve its untrammeled greed and, in the process, spread frightful misery and oppression, has now run its productive course; it has reached the point at which its technology now threatens the entire world with destruction.

One of the worst by-products is that in its decline it has poisoned the minds of many with cynical convictions as to the futility of life and with the belief that barbarism is the law of human relations. It is as if this society recognized that it could promise only destruction from now on, and then took refuge in the thought that this was the inevitable end of all human endeavors.

In contrast to this, Shakespeare raises the reality of joy in life and love among human beings, all the more profoundly because his thinking is based not on an escape from the ugliness of life but on facing this ugliness and identifying it as the enemy of human growth and fulfillment. "Low life" is as beautiful as "high life" because it is human. The fundamental truth of his work is an inspiration and challenge to us today because it also shows the heights to which human beings can rise.

Shakespeare wrote in the dawn of capitalism and was wise enough to recognize psychological patterns in the making that he regarded with horror. We can now recognize them as an early form of what was to become the great social dominance of capitalism. If he was by no means on the side of the old order, he was equally critical of the new. For that reason, literary critics to whom capitalism meant "progress" could not understand him as a social thinker. At best, they thought, he was an abstract creator of "characters" that had a mysterious eternal life.

And so it became next to impossible to create works truly in the Shakespearian tradition in capitalist countries. In English literature perhaps the nearest to him is Dickens, with his combination of seriousness and lusty humor, his virtuosity with various forms of popular language, his love for the common artisan, his breadth in depicting humanity, and his hatred of what he saw of the capitalist mind. But Dickens could not fathom the leading economic institution of his time, the capitalist factory, nor could he grasp the reality of the way in which England was governed.

The great Shakespeare settings in opera, which a lover of the poet can attend without flinching, are Verdi's early and not altogether mature *Macbeth* and his late, ripe *Otello* and *Falstaff*. And Verdi wrote in an Italy that was engaged in breaking with feudal forms and was fighting for and establishing its independence, without having fallen as yet into the capitalist Procrustean bed. Tolstoi is Shakespearean, though he did not necessarily understand or like the English playwright. He has the Shakespearean breadth and can move from the halls of the mighty and insist on the humanity of the peasant. And Tolstoi also appreciated what was human in the old order of feudal-minded nobility, yet with equanimity saw it moving out of history; welcomed the fresh current of of ideas in Russia, yet hated what he saw of oncoming capitalism.

Today, with all the fine Shakespearean scholarship, the microscopic textual analysis, the understanding of the conditions of performance in the Shakespearean theater, the subtle tracing in his plays of every comment that might be an allusion to some person or happening of his time, there is even more misunderstanding of Shakespeare; more dogged attempts to remove him from his place in history and destroy the reality of his social thinking than ever before. It is perhaps only those who appreciate the vitality and accomplishments of capitalism, yet look with joy on its removal from the earth in its decadence and take part in its replacement by a classless society, who can appreciate Shakespeare at his full stature as poet, dramatist and thinker.

It is not that such individuals take over his views of society; it is that he educates them in the relish of life, the stature to which human beings can rise through struggle, in the ability and courage to face, grasp and talk about the entire range of their social life—from the hidden patterns of government to the lives of the workers and the poor. He can strengthen people in their movement toward creating a society in which what he hoped for can be realized. For the knowledge of how it can be done is now at hand.

BIBLIOGRAPHY

Chapter One

1. Eliot, T. S.: A Talk on Dante, in *Selected Prose,* ed. John Hayward, Middlesex: Harmondsworth, 1953. p. 100.
2. Bindoff, S. T.: *Tudor England.* Middlesex: Harmondsworth, 1950. p. 130.
3. Tawney, R. H.: *Religion and the Rise of Capitalism:* London, 1942. pp. 70–71.
4. Panofsky, Erwin: Art as a Humanistic Discipline, in *Meaning in the Visual Arts:* Garden City, N. Y., 1955. p. 76.
5. Traversi, D. A.: *An Approach to Shakespeare;* Garden City, N. Y., 1956. p. 291.
6. This and all subsequent quotations from Shakespeare are from *The London Shakespeare,* ed. John Munro, London, 1957.

Chapter Two

1. Eliot, T. S.: Hamlet, in *Selected Essays;* New York, 1932, pp. 124–125.

Chapter Three

1. Machiavelli, Niccolo: *Florentine History,* trans. W. K. Marriott, Everyman, London. p. 57.
2. Hegel, G. W. F.: *The Philosophy of Fine Art,* trans. F.P.B. London, 1920. Vol. 1, pp. 275–276.

Chapter Four

1. Coulton, G. G.: *Medieval Panorama,* New York, 1947. pp. 337–338.
2. Tawney, R. H.: *Religion and the Rise of Capitalism,* New York, 1947, 50. pp. 95–96.
3. Weber, M: *The Protestant Ethic and the Spirit of Capitalism,* New York, Scribners, 1958. p. 261.
4. Wilson, J. D.: *Life in Shakespeare's England,* Harmondsworth, 1949. p. 232.
5. Foner, P., ed.: *Complete Works of Thomas Paine,* New York, 1969, Vol. 1, p. 257.

Chapter Five

1. Hazlitt, William, *Characters of Shakespeare's Plays,* London, 1955. p. 158.
2. Chambers, E. K.: *Shakespeare, A Survey,* New York, p. 143.

Chapter Six

1. Coleridge, S. T., *Shakespearean Criticism,* New York, 1960. Vol. 2, p. 150.
2. Marx, Karl, and Engels, Frederick: *Literature and Art,* New York, International Publishers, 1947, p. 82.
3. Metcalf, J. C., Introduction to Coleridge, S. T., *Biographia Literaria,* New York, Macmillan, 1926, p. xi.
4. Wilson, J. D., *What Happens in Hamlet,* New York, 1967, p. 217.

Chapter Eight

1. Bohannan, Paul, *Africa and Africans:* Garden City, N. Y., American Museum Science Books, 1964. p. 102.
2. Coleridge, S. T., *Shakespearean Criticism,* New York, 1960, Vol. 1, p. 42.
3. Van Doren, Mark, *Shakespeare,* Garden City, N. Y. 1953. p. 202.
4. Knight, G. Wilson, *The Wheel of Fire,* New York, 1957, p. 105.
5. Packard, Vance, *The Hidden Persuaders,* New York, 1958. p. 1.
6. Werfel, F., and Stefan, P. *Verdi.* New York, 1942. p. 361.
7. Ibid. p. 290.
8. Ibid. p. 335.

Chapter Nine

1. Bradley, A. C., *Shakespearean Tragedy,* Greenwich, Conn. 1968. p. 234.

Chapter Ten

1. Palmer, John, *Political and Comic Characters of Shakespeare,* London, 1962. pp. 259–260.
2. Ibid., p. 274.
3. Marx, Karl, *Economic and Philosophic Manuscripts of 1844,* New York, International, 1964. p. 169.

Chapter Twelve

1. Engels, Frederick, *Anti-Dühring,* New York, International, 1972. p. 125.
   Engels, Frederick, *Origin of the Family, Private Property and the State,* in *Marx and Engels, Selected Works,* New York, International, 1972, p. 236.
   Marx and Engels, *The German Ideology,* New York, International, 1970. p. 66.

4. Marx, Karl, *Capital*, New York, International, 1947, Vol. 1, p. 783.
5. Ibid., p. 781.
6. Ibid., p. 255.
7. Ibid., p. 788.
8. Ibid., p. 603.
9. Marx, Karl, *The Economic and Philosophic Manuscripts of 1844*, New York, International, 1964. pp. 140–141.
10. Rosenthal, M. L., *The New Poets*, Oxford, N.Y., 1967, p. 5.
11. Marx, Karl, Op. cit., pp. 100–101.
12. Marx, Karl, *Capital.* p. 787.
13. Marx, Karl, *Economic and Philosophic Manuscripts*, p. 111.
14. Marx, Karl, *Capital*, p. 354.
15. Ibid, pp. 472–473.
16. Marx, Karl, *Economic and Philosophic Manuscripts*, p. 139
17. Ibid, p. 150.
18. Ibid, p. 156.
19. Ibid., p. 213.
20. Ibid., p. 134.
21. Ibid., p. 111.
22. Ibid., p. 155.
23. Ibid., p. 137.
24. Marx, Karl, *Capital*, p. 43